Although Jesse Applegate is my 2nd cousin, fifth generation removed, I was intrigued by the author's depiction of that outstanding Oregon pioneer and statesman of Lincolnesque stature...garnered from Jesse's correspondence and from thorough, exhaustive research of a huge number of documents pertaining to his life and times. It was especially interesting to discover how a political machine can override the honest intentions of a man who wants only the best for the good of the people he serves. This book should be recommended reading in the Oregon school system and, for that matter, it is a work that will enlighten anyone interested in serving his or her country.

—Richard Applegate
Retired newspaper executive and
author of published historical novels

JESSE APPLEGATE

JESSE APPLEGATE

A Dialogue with Destiny

Leta Lovelace Neiderheiser

Enjoy!

LETA LOVELACE NEIDERHEISER

TATE PUBLISHING *& Enterprises*

Published by Tate Publishing & Enterprises, LLC
127 E. Trade Center Terrace | Mustang, Oklahoma 73064 USA
1.888.361.9473 | www.tatepublishing.com

Tate Publishing is committed to excellence in the publishing industry. The company reflects the philosophy established by the founders, based on Psalm 68:11,
"The Lord gave the word and great was the company of those who published it."

Book design copyright © 2010 by Tate Publishing, LLC. All rights reserved.
Cover design by Kellie Southerland
Interior design by Nathan Harmony

Published in the United States of America

ISBN: 978-1-61739-229-0
1. Biography & Autobiography: Adventurers & Explorers
2. History: United States: 19th Century
11.01.25

Acknowledgment

There are a number of people I must say thank you to on the long journey to bring this book to completion. First and foremost, a special thank you to my husband, Joe. Early on in this process he drove me across the state to one library or history museum after another and patiently waited while I spent hours in the dark dungeons of "historical document depositories." He read the manuscript at each stage of development and gave advice and encouragement.

My sister Denise and her husband, Earl, were the first to encourage me to write a book and then continued to give encouragement each time I met a road block along the way. I also must say thank you to three cousins: Dorothy, Shannon, and Richard for their encouragement and help on this long journey. All three cousins read the manuscript at one stage or another, and gave advice and insight into family history. A big thank you is due my friend and fellow historic trail buff, Stafford, for all the documents and leads he sent me and his frank critique of where I needed to dig a little deeper and where I needed to edit.

Without the encouragement of a local bookstore owner, Robert Moore, I would never have had the courage to submit my manuscript to a publisher.

All the beautiful pen and ink drawings are drawn by my niece, Cynthia Howard; without the help of her daughter, Jessica Olsen, I would never have mastered some of the finer points of the computer. So thank you to one and all!

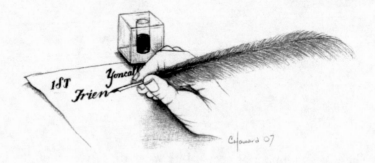

Table of Contents

Introduction

Over the years, like many an Applegate before me, I have hungrily sought information concerning my forefathers. Jesse Applegate always held a special fascination for me: the more I learned, the more I wanted to know. I began to see that his story was the story of early Oregon. Much has been written about Jesse Applegate over the years, but this book is an attempt to give a comprehensive, historical perspective to the life of this interesting, complicated man. At the death of his dear wife, Cynthia, Jesse helped his son prepare a simple, sandstone marker for the gravesite he would share with his wife. He told his son that the stone should be blank but for their names and dates of death. "Nothing else; if anyone wants to know more, let him consult the records." Those compelling words have in fact led me to consult and present "the record."

Hundreds of Jesse's letters have survived over time because many of his friends saved them; the more of them one reads, the more one sees the complexity of his mind. One theme that haunts his letters is what he calls "his lack of self esteem," and yet we see him repeatedly embark on endeavors requiring a strong sense of self. His letter to Judge Matthew Deady in March of 1862 explains his many self-doubts:

> I lack the self esteem necessary to give me confidence, it is not so much lack of ideas that I cannot speak in public, as a fear that I shall fail to give them proper expression. I am not satisfied with my personal appearance and for that reason have never suffered any likeness to be taken. The work neither of my hand nor my head give me satisfaction, and I have thought none of them worth preserving for their design or finish and one reason why I have no copy of anything I have written is that I see in copying so many necessary additions and corrections to make that the copy is used as the original and have in the first paper only the substance or tenor of it. [1]

Since Jesse had so low a value of his writing, his many letters, which can be found in libraries across the country, come not from his own files but from those of friends and even rivals who saw the value in them. In March of 1862, Judge Deady, one of Jesse's most frequent correspondents, asked Jesse to return a letter for the file he was keeping for posterity. To this Jesse responds:

> I would remark however that writing designed to be preserved does not give an insight into the feelings, impulses, and moods of ones thoughts for which the private correspondence of great men are most valued, and sought for. What is intended to form a lustrous in our memories is written and revised with care and under the latter process it loses all its freshness and all its truth as a reflection of the mind without a fig leaf. [2]

In another letter to Deady, Jesse expresses concern about his letters being saved: "Since being the mode in which your own letters cannot well appear without those of mine calling them forth, I perceive I am likely to 'live' on in print in spite of myself. This to me is rather vexatious…"

Those of us who wish to better understand Jesse Applegate and Oregon's early history are very fortunate that those letters were not in the end thrown aside, but have lain in dusty drawers awaiting discovery.

Jesse once said, "I believe God has made the human mind capable of understanding all things, except himself." Through his letters, along with numerous secondary sources, I have come to a deeper understanding of this complex man and his impact on the history of Oregon. Come join me on this fascinating journey.

"Jesse Applegate—The Man" by Dean and Maud Deaver, reprinted in *This Was a Man*, states that "a history of Oregon without Jesse Applegate would be like an Exodus without Moses. Like Moses, he had led the pioneers through the wilderness, pockmarked on early maps as the Great American Desert. Like Moses, he was a law-giver, and, like Moses, when proper provocation occurred, he sometimes threw down the tablets."

Descendents of Daniel Applegate and Rachel Lindsey Applegate

1. Mary Applegate b. 1792, d. 1796.

2. Lydia Applegate b. 1794, d. 1810.

3. Elisha Applegate b. 1796, d. 1815.

4. Lucy Applegate b. 1798, d. 1860.

5. John Milton Applegate b. 1800, d. 1835.

6. Lisbon Applegate b. July 27, 1803, d. Jan.23, 1875.

7. Charles Applegate b. Jan. 24, 1806, d. Aug. 9, 1879.

8. Anthony Lindsay Applegate b. Sept. 18, 1808, d. Nov. 28, 1892.

9. Jesse Applegate b. July 5, 1811, d. April 22,1888.

Generation Two
Children of Jesse Applegate and
Cynthia Ann Parker Applegate

1. Rozelle Applegate b. March 30, 1832, m. Dec. 27, 1847 (Charles F. Putnam) d. May 16, 1861.

2. Edward Bates Applegate b. Nov. 1833, d. Nov. 6, 1843.

3. William Milburn Applegate b. Jan. 7, 1836, d. May, 1839.

4. Alexander McCellan Applegate b. March 11, 1838, m. Nov. 1, 1863 (Isabelle Estes) d. Feb. 1, 1902.

5. Robert Shortess Applegate b. Dec. 29, 1839, m. Dec. 5, 1858 (Melinda A. Miller) d. Oct. 17, 1893.

6. Gertrude Applegate, b. Dec. 23 1841, m. Oct 22, 1864 (James D. Fay) d. Sept. 5, 1867.

7. William Henry Harrison Applegate, b. Feb. 7, 1844, m. March 8, 1873 (Nancy Elizabeth Grubb) d. Jan. 3, 1913.

8. Daniel Webster Applegate, b. Nov. 23, 1846, m. Sept. 9, 1866 (Virginia Estes) d. March 13, 1896.

9. Sara (Sallie) Applegate, b. March 4, 1848, m. July 7, 1873 (John J. Long) d. Oct. 31, 1912.

10. Peter Skene Ogden Applegate, b. Nov. 8, 1851, m. Feb. 4, 1872 (Josephine Estes) d. Feb. 21, 1916.

11. Alenia Ellen Applegate, b. May 26, 1854, m. June 13,1870 (Martin Alexander McCall) d. Oct 5, 1921.

12. Flora Applegate, b. Feb.1857, m. Oct 18, 1874 (Henry Clay Long), d. July 22, 1916.

Generation three
Grandchildren of Jesse Applegate and Cynthia Ann Parker Applegate

Rozelle Applegate Putnam and Charles F. Putnam

1. Charles Putnam, b. Dec 10, 1848, m. Oct. 29, 1874 (Elizabeth Ann Hutchinson) d. Aug. 18, 1908.

2. Lucinda Putnam, b. Mar. 20, 1851, m. June 25, 1871 (Royce J. Delaunay) d. Oct. 26, 1874.

3. Horace Greeley Putnam, b. April 20, 1852, m. July 11, 1878 (Aurilla Marie Hedrick) d. Dec. 24, 1936.

4. Edward Putnam, b. May 7, 1854, m. July 10, 1917 (Julia Wallace) d. Dec. 23, 1936.

5. Cynthia Gertrude Putnam, b. April 1, 1856, m. July 1, 1877 (Henry Clay Hedrick) d. May 10, 1941.

6. Susan Hull Putnam, b. Feb. 14, 1858, m. July 14, 1887 (George W. Hedrick) d. March 12, 1942.

7. Joseph P. Putnam, b. Feb. 14, 1858, m. April 1883 (Angeline Bristow) d. May 12, 1918.

8. Ada Putnam, b. Feb. 29, 1860, m. April 16, 1878 (T. Benton Mires) d. July 22, 1904.

Alexander McCellan Applegate and Isabelle Estes Applegate

1. Harry Applegate, b. Oct. 16, 1865, d. April 24, 1871.

2. Winfield Scott Applegate, b. May 6, 1867, m. Oct. 1,1890,(Mignon Cawlfield) d. Sept. 16, 1843.

3. Theresa Blanche Applegate, b. June 16, 1871, d. Sept. 8, 1873.

Robert Shortess Applegate and Melinda A. Miller Applegate

1. Aaron Purcell Applegate, b. Sept. 13, 1858, d. Sept. 17, 1931.

2. William Hayhurst Applegate, b. Sept. 26, 1861, d. April 22, 1916.

3. Oscar Cromwell Applegate, b. Sept. 21, 1863, m. Feb. 18, 1894 (Matilda Peterson) d. Feb. 23, 1929.

4. Anna Laura Applegate, b. Sept. 26, 1865, m. April 26, 1900 (John McKirdy) d. Nov. 27, 1941.

5. Catherine (Kitty) Applegate, b. Dec. 29, 1867, m. May 17, 1892 Joseph Frances. Nov. 9, 1939.

6. Edna Applegate, b. Aug. 10, 1870, m. 1905(Michael Damrose) 2nd husband 1918(John Craighead), d.1951.

7. Jesse Applegate, b. Aug.21, 1873, m. Feb. 16, 1904(Isaac Ohlsen) d. April 3, 1927.

8. Ira Applegate, b. 1876, d. Dec. 4, 1930.

Gertrude Applegate Fay and James D. Fay

1. James D. Fay, b. 1865, d. Jan. 11, 1930.

William Henry Harrison Applegate and
Nancy Elizabeth Grubb Applegate

1. Henry Ernest Applegate, b. Aug. 8, 1874, d. Feb. 13, 1944.

2. Herbert Henry Applegate, b. Feb. 1876, d. Aug. 29, 1898.

3. Zoe Applegate, b. March 12, 1878, d. April 26, 1902.

4. Clarence Applegate, b. May 1880, d. 1880.

5. Walter Thayer Applegate, b. Feb 9, 1881, m. 1916(_____), d. March 3, 1943.

6. Chester A. Applegate, b. Dec 16, 1884, m. (Hazel Schafer) d. Nov. 22, 1963.

7. Roscoe Applegate, b. Feb.26, 1888, m. Oct. 19, 1910(Luella Barton) d. April 11, 1963.

Daniel Webster Applegate and Virginia Estes Applegate

1. Daniel A. Applegate, b. Jan. 28, 1868, m. April 6, 1892(Ella Amelia Cellers) d. Sept. 27, 1929.

2. Minnie Applegate, b. Feb. 2, 1870, m. Dec. 15, 1891(Lee Barker) d. Jan. 11, 1960.

3. Ralph Lore Applegate, b. abt 1872, d. Nov. 25, 1920.

4. Edwin Roy Applegate, b. July 24, 1873, m. April 6, 1892(Ella Violet Fisher) d. Oct. 2, 1943.

5. Jennie May Applegate, b. May 25, 1875, m. Jan. 5, 1898(Thomas Scott) d. July 22, 1953.

6. Chester Launcelot Applegate, b. May 22, 1878, m. May 13, 1902(Evelyn Louisa Hedrick) d. July 22, 1949.

7. Cynthia Delithe Applegate, b. Aug. 27, 1881, m 1904(Milton B. Germond).

Sarah(Sallie) Applegate Long and John J. Long

1. Mary Long, b. 1874, d. abt 1877.

Peter Skeen Ogden Applegate and Josephine Estes Applegate

1. Mark Applegate, b. 1872, m. (Sarah McClanahan) d. April 3, 1938.

2. Benton Applegate, b. 1874, d. 1874.

3. Daisy Applegate, b. 1875, m. 1899(Krofft) 3rd husband (Edgar Walter Voyle) d. 1916.

4. Karl Applegate, b. Feb.15, 1879, d. 1879.

5. Sue Applegate, b. Feb. 15, 1879, (Sutherlin) d. 1960.

6. Laura Applegate, b. 1881, d. 1881.

7. Clyde E. Applegate, b. Sept 1883, m. July 11, 1904(Della May Gillette) d. Aug. 24, 1937.

8. Jesse Carr Applegate, b. Jan. 15, 1886, m.(Lola Payne) d. Jan. 1, 1936.

9. Vernon Applegate, b. 1891, d. 1895.

10. Blanche Enid Applegate, b. July 20, 1895, m. (S.H. Isherwood) (Charles Healy) d. aft. 1962.

Alenia Ellen Applegate McCall and Martin Alexander McCall

1. Jesse Applegate McCall, b. 1871, m. Nov. 16, 1898(Lula May Throp) d. 1911.

2. Laura Adelaide McCall, b. 1873, m. Dec 9, 1891(Charles Winnings)

3. Alma McCall, b. 1875, d. March 22, 1878.

4. Guert Laurence McCall, b. May 16, 1878, m. Aug 9, 1903 (Kate Howard).

5. Violet McCall, b. 1879.

6. Stella McCall, b. May 5, 1881.

7. Muriel McCall, b. 1883.

8. Lillian McCall, b. Feb 1885.

Flora Applegate Long and Henry Clay Long

1. Henry Clay Long Jr., b. Aug. 18, 1875, d. April 23, 1933.

2. Annie Long, b. Feb. 1877, m. (Ben Bass)

3. Peter Long, b. Dec. 23, 1878, d. March 5, 1893.

4. Rachel Long, b. Nov. 20, 1880.

5. Girl child, b. 1887, d. March 16, 1888.

Jesse Applegate, a sketch drawn by his nephew George 'Buck' Applegate. (Applegate family photographs, Courtesy of Douglas County Museum.)

Cynthia Ann Parker Applegate-wife of Jesse Applegate. (Applegate family photographs, Courtesy of Douglas County Museum.)

Jesse's Forefathers

Most Applegate historians record the first Applegate in America as Thomas Applegate, who arrived from Holland at Plymouth on Boston Bay sometime before 1632. The *Early Families of Weymouth, Mass.*, published by the Genealogical Society of Baltimore, shares an interesting story about the pagan pilgrim, Thomas Morton, and his pagan Maypole celebration at Merrymount on May 1, 1627.

> The inhabitants of Merrymount … did devise amongst themselves to have … Revels, and merriment after the old English custom … & therefore brewed a barrel of excellent beer, & provided a case of bottles of excellent beer, & good cheer to all comers of that day. And upon Mayday they brought the Maypole to the place appointed … and there erected it with the help of the Savages.

Morton was arrested by the Puritans shortly after this incident and jailed. Some years later, he wrote a book, eventually published in 1883, listing some of his friends from Merrymount, and a Thomas Applegate is included among them. Perhaps this is Jesse's ancestor; if so, it would place him in America as early as 1627, possibly as early as 1624.

Records indicate that Thomas Applegate had a ferry license suspended in 1632 in the town of Braintree, Massachusetts. From this record we can begin to trace Jesse's family. The Applegate "itchy foot," which would repeatedly drive Applegates toward the new frontier, soon drove Thomas to Weymouth, Massachusetts—a forested, sparsely settled frontier area north of Plymouth.

The next Applegate in the records that is of interest to us is Thomas Applegate, great-grandson of the first Thomas and great-great grandfather of Jesse Applegate. This Thomas Applegate lived near the French Fort Duquesne (later Pittsburg) prior to the French and Indian War and served in the war under Captain Thomas Caton. Evidence suggests that Thomas may have been a teamster under Major General George Braddock before the battle of the Monongahela. A young Colonel George Washington served as an aide-de-camp, and a young Daniel Boone was a fellow teamster.[3] After the war, Thomas made at least a portion of his living as a surveyor, just as Jesse would many years later.[4]

Daniel Applegate

In order to place Jesse's life in context and to get a better feel for the man he came to be, it may be useful to look briefly at the life of Daniel Applegate, Jesse's father. Daniel was born near what would later be known as Albany, New York, in 1768. His mother, Catherine, was often left alone with her children while Daniel's father, Richard, was off fighting—first in the French and Indian War (in western Pennsylvania), and later in the Revolutionary War.

In 1778, when Daniel was just eleven, his mother died. At that time, his father and his older brothers, William and Benjamin, were all serving in the Revolutionary War. According to family history, Daniel went to live with his brother-in-law's uncle. Daniel found this Dutch farmer to be very strict and soon ran away. He headed due south towards Valley Forge, expecting to find his father or older brothers there, under the command of George Washington. Young Daniel had grown up hearing stories of his father's service under Washington in the 1750s around Fort Duquesne. Now Daniel traveled some eighty miles cross-country from Northhampton County to reach Washington's Valley Forge camp. Neither his father nor his older brothers were at the camp, but Colonel Shreeve, the commanding officer, took pity on the young lad; Daniel became his messenger boy. Alice Williams, a descendent of Jesse's sister, Lucy, states in her records that Daniel did not stay in the camp but lived in the Shreeve family home for some time. Daniel arrived at the camp unable to read, write, or do simple math, but while in the Shreeve home, he received the rudiments of schooling and soon became something of a camp mascot.

At age fourteen, Daniel enlisted as a private in the Continental Line at Battle Hill (Morris County, New Jersey) in the company of Captain Ballard of the Second Jersey Regiment, commanded by Colonel Israel Shreeve.[5] In a letter Jesse wrote in 1863 requesting a West Point appointment for his son, Dan, Jesse states that his father fought at Brandywine, Trenton, and Princeton, adding that Daniel received a bayonet wound at Monmouth Courthouse and was present at the siege of Yorktown, where he saw Cornwallis deliver up his sword.[6] Daniel's official army discharge papers of 1783 at Snake Hill mention only his presence at the siege of Yorktown, the site of Cornwallis' surrender. The discharge papers list him as a musician and flag bearer. The drum Daniel had used in the war became a family heirloom and was brought West years later by Jesse and his older brothers Charles and Lindsay. It was almost lost in a terrible mishap on the Columbia River in 1843. As the Applegate family navigated the river on the last leg of their journey to the "promise land," a raft capsized, throwing all aboard into the raging river and claiming the lives of two of the brothers' sons. Fortunately, however, the drum was saved, and it now hangs in the old Charles Applegate house in Yoncalla, Oregon.

Daniel Applegate's Revolutionary War Drum

At the end of the Revolutionary War, men were paid in land grants; therefore, many migrated to the newest frontier of the time. The Applegate family was part of this population shift. Daniel's father, Richard, went by way of the Ohio River to Kentucky, and Daniel went over the Cumberland Gap; both ended up in the Fayette County area of Kentucky. Daniel's older sister, Alletta, and her husband Peter Lanterman are also listed on the Kentucky tax rolls of 1789. Daniel took a fifty-three-acre land grant and soon married the lovely Rachel Ann Lindsay, on June 10, 1790. Rachel was the daughter of Anthony and Rachel Dorsey Lindsay, both from prominent colonial families. As the prevailing sentiment of the day in Kentucky was that a man's deeds were more important than his social background, Daniel's service in the Revolutionary War found him favor with his new in-laws.

The young couple's land was in the Buffalo Stomping Ground area of Kentucky, and all of Daniel and Rachel's children were born near there, in Woodford County. The county tax records make it seem as though the young family moved several times, but this was not, in fact, a case of the "Applegate itchy foot." In reality, as the area's population increased, the county divided three times: Woodford County became Shelby County, then Henry County. Daniel sold his first fifty-three acres in 1797 to Harry Toulmin[7] and then received one hundred acres of bounty land issued March 13, 1799.[8]

Jesse's Early Childhood

Jesse Applegate was born July 5, 1811, the youngest of Daniel and Rachel's nine children. We do not know a great deal about Jesse's early life in Kentucky. His father kept an inn at their home for a time and ran a school on the second floor of the home. It seems that Daniel did not like farming and, because he was so far from Eastern markets, found it hard to eke out a living for his family. Records indicate that he applied for a Revolutionary War pension in 1819 at the age of fifty-one while the family was still in Kentucky.[9]

After his death, Jesse's children would state that Jesse so seldom spoke of his early youth that they knew very little about that part of his life.[10] Susannah Applegate, in her unpublished manuscript about Jesse Applegate, gives some information about Jesse's family. She writes that Charles, Jesse's older brother, remembered their oldest brother Elisha as tall and strong like their father, handsome, and anxious to go off and do his patriotic duty at New Orleans with Jackson's army. Young Elisha never came home; he died of yellow fever and was buried in Baton Rouge, Louisiana.

When he was an adult, Jesse would say that he had no memory of Elisha or his older sister Lydia. However, Charles said he would never forget his mother and sister Lucy's grief when they "laid Lydia away in her wedding dress" at the tender age of eighteen. Charles, Lindsay, and Jesse all described their mother as a "gentle mother": somber and sad, "a woman of sorrows." This description cannot come as a surprise, since Rachel had endured the deaths of three of her children: first her little Mary at age four, then Elisha and Lydia just at the prime of their lives. Jesse, in his old age, also became a "man of sorrows" after the death of four of his own children: little Milton before they left Missouri, his treasured son, Edward Bates, on the Columbia River in 1843, his favorite, idolized daughter, Rozelle, at the tender age of twenty-nine, and, four years later, his rebellious daughter, Gertrude.

Charles, Lindsay, and Jesse described their father as a powerful man who was muscular and over six feet tall. He was "soldierly and exacting." Years later, Jesse's daughter, Sallie, would describe her father as very precise and exacting, perhaps a trait he learned from his father.[11]

By 1820, Kentucky was becoming too crowded for the early pioneers, so many began to look westward to the newest frontier. In 1821, Daniel moved his young family to the small French village of St. Louis, Missouri. Shortly after the move, he notified the Military Pension Board of his new address. His brother, Benjamin, who was living in Ohio, sent an affidavit to the pension board verifying that Daniel had served in the Revolution. Daniel died on February 11, 1826, with his family gathered about him. His last words were, "I am ready. Let it be so." Daniel was buried in the old St. Louis Cemetery.[12] He had been a great source of authority and wisdom for his family, and he was greatly missed.

After Daniel's death, it is unclear what became of Jesse's mother, Rachel, but family tradition holds that she went to live with her daughter, Lucy Wingfield. There is not much evidence for this, although Jesse mentions in an 1841 letter to his brother Lisbon that Lucy and her husband, James, lived in the Osage Valley; he does not mention his mother. Jesse does mention in an 1830 letter to Lisbon that, "Mamma has been very sick, and was just recovering." He then states in the same letter that he wanted to send a treat to his mother, "who has ever been treated more like a slave than a mother." In a letter written to Lindsay after the death of their older brother, Charles, in 1879, Jesse writes that in his youth, Charles and his mother were his best friends.

Daniel's sister, Alletta Lanterman, moved to Spring Creek, Illinois, in 1819. Colonel Rex Applegate in his family history *The Applegates of Oregon-Their Ancestors and Descendants* shares an interesting story told by Lindsay's son, Elisha Applegate. According to Elisha, his father, Lindsay, was allowed as a lad of about fifteen to go visit Aunt Hettie (Alletta.) During his visit, he made the acquaintance of the neighboring boys, among who was a gangly fellow called Abe. Raccoons were plentiful in the bottoms, and hunting them was a common pastime. One fine Sunday morning in the winter of 1820–21, a squad of boys and a pack of dogs gathered at Aunt Hettie's woodpile to plan a raid upon the raccoons.

"The gangly boy," two years Lindsay's senior, was there dressed in patched butternuts (overalls) and coonskin cap and bubbling over with irrepressible fun. The chatter and guffaws soon provoked Mrs. Lanterman to issue a mild rebuke: "Boys, I do not like such levity on the Lord's sacred Sabbath day." However, the hunt went on, and in due time the pack treed the coons in a big, hollow oak. The boys proceeded to smoke the coons out, and when the astonished coons poked their heads out of the tree, they looked so comical that the boys began to howl with laughter. Young Abe said with a comic, drawling gravity, "Boys, we oughtn't to have so much levity on the Sabbath day." This was Lindsay's introduction to future president Abraham Lincoln. Lindsay and Lincoln's paths would cross again when they served together in the Black Hawk War in 1832 under the command of General Whiteside.

This short history of Jesse's ancestors makes it clear that he and his brothers had the blood of many generations of pioneers flowing through their veins, calling them ever westward.

Jesse's Youth

Soon after Daniel's death, Jesse was sent to the Rock Springs Seminary in Shiloh, Illinois. Family history indicates that his brothers, Charles and Lindsay, decided that the young Jesse was exceptionally bright and deserved a chance at a better education than the one his frontier life had afforded him. They were able to earn a little extra money to help pay for Jesse's education; Charles, through his blacksmithing, and Lindsay by splitting rails. It is possible that the newly founded Rock Springs Seminary (later Shurtleff College) was chosen because Mr. Peck, its founder, was a Baptist; Jesse's mother was a lifelong member of the Baptist Church. A letter that J.M. Peck wrote in March of 1852 to General Joseph Lane, a member of Congress from Oregon, gives us the only record of Jesse's time at Rock Springs:

Sir:

Apologies take up a gentleman's time and do no good. I write to make some special inquiries about one of your constituents, Jesse Applegate, Esq., whose name I see in your communication to the President of December 12, 1851, as having done much to open up a new route for emigrants, explore the country, etc. My object is to learn what I can about his circumstances, his family, his habits, and his pursuits in life. The following brief sketch will explain my motives, and the reasons why I take the interest in his welfare. In 1827, "Rock Spring Seminary" (from which subsequently originated Shurtleff College) was opened at this spot, and Mr. Applegate, then about sixteen or seventeen years of age, one of its first pupils. It is no disparagement to him, or any American, to state he was then a poor boy, had but a single dollar in his pocket, which he paid for entrance fee, and clothing barely sufficient for the winter. His chance for education had been poor—nothing superior to a "back-woods" log-cabin and a little instruction in the elements of English common school education. He soon discovered unwearied industry, incessant application, and an inclination to learn beyond all ordinary students. One of the teachers was the late John Messenger, Esq., an old surveyor, a most expert and self-taught mathematician, & a singular, mechanical genius. He devoted extra attention to Applegate at night, and he made such proficiency that in the spring of 1828, the trustees made him a tutor, while he continued his lessons. On leaving the institution, after a period of some twelve or fifteen months, he had paid all his expenses, procured clothing, and had some $8.00 or $10.00 left for pocket money. He then taught school in the interior of St. Louis County, and pursued his mathematical studies with the late Col. Justus Post with the same untiring industry and success. After that he got a berth in the surveyor general's office in St. Louis, under Colonel McRae. Thus he arose step by step by the most singular industry, sobriety, and good conduct. He has put on his hands as skill some of the most difficult contracts surveying Missouri, and I understood that before he left Missouri he was worth perhaps $10,000. I have thus given you a mere sketch to explain why I feel no ordinary interest in the prosperity of Mr. Applegate. There are many of his associates in school who often inquire about his welfare. Will you please communicate such facts as are convenient and furnish me his post-office address? I beg leave to refer you my friends Col. W.H. Bissell and Gen. James Sheilds, from this county, for information concerning the individual who, though a stranger, presumes to address you in this manner. Respectfully yours, J.M. Peck[13]

This letter provides a good overview of Jesse's time at the school and his education, but it also shows what an impression he left on his headmaster: it was clearly not easy and yet important for Mr. Peck to boldly ask for information from an important congressman.

After Jesse left the Rock Springs Seminary, he returned to the St. Louis area and taught in a small backwoods school for a short time while continuing his math education with the help of Colonel Justus Post. Colonel Post, a prominent man in St. Louis who had trained at West Point and served in the war of 1812, was interested in engineering and encouraged the young Jesse, whom he considered a prodigy in mathematics, to continue his education with an eye to that field.

St. Louis—Years of Formation

When Jesse was not quite twenty years old, he was able, with the help of Colonel Post, to obtain a job in the office of the surveyor general of the United States in St. Louis under Colonel William McRae. Colonel McRae took to the young Jesse and treated him much like a son. Years later, Jesse wrote in a letter to Hubert H. Bancroft about McRae:

> He was a man of vast and varied information and as he kept me near his own person and was a good talker, I learned more from him in one year than College students do in three. It was from him probably I imbibed a love of truth and an ardent desire to learn it on all subjects. I boarded at the Old Green Tree Tavern and spent my evenings there or in my Master's Study as I chose.[14]

Part of Jesse's job as a junior clerk at the surveyor general's office was to gather the mail each day, and he soon became acquainted with the postmaster of St. Louis, Wilson Price Hunt. Hunt had been a former partner with John Jacob Astor's Pacific Fur Company, having actually led the company's 1811 overland expedition to Oregon. One can only guess at all the questions the inquisitive young Applegate must have asked the older man.

Fred Lockley, in a series of articles titled "Sketch of the Applegate Family" printed in the *Oregon Journal*, writes that Jesse spent a good deal of his spare time with Mr. Hunt, who delighted to tell about John Jacob Astor and about his trip to Oregon in 1811. Mr. Hunt told him about the establishment of Astoria: trading with the Indians, the beauty, fertility, and richness of the Oregon country and the great opportunities for trading and commerce in this almost unknown country on the shores of the Pacific. Jesse, in his notes to Bancroft years later, wrote, "Such intimacy as may exist between an old bachelor of fifty and an inquisitive boy of nineteen soon existed between us."[15]

Hunt kept his hand in the fur business while postmaster, using the basement of the post office as a fur warehouse. There Jesse received many lessons in natural history, not only about the furs, but also about the animal's habitat, lessons that stirred a longing to go west and see these natural wonders for himself.[16]

Hunt's brother Theodore was the recorder of land titles in St. Louis. Since Theodore was a paralytic and required assistance, he had young Applegate come to his home in the evenings to help him with his work. Years later, Jesse would state that he "was exceedingly well paid for his part." Wilson P. Hunt and his wife would frequently join the two at Theodore's home, where Wilson would regale them with his personal adventures in Oregon and Mexico. Jesse, in his notes to Bancroft, said of Mrs. Hunt: "Mrs. Hunt was the best talker I ever met... and not only I but the greatest minds of the city could listen to her by the hour with profit."[17] Mrs. Hunt was the first of several very bright women for whom Jesse expressed admiration over the course of his life; despite Jesse's professed lack of self-esteem, he seems to have been confident enough not to be intimidated by bright women.

Boarding at the Green Tree Tavern allowed Jesse to rub shoulders with several members of the American Fur Company, men like William Sublette, Jedediah Smith, and David Jackson. In the fall these mountain men came to St. Louis to settle the affairs of the past year and arrange for the coming year's expeditions. Each of these men had explored vast areas of the West, so the young, eager Jesse was able to hear the details of Smith's overland trip from St. Louis to Salt Lake, across the great desert, on to Southern California, and finally up the coast to Fort Vancouver, where he wintered in 1828–29 with Dr. John McCloughlin.

Jesse volunteered to clerk for the trappers and describes the experience thus:

> I was then handy with a pen and handier with figures, and volunteered my services to these mountain heroes, my sole reward being to hear them recount their adventures. They took me to places in the city after the work of the evening was done, where no youth ought to go, and where I never would have ventured except under their powerful protection and would have taken me to the Rocky Mountains if my kind master Colonel McRae had not forbade it.[18]

All the stories of the West began to stir a desire in the young Applegate to learn more about this vast country. He sought out all the material he could find on the frontier, and the journal of the overland trip made by Lewis and Clark in 1803–06 proved to be a wonderful resource. In about 1835, Applegate had a personal meeting with Captain William Clark, and long afterwards confesses that Clark inspired in him "a genuine enthusiasm for pioneering."[19]

Edward Bates—Friend and Mentor

While Jesse was rubbing shoulders with the mountain men, he was also keeping company with some of the most distinguished and learned men in St. Louis. One of them was Edward Bates, a former congressman, leader of the Whig Party of Missouri, and a distinguished lawyer. Bates came to St. Louis at the urging of his older brother, Frederick Bates, who was the secretary of the Missouri Territory and later governor of Missouri. Years later, Bates would become attorney general in Lincoln's first cabinet.

Edward Bates was a Virginia gentleman of the old school, with all the dignity, culture, and delicate sense of honor the phrase implies. He was a conservative Quaker with the political leanings of a Federalist, as exemplified by Washington. Like most Quakers, he was strongly opposed to slavery. Exactly how the friendship between Bates and the young Jesse came about is not clear. Family tradition holds that Jesse was a clerk in Bates' law office and that Bates gave Jesse the foundations of his broad knowledge of literature, history, general science, Latin, government, and law. This association and subsequent furthering of Jesse's education is what made him one of the best-educated men in Oregon years later. His work with Bates gave him the basic knowledge of law and an advanced knowledge of engineering that would place him in good stead in the "Oregon country."[20]

After Jesse married, he and his new bride returned to St. Louis and stayed in the grand home of Mr. Bates for several days. He told his wife Cynthia that someday he would build her a home just as grand. Tradition says that Mr. Bates told Jesse, "You could have searched the whole world over and not have found a more suitable bride than Cynthia."[21] Jesse and Cynthia named their first son Edward Bates Applegate in honor of this wonderful friend and mentor. In an address to the Oregon Historical Society, Joseph Schafer expounds on this relationship:

Bates and Applegate while differing much in mental gifts—the younger man being more brilliant and original than the elder—were so congenial that the friendship formed in this unequal manner grew stronger with the passing years and endured through life. It is said that even while under the enormous stains of his cabinet duties, during the war, Bates yearly wrote one or more letters to Applegate, and those familiar with the latter's epistolary habit are well convinced that no letter failed a response.

This was one of the ways in which the "rancher" of the Oregon frontier kept himself in touch with national politics.[22]

Mr. Bates' influence became increasingly clear in Jesse's legal knowledge and political loyalties, both of which were unusual in the Oregon territory. Bates was a strong, conservative Whig and later one of the founders of the Republican Party, and Jesse maintained a lifelong faithfulness to the Whig-Republican party, even when it put him at odds with the Democratic-controlled political scene in Oregon.

The friendship between the two men continued long after Jesse went to Oregon. Indeed, in 1861, Bates unsuccessfully attempted to have Jesse appointed as surveyor general of Oregon. In the same year, Jesse cited "our long acquaintance" in asking Bates to use his influence to keep Judge Deady on the bench.[23] In a letter to Judge Deady, also written around that time, Jesse writes the following tribute to his dear friend Mr. Bates:

> Mr. Bates is the only living man for whom I have that veneration amounting to man worship for which Napoleon first seems to inspire his soldiers. When I speak or write to him I feel the same restraint imposed by an oath, and while I am almost indifferent about the good opinion of the rest of the world, in his eyes I have the greatest desire to appear well.[24]

Jesse's years in St. Louis brought him growth in education, culture, and politics. The lifelong friendships that he made in this most formative stage of his development would shape who he was as a man. Joseph Schafer, in "Jesse Applegate, Pioneer and State Builder," maintains that the relationship with Bates is what produced Jesse's "strong, clear views on government…a passion for order…and the punctilious regard he ever showed for forms and precedents in legislative matters."

But, most important, it was in St. Louis that the seeds of Jesse's move to the Oregon country were planted and watered. We discover from a letter written thirty-five years later to Judge Deady that sometime during Jesse's time in St. Louis he applied, and was turned down, for a cadetship in a military academy. He states, "It was the only position I ever sought." His failure to obtain this post certainly seems to have changed the personal course of his life and perhaps was a key factor in his lifelong lack of self-esteem.

As a deputy surveyor, Jesse was now out and about in the countryside, which strengthened the farm boy's yearnings to leave the city and return to the land. In the autumn of 1830, he asked his brother Lisbon to buy a half-quarter of land for him in Cole County, Missouri. In this letter, he explains his desire for his own land:

> My health has been very good this summer & I at the moment feel the strength of a young Lion that wants nothing but freedom from this cage to display his energies in the chase and leap in the hills as an Antelope. Did not the bane of human life, the root of all evil, bind me to this desolate wilderness this waste made barren by human ants, I would fly at once to the bosom of my friends, and roam at large in the shady groves of the Monetean—but the will of heaven be done.[25]

In this same letter, Jesse raises some concerns peculiar to his situation. "Should I come up there a bachelor would there be any chance to get a pretty, witty, *industrious*, clean, neat, *virtuous* wife, rich or poor?" Jesse's emphases give us some insight into his priorities.

Destiny, or perhaps Jesse himself, solved the problem two months after he wrote this letter, while out on a surveying trip in southwestern Missouri, he attended a logrolling bee at the home of Mrs. English, where he met Cynthia Ann Parker, a young woman of nineteen who was working for Mrs. English. Family tradition holds that Jesse first noticed Cynthia's small, deft hands—the most capable he had ever seen. Her eyes were a merry blue, her skin was fair, and her hair was fine and golden-brown. She was a little thing, with the face of a doll. Jesse would later say that her name and face persisted in his memory so that he never wanted to be where she was not. Jesse and Cynthia were married on March 13, 1831. Jesse's older brother, Lisbon, was a judge in the Cole County Circuit Court of Missouri and had officiated at both Charles and Lindsay's marriages but, oddly enough, did not at Jesse's.[26]

Cynthia and Jesse on their wedding day

The young couple returned to St. Louis, where they lived for at least the next year while Jesse continued to work in the surveyor-general's office. Their first child, Rozelle, was born on March 30, 1832, while they were still living in the city.

Cynthia

Cynthia was born on August 15, 1813, on the Cumberland River in Northeastern Tennessee, the only daughter of Jeremiah Parker and Sallie Ann Yount (or Gauhnt.) Cynthia had six older brothers and one younger brother. Her father's business as a flatboat man involved loading a flatboat with farm produce and floating it down the Mississippi to New Orleans, where both produce and boat were sold.

Cynthia's mother, who was Pennsylvania Dutch, [German] died when Cynthia was only about seven. Her father took three of her older brothers onto the flatboat with him and sent Cynthia and her younger brother, William, to live with their mother's brother, John Yount. It seems the uncle was not pleased to have the children living with him and provided them with little education. However, Cynthia did learn to spin, weave, and do housework, all skills she would later say served her well as a pioneer wife in the remote Oregon country. When she became a teenager, she earned her food and clothes by working for the neighbors, one of whom, Mrs. English, was very fond of her and treated her much like a daughter. It was, in fact, at a logrolling bee at her home where Cynthia met the young surveyor, Jesse Applegate. Three short months later, they were married.[27]

Now that Jesse had completed his education, made many influential friends, and found his life partner, he was ready to move into a new phase of his life that would lead him ever westward.

St. Clair County Gears

Sometime in the early summer of 1832, Jesse staked a claim in St. Clair County, Missouri, within three miles of the town of Osceola. Soon his wife and new daughter joined him, along with William G. Parker, Cynthia's younger brother. Jesse's brothers, Charles and Lindsay, also had farms in the area.

St. Clair County was in the southwest part of the state, near the Kansas line. The nearby forest was filled with plenty of wild game, wild plums, persimmons, grapes, papaws, and nuts, and the rivers were teeming with fish. Jesse's land lay on the fertile bottomlands of the Osage River, and his farm soon had thriving orchards, good crops, and numerous cattle.[28] The houses of the three brothers were large, frontier dwellings made of hewed logs, each a story and a half, with a porch along one full side and a fireplace on each end.

Lindsay built a gristmill on a lovely little stream where the main road from the east crossed over his property. One day a well-dressed stranger stopped by the mill, and soon he and Lindsay were deep in conversation. Lindsay discovered that the young man, Robert Shortess, had worked in a gristmill in the East, and so he hired him to operate the new mill. Jesse enjoyed many discussions with Shortess, a well-read English scholar whose judgment was sound, and one of their favorite topics was the idea of moving west to Oregon. Early in the spring of 1839, a flood took out the mill, and so Shortess took the opportunity to join up with a party from Peoria, Illinois, headed west.

In 1841, Jesse describes life on the Osage to his brother Lisbon: "If we have not much increased in wealth on the Osage, we have certainly greatly increased in number, and upon the whole prosperous for if we gain nothing we lose little and therefore keep nearly even." In the same letter he encourages Lisbon to bring his family to visit, "it will be the most agreeable journey and a change of scenery which is at all times refreshing to the mind and body—the sight of hills lifting their heads in the grand sublimity of nature, frowning in majesty over the green valley or rushing stream will be to the inhabitant of monotonous plains a sight worth five such journeys."[29]

Five children joined the family during their time on the Osage: Edward Bates, named for Jesse's dear St. Louis friend; William Milburn, also named for one of his St. Louis mentors; Alexander McCellan, named for a faithful old friend who had healed Jesse's nephew and namesake, Jesse A. Applegate; Robert Shortess, named for the friend who had already heard the call of "west to Oregon;" and little Gertrude, who got her name because her father said she looked so "Dutch."

Difficulties for the Young Applegate Family

Jesse and Cynthia's first real heartache came in May of 1839, when three-year-old Milburn died from burns caused when his woolen garments caught fire from sparks flying from the fireplace.

Throughout Cynthia's life, she was often heard to say, "My poor, poor Milburn, my poor sweet little boy." Family history holds that the last thing she did before leaving her Osage home to head west was tend Milburn's grave one last time and beg those left behind to care for the precious spot.

The Applegate brothers all prospered on their farms and added to their holdings. Jesse had surveyed the county for the federal government and used his earnings to acquire more land. The farms around them, however, had gradually become slave-tilled plantations. Jesse's farm was large and he needed hired help, but it was becoming increasingly difficult to hire free men. Jesse was bitterly opposed to slavery, due perhaps to the influence of his Quaker friend Edward Bates, yet circumstances forced him to hire his neighbor's slaves to help with his farm.[30] Sallie Applegate Long states that her father believed that slavery was more degrading to the master than to the slave; he was therefore determined to remove his children from its influence. His discomfort with this situation helped pull him westward.[31]

Sallie Long explains in her "Traditional History of the Applegate Family" that during this time in Missouri, Jesse hired a young slave girl to help Mrs. Applegate with the housework and the children. The young girl told many tales of mistreatment by her master, and Mrs. Applegate became convinced that the only way to help the girl was to buy her papers. Jesse refused at first, but Cynthia hated slavery perhaps more than Jesse did. She had seen the degradation of her uncle's slaves and was determined to help this young girl. Finally, one day Jesse bought the bill of sale and brought it to Cynthia. They explained to the girl that she was now a free woman and they would pay her a wage for her work; before she could enjoy her freedom, the young girl died of the "summer fever." That "summer fever" was something that plagued all those who lived in the bottomlands of the Missouri and Mississippi rivers. Every summer, "the fever" (cholera, typhoid, and malaria) ran rampant in the bottomlands of Missouri, claiming the lives of many, but especially of children. Robert Shortess indicated in his letters from Oregon to Jesse and Lindsay that the "summer fever" was unheard of in Oregon; here was one more reason for a father to look westward for a healthier land for his children.

The changing political climate in Missouri was also causing problems for Jesse. Jesse, a loyal Whig and abolitionist, was greatly outnumbered by slave-holding Democrats. Years later, he would say that he was in a minority of ten out of one hundred ten. The ten Whigs had to go to the polls as a group, well armed, and early in the day "before the universal beverage had its effect." His flight to Oregon did not solve this problem; since Oregon as well was heavily Democratic, Jesse would suffer for his ever-faithful allegiance to the Whig-Republican party.[32]

It was hard for the farmers on the still-remote western frontier of Missouri to get their crops to market, and the resulting shortage of money made it difficult to buy goods and keep up with mortgage payments. Jesse blamed President Tyler and the Democrats of 1842 for what he called "evils inflicted by experiments of our rulers." He believed that the nation needed to return to its old, safe currency. The nation as a whole was struggling with a depression, and the communities on the western frontier of Missouri were feeling it more than most. Looking back on this time, Jesse writes, "There was no means of transportation West of the Mississippi except the navigable rivers the remote frontiers not having this facility were the first to feel, and most to suffer from the "hard times" and depression of the prices that preceded the Mexican War."[33]

Robert Ormond Case describes these hard times:

> In Missouri, Arkansas, Illinois, and western Kentucky, hard times were knocking at the door. Wheat brought fifteen cents a bushel. Corn could not be given away. Waiting passengers could smell riverboats approaching on the Missouri and Mississippi; they were burning bacon for fuel. Jesse Applegate sold a steamboat load of bacon that year for one hundred dollars. The curing salt alone had cost him $150. Men worked on

farms for fifty cents a day, not in cash, but in orders for goods
on merchants who were themselves bankrupt.[34]

Jesse Applegate explains the conclusion he and many others
reached during this dire time: "This state of things created much
discontent and restlessness among a people who had for many generations been nomadic, and had been taught by example of their
ancestors to seek a home in a 'new country' as a sure way of bettering
their condition."[35]

The Call of Oregon

The "Oregon Fever" growing across the land was incited by several
events. Thomas Benton and Lewis Linn, two Missouri senators, had
introduced a bill in the U.S. Congress in June of 1841 giving 640 acres
of free land per man and 160 acres per child to anyone who would
go west to the Oregon Country.[36] The bill did not pass and would be
reintroduced every session until it finally passed in 1850. The question of who would control the vast Oregon Territory—England or
the United States—had not been settled, and many understood that
a large influx of American citizens in the territory would help decide
the question in America's favor. Yet, Jesse Applegate would always
maintain that his motivation for going west was not to secure the
Oregon country for the United States, but simply to better himself. In a letter written to John Minto in 1883, Jesse states: "The
people with whom I crossed the Plains in 1843 I think as a body
were upright and moved by as pure, and high motives, as any people
that came before or followed after them to Oregon ... I do not think
a single man, woman, or child made the long and arduous journey
across the plains, to secure their ideal Oregon only to their country,
but to possess it themselves."[37]

Prospective settlers read newspaper accounts from missionaries
like Jason Lee and Marcus Whitman who sang the praises of Oregon
for its mild climate, free land, and lack of sicknesses such as malaria

and cholera. Letters from Mrs. Whitman showed that women could make the trip over the mountains and deserts to the Oregon frontier. Mary Patricia Rawe, in her essay on the Oregon Trail, says of these letters: "They influenced others until the word 'Oregon' became like a magic incantation that conjured up wealth and happiness."[38] Political leaders and newspaper editors saw it as their duty to publish material that encouraged emigration to Oregon. This could be seen in the New Orleans *Picayune* of Saturday, June 3, 1843:

THE OREGON CIRCULAR
We have received from Cincinnati a circular in
relation to the occupation of the Oregon Territory,
which we deem as important as being expressive of the views
of the West on the subject that we give it in entire:
(Circular)

"Cincinnati'
May 22, 1843
Dear Sir: It having been determined to hold a convention at this place on the third, fourth, and fifth days of July next, to urge upon congress the immediate occupation of the Oregon Territory by the arms and laws of the Republic, and to adopt such measures as may seem most conductive to its immediate and effectual occupation, whether the government acts or not in the matter; we most respectfully request your attendance at the convention or such as expression of your views on the subject as you may deem most expedient.

It will be proposed to base the action of the convention on Mr. Monroe's declaration of 1823—that the American continents are not to be considered subject to the colonization by any European powers—and that we should consider any attempt on their part to extend their systems to any portion of this hemisphere as dangerous to our peace and safety.

Very respectfully…
Oregon General Committee
of Ohio[39]

This notice was only one of many that appeared in the newspapers along the frontier, but by this time, Jesse's "itchy foot" and call to go west had already taken hold. In March of 1843, Jesse and Lindsay published in the local Missouri newspaper, the *Bonneville Herald,* their own call to raise a company to migrate to Oregon. Jesse then sent the following letter to his brother Lisbon.

St. Clair Co., Mo.
April 11th, 1843

Dear Brother:

I will start with my family to the Oregon Ty. this spring—Lindsay and perhaps Charles will go with me. This resolution has been conceived and matured in a very short time, but it is probably destiny, to which account I place it having neither time nor good reasons to offer in defense of so wild an undertaking—We are all well—and I only snatch this opportunity to write to you for the purpose of ascertaining if the same species of madness exists on your side of Mo.

If you are going to Oregon by all means go this spring for if Linn's Bill pass next year every man and every man's neighbor will move in that direction.

Write immediately—and meet us if possible at the rendezvous, armed and equipped as the journey requires.

Your affectionate Brother,

Jesse Applegate[40]

Lisbon did not answer the call to go west that spring of '43, but Charles, Lindsay, and Jesse did. Lisbon came west to California for a short time during the gold rush, but returned to Missouri in 1852 because his wife was never willing to make the move. His son, George, came west with his father and stayed to found the town of Applegate in the mountains east of Sacramento.

While western newspapers were encouraging migration and writing many glowing accounts of the "Oregon country," most eastern newspapers were consistently negative about the western migration. The best example is Horace Greeley, editor of the New York *Daily Tribune*. Greeley, in 1843, began to use his paper to promote the idea that the land in Oregon was not as valuable as many maintained and that the distance was too great for effective incorporation into the Union.[41] In July of 1843, Greeley wrote a long article in his paper condemning the large migration of emigrants that had recently left Missouri. He suggested that the whole endeavor bore "an aspect of insanity...For what, then do they brave the desert, the wilderness, the savage, the snowy precipices of the Rocky Mountains, the weary summer march, the storm-drenched bivouac, and the gnawing of famine? Only to fulfill their destiny! There is probably not one among them whose outward circumstances will be improved by this perilous pilgrimage." Greeley feared they would only wake from their "cherished delusions" when it was too late. "We do not believe nine-tenths of them will ever reach the Columbia alive."

The New York *Aurora* echoed Greeley's view of the endeavor by stating that the children of 1843 were the "tender offerings to the mad ambitions of their parents," and that not one in ten would survive.[42]

Greeley's views turned out to be overly pessimistic, but the journey west was indeed perilous, and Oregon was not always the promised land for its new settlers. Many did lose their lives on the long, slow trek west, and many more came to feel it was indeed a "cherished delusion." Yet, over the next twenty years some 55 to 60,000 made the long, hard trip over the trail to Oregon. The total number that headed west over the Oregon and California Trail is somewhere between 300,000 and 450,000. The exact number may never be known because there was no central register where people signed up for the journey west; they just packed up their wagons, joined other like-minded people and headed west.

Across the Wilderness

So it was that in the spring of 1843, the three Applegate brothers and their families, along with Cynthia's brother, William G. Parker, Jesse's niece, Harriet Wingfield Williams (the daughter of Jesse's sister Lucy), and her husband Benjamin, all prepared to leave their homes behind. They packed their wagons and prepared to go to the rendezvous point near Independence, Missouri, in late April. According to Joseph Schafer, Jesse took four wagons loaded with the family's belongings; the three brothers also brought a herd of livestock that included about 800 cattle. The wagons were packed with flour, bacon, coffee, sugar, salt, and such fruit and vegetables as were suitable for transportation.[43] Cynthia slipped in an old, brown crock full of peaches that she would use en route to bake a peach pie for Jesse's birthday on July 5, 1843.[44]

Along with foodstuffs, the wagons were packed with tools of all kinds. They would be needed on the trail and at the end of the journey to help the family build new homes and start farms. Jesse's trusty surveying instruments were carefully wrapped and placed in the wagon. Added to the cargo were a year's clothing, some household goods, and a few precious books, including a dictionary, a copy of Shakespeare, some mathematical works, *The Federalist* (which Jesse donated to the Multnomah Circulating Library at Oregon City on his arrival in 1843), several scientific works, the children's schoolbooks, and the small Bible given to Jesse by his mother. A final addition to the wagon's load was the slip of the lovely 'Gloria de Dijon' climbing rose bush.

Jesse was forced to leave behind barns full of much of the previous year's crops and a smokehouse filled with the bacon from three hundred hogs. He left this and his land in the care of a neighbor with instructions to sell the land the next spring and send the money to Oregon. The neighbor, a Mr. Story, died and Jesse then appointed his brother Lisbon as his agent for the land.[45] However, there is no evidence that Jesse ever received any money from his property in Missouri. No matter, he had turned his back on this home of his youth, the farm on the Osage. The government had not settled the question of free land, nor had the war department accomplished its desire to open a road into the vast west, but frontiersmen like Jesse would not wait. They were ready and eager to take matters into their own hands.

The wagon train of 1843 was not the result of an organized movement by any one person or group, but the combined forces of various restless and adventurous men from all parts of the country, especially from Missouri and Illinois. The word *men* is intentional, for it was the men who had made up their minds to go; their wives and children had little or no choice but to pack up and follow along. The Applegate women were more blessed than most, for they were each other's best friends; in fact, Charles and Lindsay's wives were sisters. All three would rely upon each other on this long journey into the unknown. The large family group assembled at Fitzhugh's Mill west of

Independence, Missouri, because they had heard rumors that a wagon train would leave there for Oregon as soon as the weather permitted.

The group that assembled there in the spring of 1843 tended to be western frontiersmen, most with little formal education, but well schooled in the skills they would need to survive the long trek west. There were a few with college degrees; some, like Jesse, were self-educated men. Some were strongly law-abiding, upstanding men, while others were lawless men unaccustomed to cooperation of any kind, men who would rebel against any formal structure. The cost of outfitting for the journey prevented many who might have sought free land in the West from joining that great migration. The migration of 1843 was a migration of the middle class; the wealthy had no need to go, and the poor could go only as hired help for the middle-class emigrant.

Some historians have credited Dr. Marcus Whitman with organizing what was later called the "Great Migration of '43." However, Jesse in his "Views of Oregon History," written as comments on Frances Fuller Victor's *River of the West*, states the following:

> Dr. Whitman made no stay in Missouri and arrived at Washington in March of 1843. The emigrants of that year were moving to the rendezvous in April, that they did so through the influence of Dr. Whitman is simply absurd. Dr. Whitman did not overtake my party until it reached the South Platte—his presence in my camp was the first intimation I had that he was in the States, except a few families with Daniel Waldo the whole emigration had traveled together to the crossing of the Big Blue. If Dr. Whitman had influenced any of them to migrate, they kept it to themselves. If any of them knew he was in the states and was to be our guide upon the journey they were equally reticent—there could be no motive to keep such a thing secret, so I conclude the mass of emigrants were as innocent of knowing his whereabouts as myself... Dr. Whitman was an ardent and sincere Christian not on the outside only, but in every impulse of his heart—in

every thought of his brain. As a missionary, he had undertaken to civilize and Christianize a tribe of savages, and his
whole soul was enlisted in the work...He talked with me
many times on the journey...He was a true patriot and as
ardent in his wishes to see Oregon secured to the U.S. as any
American in it. Nevertheless, he did not attach any special
importance to his own visit to Washington as having any
weight in bringing about the event.

From the time he joined us on the Platte until he left us at
Fort Hall, his great experience and indomitable energy were of
priceless value to the emigrating column. His constant advice,
which we knew was based upon his knowledge of the road was
travel, travel, TRAVEL—nothing else will take you to the end
of your journey, nothing is wise that does not help you along,
nothing is good for you that causes a moment's delay.[46]

Dr. Whitman was not given money or supplies by the American
Board of Commissioners for Foreign Mission to help cover the
expenses of his journey back to the Oregon country. He left the
Missouri border country with little in the way of provisions for his
return journey. Once he joined up with the train on the Platte, Jesse
would invite him to join the family encampment each evening. Thus,
while the good doctor was assured the aid and protection of the emigrants, he in turn gave sound, knowledgeable advice and medical
assistance to the emigrants of '43.

James Nesmith, in his diary of 1843, states that the Oregon
Company met at Fitzhugh's Mill for an organization meeting on
Thursday, May 18, 1843. Mr. Layson was the chair and Peter Burnett
the secretary. A committee of nine was appointed to draft rules and
regulations to govern the company, and a committee of seven was
appointed to inspect the outfits of individuals to see if they were
sufficient for the journey ahead.

An excerpt of the rules drawn up by the committee follows. They
are brief and to the point:

The following are the rules and regulations for the government of the Oregon Emigrating Company:

RESOLVED, Whereas we deem it necessary for the government of all societies, either civil or military, to adopt certain rules and regulations for their government, for the purpose of keeping good order and promoting civil and military discipline. In order to insure union and safety, we deem it necessary to adopt the following rules and regulations for the government of the said company:

Rule 1. Every male person of the age of sixteen or upward, shall be considered a legal voter in all affairs relating to the company.

Rule 2. There shall be nine men elected by the majority of the company, who ... shall ... settle all disputes arising between individuals and to try and pass sentences on all persons for any act for which they may be guilty, which in subversive of good order and military discipline ... A majority of two-thirds of the council shall decide all questions that may come before them.

Rule 3. There shall be a captain elected who shall have supreme military command of the company. It shall be the duty of the captain to maintain good order and strict discipline, and as far as practicable, to enforce all rules and regulations adopted by the company....

Rule 4. There shall be an orderly sergeant elected by the company, whose duty it shall be to keep a regular roll, arranged in alphabetical order, of every person subject to guard duty in the company; and shall make out his guard details by commencing at the top of the roll and proceeding to the bottom, thus giving every man an equal tour of guard duty ...

Rule 5. The captain, orderly sergeant, and members of the council shall hold their offices at the pleasure of the company....

Rule 6. The election of officers shall not take place until the company meets at the Kansas River.

Rule 7. No family shall be allowed to take more than three loose cattle to every male member of the family of the age of sixteen or upward.[47]

This last rule did not please the Applegate brothers since they had several hundred head of loose stock between them that they had planned to take to the Oregon country. Although others in the company had loose stock, the Applegates probably had the most. It is unclear just what transpired concerning this rule, but we do know that the Applegate brothers started west with their cattle.

The Journey Begins

Peter Burnett shares in "Recollections of an Old Pioneer" that Captain John Gantt was secured to pilot the emigrants as far as Fort Hall. The spring of 1843 had been very late; the ice on the Missouri River was still breaking up as late as April 11, and it was therefore assumed that the grass would be too short to support the stock. On the beautiful clear morning of May 22, the wagons, dressed in their new white covers, began their slow, undulating westward trek on this epic journey. Most of those hardy souls would never again see their homelands or the "states."[48]

Thirty-three years later Jesse Applegate summarizes the journey in the following words:

> The migration of a large body of men, women, and children across the continent to Oregon was, in the year of 1843, strictly an experiment; not only in respect to the members, but to the outfit of the migrating party...The migrating body numbered over one thousand souls, with about one hundred twenty wagons, drawn by six-ox teams, averaging about six yoke to the team and several thousand loose horses and cattle...[49]
>
> No other race of men with the means at their command would undertake so great a journey, none save these could

successfully perform it, with no previous preparation, relying only on the fertility of their own invention to devise the means to overcome each danger and difficulty as it arose.[50]

Peter Burnett was elected captain of the wagon train and James W. Nesmith orderly sergeant. Nesmith recorded in his diary 254 men of age to do guard duty and 111 wagons. In his address to the Oregon Pioneer Association in 1876, Jesse claimed there were 120 wagons.

The migration started out with good weather; the trail was in good condition and all were in fine spirits. At last they were beginning the journey that had occupied their every waking thought for months. A letter by Peter Burnett printed in the *New York Herald* describes the following: "Our usual mode of encampment was to form a hollow square with the wagons ... of camping on a level prairie, dry and beautiful. In the night, a huge thunderstorm with torrents of rain came upon the camp. Half the tents blew down and nearly all were wet in the morning." [51]

Charles Applegate wrote a short account of the trip west some thirty-three years later, adding some detail to the description above.

It was late in the evening when we campt on a prairie. After nite there came one of the most tremdous horrifying thunder storms I ever saw. The rain came down in torents the wind upset the wagons and tents. There was no intermission in the flash of lightning. A continual crash and roar of thunder in fact it looked like the hole thing was going back to its original caus ... when the world was a void and without form. We had a coral with our wagons put work cattle inside and when the storm came on the cattle went perfectly crazy. Broke through the coral in every direction, breaking wagon tongues, upsetting wagons making a mash of everything. There was nobody killed or badly hurt in the morning. There were no cattle to be seen in any direction. A party took the trail of the cattle and proceeded getting all of them but they had rambled for miles a way. The men was all day collecting them.[52]

Jesse Takes the Lead

This was one of several events that led to discontent among the settlers without loose cattle. By June 7, dissention and grumbling accelerated among the emigrants. They had by now reached buffalo country and many wanted to do nothing but go out "on the hunt." Those who did not own loose livestock resented being required to do night guard duty. They also felt that the large numbers of loose stock were slowing the train down, and so Jesse Applegate and his friends came under severe criticism. There were attempts to resolve the issue, but in the end, Peter Burnett resigned as captain and the train was divided into a "light column" captained by William Martin and a slow column, or "cow column," captained by Jesse Applegate.[53] Now Jesse would have the responsibility to determine each day's route, each night's camping places, the order of march, and the enforcement of all regulations. Years later, Charles would remember Jesse saying, "If you make me Captain I will be your Captain. You will need to elect a court composed of three men. The court will settle all disputes and their decision will be final without interference from me or any other man. Any man that wants to leave the company is free to do so. But any man that rebels against the decision of the court can expect no protection from the company."[54]

The Applegate brothers owned the most loose stock, so it was logical that one of them would be elected captain of the "cow column." What is less clear is why Jesse was chosen. He was the youngest of the three brothers at only thirty-two, but the westerners on the journey instinctively recognized Jesse as a leader. He was well suited to the frontier life, as he had spent his entire life on one frontier or another. He was over six feet tall, strong, and a man of great endurance: he could walk sixty miles in a day, get up, and do it again the next day. He knew more about the country they would be traveling over than most because of his associations in St. Louis with men like Jedediah Smith, William Sublette, and Wilson Price Hunt. He had spent a good deal of his youth wandering the wilderness of Missouri as a surveyor. James

Nesmith would say of Jesse years later: "…more by his silence that by what he said [he] gave character to our proceedings. As a frontiersman in courage, sagacity, and natural intelligence he is the equal of Daniel Boone. No man did more upon the rout[e] to aid the destitute and encourage the weak. He divided his rations with the same reckless liberality with which he signed the bonds of those who have victimized and reduced him to poverty in his old age."[55]

Jesse numbered and marked all wagons and gave instructions that they would change places every day so that every wagon would take the lead and do its share in breaking the trail. If he was to be the leader, he would take the lead in all matters that benefited the emigrants: determining the campsites, fighting Indians, sending out hunting parties, and any other matter that might arise.

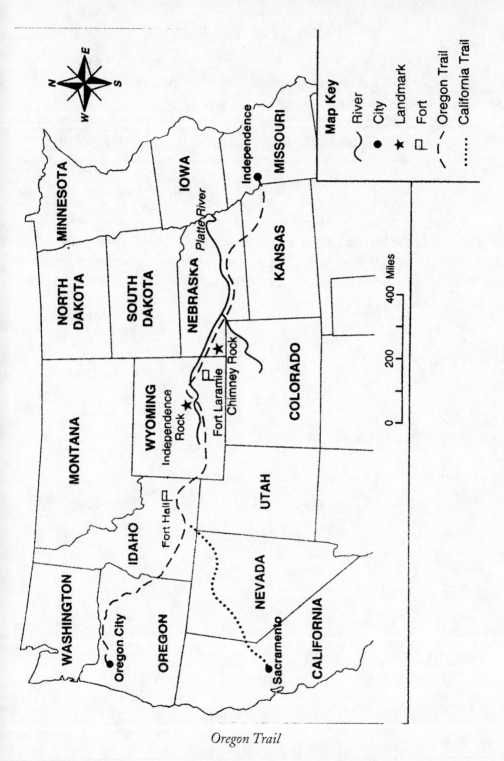

Oregon Trail

The following portion of a letter in the *Iowa Territorial Gazette* of June 10, 1843 describes the division of the company:

> We are now some two or three hundred miles west of Independence on the Blue rivers, tributaries of the Kansas, in good health and spirits. I regret to say that a division has taken place in the company in consequence of the number of cattle driven by some, those having no cattle refusing to stand guard at night over stock belonging to others. The result of all this was, that Capt. Burnett resigned the command of the company—Almost 50 wagons, those who had large droves of loose cattle, now left, with a general request that all in favor with them should fall back.

Much has been written about the overland journey of 1843, but a few details about the Applegates and the "cow column" are in order, and the best person to share these details would be Jesse himself. Jesse's "A Day with the Cow Column" was originally prepared as an address to the Oregon Pioneer Association in 1876 and later published in the *Overland Monthly* magazine. Professor Joseph Schafer pronounces it "a most intimate and delightful account of a typical day on the dreary overland march."

A Day with the Cow Column
in 1843
By Jesse Applegate

The migration of a large body of men, women, and children across the continent to Oregon was, in the year 1843, strictly an experiment not only in respect to the numbers, but to the outfitting of the migrating party.

Before that date, two or three missionaries had performed the journey on horseback, driving a few cows with them. Three or four wagons drawn by oxen had reached Fort Hall on the Snake River, but it was the honest opinion of most of those who had traveled the route down the Snake River that no large number of cattle could be subsisted on its scanty pasturage, or wagons taken over a route so rugged and mountainous.

The emigrants also were assured that the Sioux would be much opposed to the passage of so large a body through their country, and would probably resist it on account of the emigrants destroying and frightening away the buffalos, which were then in diminishing numbers.

The migrating body numbered over one thousand souls, with about one hundred and twenty wagons, drawn by six-ox teams, averaging about six yokes to the team, and several thousand loose horses and cattle.

The emigrants first organized and attempted to travel in one body, but it was soon found that no progress could be made with a body so cumbrous, and as yet so adverse to all discipline. And at the crossing of the "Big Blue" it divided into two columns, which traveled in supporting distance of each other as far as Independence Rock on the Sweet Water.

From this point, all danger from Indians being over, the emigrants separated into small parties better suited to the narrow mountain paths and small pastures in their front. Before the division on the Blue River there was some just cause for discontent in respect to loose cattle. Some of the emigrants had only their teams, while others had large herds in addition which must share the pasture and be guarded and driven by the entire body.

This discontent had its effect in the division on the Blue. Those not encumbered with or having but few loose cattle attached themselves to the light column; those having more than four or five cows had of necessity to join the heavy or cow column. Hence the cow column, being larger than the other and encumbered with its large herd, had to use greater exertion and observe a more rigid discipline to keep pace with the more agile consort.

It is with the cow or more clumsy column that I propose to journey with the reader for a single day.

MORNING

It is four o'clock a.m. The sentinels on duty have discharged their rifles—the signals that the hours of sleep are over. Every wagon and tent is pouring forth its night tenants. The slow-kindling smokes begin largely to rise and float away on the morning air. Sixty men start from the corral—spreading as they make their way through the vast heard of cattle and horses that form a semi-circle around the encampment, the most distant perhaps two miles away.

The herders pass to the extreme verge and carefully examine for trails beyond to see that none of the animals have strayed or been stolen during the night. This morning no trails lead beyond the farthest animals in sight, and by five o'clock the herders begin to contract the great moving circle and the well-trained animals move slowly toward the camp, clipping here and there a thistle or tempting bunch of grass on the way. In about an hour five thousand animals are close up to the encampment, and the teamsters are busy selecting their teams and driving them inside the corral to be yoked. The corral is a circle one hundred yards deep, formed with wagons connected with each other; the wagon to the rear being connected with the wagon in front by tongue and ox chains. It is a strong barrier that the most vicious ox cannot break, and in case of an attack of the Sioux would be no contemptible entrenchment.

From six to seven o'clock is a busy time. Breakfast is to be eaten, the tents struck, and the teams yoked and brought up in readiness to be attached to their respective wagons. All know when, at seven o'clock, the signal to march sounds, that those not ready to take their proper places in the line of march must fall into the dusty rear for the day.

There are sixty wagons. They have been divided into fifteen divisions or platoons of four wagons each, and each platoon is entitled to lead in its turn. The leading platoon of today will be the rear one of tomorrow, unless some teamster, through indolence or negligence, has lost his place in line and is condemned to that uncomfortable post. It is within ten minutes of seven. The corral before now a strong barricade is everywhere broken, the teams being attached to the wagons. The women have taken their places in them. The pilot (a borderer who has passed his life on the verge of civilization and has been chosen to the post of leader from his knowledge of the savage and his experience in travel through roadless wastes) stands ready in the midst of his pioneers and aids to mount and lead the way.

Ten or fifteen young men, not today on duty, form another cluster. They are ready to start on a buffalo hunt, are well mounted and well armed, as they need to be, for the unfriendly Sioux have driven the buffalo out of the Platte, and the hunters must ride fifteen to twenty miles to reach them. The cow-drivers are hastening, as they get ready, to the rear of their charge to collect and prepare them for the day's march.

It is on the stroke of seven; the rushing to and fro, the cracking of whips, the loud commands to oxen, and what seemed to be the inextricable confusion of the last ten minutes has ceased. Fortunately everyone has been found and every teamster is at his post. The clear notes of a trumpet sound in the front; the Pilot and his guards mount their horses. The leading division of wagons moves out of the encampment and takes up the line of march, the rest fall into their places with the precision of clockwork, until the spot so lately full of life sinks back into the solitude that seems to reign over the broad plain and rushing river as the caravan draws its lazy length toward the distant El Dorado.

It is with the hunters we will briskly canter toward the bold but smooth and grassy bluffs that bound the broad valley, for we are not yet in sight of the grander but less beautiful scenery of the Chimney Rock, Court House and other bluffs so nearly resembling giant castles and places made by the passage of the Platte through the Highlands near Laramie. We have been traveling briskly for more than an hour. We have reached the top of the bluff, and now have turned to view the wonderful panorama spread before us. To those who have never been on the Platte, my powers of description are wholly inadequate to convey an idea of the vast extent and grandeur of the picture, and the rare beauty and distinctness of its detail.

No haze or fog obscures objects in the pure and transparent atmosphere of this lofty region. To those accustomed only to the murky air of the seaboard, no correct judgment of distance can be formed by sight, and objects which they think they can reach in a two hour's walk may be a day's travel away. And though the evening air is better conductor of sound, on the high plains during the day the report of the loudest rifle sounds little louder than the bursting of a cap; and while the report can be heard for but a few hundred yards, the smoke from the discharge may be seen for miles.

So extended is the view from the bluff on which the hunters stand, that the broad river glowing under the morning sun like a sheet of silver, and the broader emerald valley that borders it, stretch away in the distance until they narrow at two points in the horizon. And when first seen, the vast pile of the Wind River Mountains, though hundreds of mile away, looks clear and distinct as a white cottage on the plain.

We are six miles away from the line of march. Everything is dwarfed by distance, but it is seen distinctly. The caravan has been about two hours in motion and is now extended as widely as prudent safety permits.

First, near the bank of the shining river, is a company of horsemen. They seem to have found an obstruction, for the main body has halted, while three or four ride rapidly along the bank of the creek or slough. They are hunting a favorable crossing for the wagons. While we look, they have succeeded. It apparently required no work to make it passable, for all but one of the party has passed on, and he has raised a flag, no doubt a signal to the wagons to steer their course to where he stands. The leading teamster sees him, though he is yet two miles off, and steers his course directly toward him, all the wagons following in his track. The wagons form a line three quarters of a mile in length. Some of the teamsters ride upon the front of their wagons, some march beside their teams. Scattered along the line, companies of women and children are taking exercise on foot. They gather bouquets of rare and beautiful flowers that line the way. Near them stalks a stately greyhound or an Irish wolf dog, apparently proud of keeping watch and ward over the master's wife and children.

Next comes a band of horses. Two or three men or boys follow them, the docile and sagacious animals scarce needing this attention, for they have learned to follow to the rear of the wagons, and know that at noon they will be allowed to graze and rest. Their knowledge of the time seems as accurate as of the place they are to occupy in the line, and even a full-blown thistle will scarcely tempt them to straggle or halt until the dinner hour has arrived. Not so with the great herd of horned beasts that brings up the rear. Lazy, selfish and unsocial, it has been a task to get them back in action. The strong, always ready to domineer over the weak, halt in front and forbid the weaker to pass. They seem to move only in fear of the driver's whip; though in the morning, full to repletion, they have not been driven an hour before their hunger and thirst seem to indicate a fast of day's duration. Through all the day their greed is never sated nor their thirst quenched, nor is there a moment of relaxation of the tedious and vexatious labors of their drivers, although to all others the march furnishes some season of relaxation or enjoyment. For the cow-driver there is none.

But from the standpoint of the hunters the vexation are not apparent. The crack of whips and loud abjurations [sic] are lost in the distance. Nothing of the moving panorama, smooth and orderly as it appears, has more attractions for the eye than the vast square column in which all colors are mingled, moving here slowly and there briskly, as impelled by horsemen riding furious in front and rear.

But the picture in its grandeur; its wonderful mingling of colors and distinctness of detail, is forgotten in contemplation of the singular people who give it life and animation. No other race of men with means at their command would have undertaken so great a journey. None save these could successfully perform it, with no previous preparation, relying only on the fertility of their invention to devise means to overcome each danger and difficulty as it arises.

They have undertaken to perform, with slow-moving oxen, a journey of 2000 miles. The way lies over trackless wastes, wide and deep rivers, rugged and lofty mountains, and is beset with hostile savages. Yet, whether it is a deep river with no tree upon its banks, a rugged defile where even a loose horse could not pass, a hill too steep for him to climb, or a threatened attack of an enemy, they are found ready and equal to the occasion, and always conquer. May we not call them men of destiny? They are people changed in no essential particulars from their ancestors, who have followed closely the footsteps of the receding savage, from the Atlantic Seaboard to the great valley of the Mississippi.

But while we have been gazing at the picture in the valley, the hunters have been examining the high plain in other directions. Some dark moving objects have been discovered in the distance, and all are closely watching them to discover what they are. For in the atmosphere of the plains a flock of crows marching miles away, or a band of buffaloes or Indians ten times the distance look alike and ludicrous mistakes occur. But these are buffaloes. For two have struck their heads together and are, alternately, pushing each other back. The hunters mount and away in pursuit and I, a poor cow-driver, must hurry back to my daily toil, and take a scolding from my fellow herders for so long playing truant.

NOON

The Pilot, by measuring the ground and timing the speed of the wagons and the walk of his horse has determined the rate of each, so as to select the nooning place, as nearly as the requisite grass and water can be had at the end of five hours' travel of the wagons. Today, the ground being favorable, little time has been lost in preparing the road. He and his pioneers are at the nooning place and hour in advance of the wagons, which time is spent in preparing convenient watering places for the animals and digging little wells near the bank of the Platte. As the teams are not unyoked, but simply turned loose from the wagons, a corral is not formed at noon, but the wagons are drawn up in columns, four abreast, the leading wagon of each platoon on the left—the platoons being formed with that view. This brings friends together at noon as well as at night.

Today an extra session of the Council is being held, to settle a dispute that does not admit of delay between a proprietor and a young man who has undertaken to do a man's service on the journey for bed and board. Many such engagements exist and much interest is taken in the manner this high court, from which there is no appeal, will define the rights of each party in such engagements. The Council was a high court in the most exalted sense. It was a Senate composed of the ablest and most respected fathers of the emigration. It exercised both legislative and judicial powers and its laws and decisions proved it worthy and equal [to] the high trust reposed in it.

Its sessions were usually held on days when the caravan was not moving. It first took the state of the little commonwealth into consideration; revised or repealed rules defective or obsolete, and exacted such others as the exigencies seemed to require. The commonwealth being cared for, it next resolved itself into a court to hear and settle private disputes and grievances. The offender and the aggrieved appeared before it. Witnesses were examined and the parties were heard by themselves and sometimes by counsel. The judges thus being familiar with the case, and being in no way cramped or influenced by technicalities, decided all cases according to their merits. There was but little use for lawyers before such a court, for no plea was entertained which was calculated to hinder or defeat the ends of justice. Many of these judges have since won honors in higher spheres. They have aided to establish on the broad basis of right and universal liberty two of the pillars of our great Republic in the Occident. Some of the young men who appeared before them as advocates have themselves sat upon the highest tribunals, commanded armies, been Governors of States, and taken high positions in the Senate of the nation.

AFTERNOON

It is now 1 o'clock; the bugle has sounded, and the caravan has resumed its westward journey. It is in the same order, but the evening is far less animated than the morning march; drowsiness has fallen apparently on men and beast. Teamsters drop asleep at their perches, and even when walking by their teams—and the words of command are now addressed to the slowly creeping oxen in the softened tenor of women or the piping treble of children, while the snores of the teamsters make a droning accompaniment.

But a little incident breaks the monotony of the march. An emigrant's wife whose state of health has caused Dr. Whitman to travel near the wagon for the day is now taken with violent illness. The doctor has had the wagon driven out of the line, a tent pitched and a fire kindled. Many conjectures are hazarded in regard to this mysterious proceeding and as to why this lone wagon is to be left behind.

NIGHT

And we too must leave it, hasten to the front, and note the proceedings, for the sun is now getting low in the West. At length the painstaking Pilot is standing ready to conduct the train into the circle which he has previously measured and marked out, which is to form the invariable fortification for the night. The leading wagons follow him so nearly around the circle that but a wagon length separates them. Each wagon follows in its track, the rest closing on the front, until its tongue and ox-chains will perfectly reach from one to the other. And so accurate are the measurements, and perfect the practice that the hindmost wagon is brought into position. It is dropped from its team, the teams unyoked, and the yokes and chains used to connect the wagon strongly with that in its front. Within ten minutes from the time the leading wagon halted, the barricade is formed, the teams unyoked and driven out to pasture.

Everyone is busy preparing fires of buffalo chips to cook the evening meal, pitching tents and otherwise preparing for the night. There are anxious watchers for the absent wagon, for there are many matrons who may be afflicted like its inmate before the journey is over; and they fear the strange and startling practice of this Oregon doctor will be dangerous. But as the sun goes down, the absent wagon rolls into camp, the bright, sparkling face and cheery look of the doctor, who rides in advance, declare without words that all is well and mother and child are comfortable.

I would fain now and here pay a tribute to that noble and devoted man, Dr. Whitman. I will obtrude no other name upon the reader, nor would I his, were he of our party or even living. But his stay with us was transient, though the good he did was permanent, and he has long since died at his post.

From the time he joined us on the Platte until he left us at Fort Hall, his great experience and indomitable energy were of priceless value to the migrating column. His constant advice, which we knew was based on knowledge of the road before us, was—"travel, travel, TRAVEL! Nothing else will take you to the end of your journey; nothing is wise that does not help you along. Nothing is good that causes a moment's delay." His great authority as a physician and complete success in the case above referred to saved us from many prolonged and perhaps ruinous delays from similar causes. And it is no disparagement to others to say to no other individual are the emigrants of 1843 so much indebted for the successful conclusion of their journey as to Dr. Marcus Whitman.

All able to bear arms in the party have been formed into three companies, and each of these into four watches. Every third night it is the duty of one of these companies to keep watch and ward over the camp, and it is so arranged that each watch takes its turn of guard duty through the different watches of the night. Those forming the first watch tonight will next be second on duty, then third and forth, which brings them through all the watches of the night. They began at eight o'clock p.m. and end at four o'clock a.m.

It is not yet eight o'clock, when the first watch is to be set. The evening meal is just over, and the corral now free from the intrusion of cattle or horses. Groups of children are scattered over it. The larger are taking part in a game of romps. The "wee toddling things" are being taught that great achievement that distinguishes man from the lower animals. Before a tent near the river a violin makes lively music, and some youths and maidens have improvised a dance upon the green; in another quarter a flute gives its mellow and melancholy notes to the still night air; which, as they float away over the quiet river, seem a lament for the past rather than a hope for the future.

It has been a prosperous day. More than twenty miles have been accomplished of the great journey. The encampment is a good one. One of the causes that threatened much future delay has just been removed by the skill and energy of the "good angel" of the emigrants, Dr. Whitman, and it has lifted a load from the hearts of the elders. Many of these are assembled around the good Doctor at the tent of the Pilot (which is his home for the time being) and are giving grave attention to his wise and energetic counsel. The care-worn Pilot sits aloof, quietly smoking his pipe, for he knows the brave Doctor is "strengthening his hands."

But time passes; the watch is set for the night, the council of old men has broken up, and each has returned to his own quarter. The flute has whispered its last lament to the deepening night. The violin is silent, and the dancers have dispersed. Enamored youth have whispered a tender "good night" in the ear of the blushing maiden, or stolen a kiss from the lips of some future bride—for Cupid, here as elsewhere, has been busy bringing together congenial hearts, and among these simple people he alone is consulted in forming the marriage tie. Even the Doctor and the pilot have finished their confidential interview and have separated for the night. All is hushed and repose, from the fatigues of the day, save the vigilant guard and the wakeful leader who still has cares upon his mind that forbid sleep.

He hears the ten o'clock relief taking post, and the "all well' report of the returned guard; the night deepens, yet he seeks not repose. At length a sentinel hurries to him with the welcome report that a party is approaching—as yet too far away for its character to be determined, and he instantly hurries out in the direction seen. This he does both from inclination and duty, for in times past the camp had been unnecessarily alarmed by timid or inexperienced sentinels, causing much confusion and fright amongst the women and children, and it had been made a rule that all extraordinary incidents of the night should be reported directly to the pilot, who alone had the authority to call out the military strength of the column, or so much of it as was in his judgment necessary to prevent a stampede or repel an enemy.

Tonight he is at no loss to determine that the approaching party is our missing hunters, and they have met with success, and he only waits until by some further signal he can know that no ill has happened to them. This is not long wanting. He does not even wait their arrival, but the last care of the day being removed, and the last duty performed, he too seeks the rest that will enable him to go through the same routine tomorrow. But here I leave him, for my task is also done, and unlike his, it is to be repeated no more.[56]

This essay clearly shows why Jesse succeeded as a captain for the 1843 wagon train. He was well organized, had a system in place to address all issues that might arise, and was deeply involved with his charges. He still held the job of captain of the "cow column" when they reached the end of their journey. Schafer remarks:

It is a trite but true remark among far west pioneers that no severer test of a man's fitness for leadership was ever devised than the captaincy of an Oregon or California emigrating company; and it is the universal testimony of the 1843 immigrants that Applegate more than met the requirements of the exacting office. By his accurate knowledge of the difficulties to be encountered, his resourcefulness in overcoming them, his tact and courage, his commanding personality, and with the kind, helpful spirit he always manifested, he not only held the uniform respect of all these staunch frontiersmen but won their loyal affection.[57]

Jesse Applegate was a born leader and he clearly proved this as wagon master for the "cow column." Separating the slow moving wagons from those less encumbered by loose stock reduced friction, but there would always be a few ruffled feathers in a group as independent as these western frontiersmen. No one forced these people to go west, and no one could force them to conform to rules or personalities they did not agree with on a given day.

Peter Burnett, in his "Recollections," shares an amusing story about the greyhound mentioned in Jesse's "Day with the Cow Column." The greyhound, named Fleet, belonged to Lindsay, who was very proud of the animal. It seems that an antelope appeared on the trail one day about a half mile off to the right, approaching at a right angle. Fleet noticed and ran to meet it, regulating his pace to intercept the antelope at the point where it crossed the road. Since the antelope was focused on the train, it did not see the greyhound until the latter was within twenty feet. Then the race began, each animal running at his utmost speed. The greyhound was able to give chase for only about a quarter of a mile; he seemed astonished that another animal could outrun him. Whenever Lindsay told the story, he would exclaim, "The antelope ran a mile before you could see the dust rise." Fleet never again chased an antelope.[58]

While the caravan was crossing the open prairie, Jesse advised the members of his column to pick up driftwood whenever they happened upon it during the day, but sometimes they were forced to burn dried buffalo chips in place of wood. Matches were precious, and the wind on the prairie proved tiresome, but the pioneers soon discovered that cooking could be nicely managed over a trench six inches wide, ten inches deep, and about twenty-four inches long.

Once the company had divided, the light column was usually in the lead, but the two columns were often in sight of each other, and rarely were they more than four or five miles from each other. However, James W. Nesmith notes in his journal several times when Applegate's company was in the lead: "Saturday, June 17…Mr.

Applegate's company passed us in the evening. Sergeant Ford on guard July 1...Captain Applegate and Dr. Whitman came into camp this evening, their company camped eight mile below this place. Friday, July 14—Arrived at Fort Laramie about 10:00 o'clock where we found Childs and Applegate's company. July 16 ... Camped with Childs. Applegate's company having gone ahead."[59]

Jesse's company left Ft. Laramie ahead of the light column. A few miles west of the fort, the first death of the trip occurred: Joel Hembree, six-year-old son of Joel J. Hembree, was killed when a wagon ran over him. A note marking the grave was left for those following.[60]

At the crossing of the Platte River near Red Buttes the cow column crossed ahead of the main company because a number of men in the main company were sick. Nesmith's diary reveals that it was more than just a physical illness:

> The company discontented and strong symptoms of mutiny.
> Some anxious to travel faster, some slower, some want to cross
> the river here, some want to go ahead, and others want to go
> any way but the right way. This will always be the difficulty
> with heterogeneous masses of emigrants crossing these plains.
> While every man's will is his law, and lets him act or do as
> he pleases, he will always find friends to support him.... They
> have the elements of destruction within themselves.[61]

Captain Applegate and his column camped under the famous landmark, Independence Rock, late in July, perhaps the twenty-eighth. Some of the members of the company indulged in the favorite pastime of those who passed by the Rock: after mixing together a paint from gunpowder, tar, and bear grease, they climbed as high as they dared and painted their names on the face of that landmark.[62]

On the fifth, sixth, and seventh of August, Captain Applegate led his column past the headwaters of the Sweet Water and up the long, gradual slope of the Continental Divide. The emigrants had reached the Oregon country, but were a long way from the end of their journey.[63]

Perils of the Oregon Country

The "cow column" arrived on August 27 at Fort Hall, where the weary emigrants rested for several days while repairs were made on equipment and supplies were secured from the fort. Fort Hall at this time was a Hudson's Bay trading post. Captain Richard Grant, the officer in charge of the post, advised the emigrants that they should either turn aside towards California with their wagons or leave them with him and go on to the Columbia on horseback. Sixteen men did decide to go on to California, with John Gantt, the hired scout, among them. Gantt insisted it was madness to try to take the wagons on to Oregon from this point. According to Nesmith, "part of the company went on with pack animals leaving their wagons behind."

One can only speculate how different the history of Oregon might have been if the pioneers had chosen to believe Grant and Gantt and leave their wagons behind, but it is doubtful that many families would have ventured on such a long and perilous journey without hope of arriving with their wagons and possessions intact. Dr. Whitman had taken a wagon reduced to a cart as far west as Fort Boise, and he believed that wagons could make the entire trip. It was his knowledge of the road ahead that persuaded most of the emigrants to proceed with their wagons.

From Fort Hall on, Jesse was out in advance of the wagon train with his compass each day, determining the route to be taken at certain critical points as they moved forward across the Snake River into the Burnt River Canyon. This is the first time the emigrants had to double team to move the wagons. Sarah Jane Hill shared, years later, that it took eight or nine yoke of oxen to pull each wagon over the steep hills. At other times several men would attach ropes to the wagons and slowly lower the wagons to keep them from tipping over.[64]

When the emigrants arrived in the Powder River Valley they began to see the 'Eden' of Oregon they had been looking forward to with each weary mile of the journey. The next valley, Grande Rhonde Valley, Peter Burnett described as, "One of the most beautiful valleys in the world, embosomed among the Blue Mountains, which are covered with magnificent pines." [65]

Dr. Whitman helped guide the wagons as far as the Grande Ronde Valley at the eastern foot of the Blue Mountains. There he received a message that two of his fellow missionaries, Reverend and Mrs. Spalding, were gravely ill, and he felt it was his duty as a doctor to hurry on to their aid. In his stead, a trusted Indian convert from the mission named Stickus helped the company on their way.

Peter Burnett would describe the Blue Mountains as "terrible hills," and Ninevah Ford shared that they often moved such a short distance in a day that they could see the former night's camp. "We found it very laborious and very hard cutting that Tamarisk timber with our dull axes that we had not ground since we left Missouri."[66]

It was difficult for the cow column to keep the cattle from straying in the rough, forested country. The trail over the Blue Mountains was so narrow that a party of ax-men had to go in advance of the wagons to clear the way. Jesse was one of those who helped cut the trail and thereafter was known as an "excellent hand with an ax."[67]

Over a period of about five days, October fifth to tenth, the emigrants began to straggle into Whitman's mission. They were able to replenish their supplies from the mission's store; however, many complained bitterly about the prices, as Burnett reports:

> The exhausting tedium of such a trip and the attendant vexation have a great effect upon the majority of men, making them become childish, petulant, and obstinate.
>
> I remember that while we were at the mission of Doctor Whitman, who had performed such hard labor for us, and was deserving of our warmest gratitude, he was most ungenerously accused by some of our people of selfish motives in conducting us past his establishment, where we could secure fresh supplies of flour and potatoes. This foolish, false, and ungrateful charge was based upon the fact that he asked us a dollar a bushel for wheat, and forty cents for potatoes.

As our people had been accustomed to sell their wheat from fifty to sixty cents a bushel and their potatoes as from twenty to twenty-five cents in the Western States, they thought the prices demanded by the doctor amounted to something like extortion, not reflecting that he had to pay at least twice as much for his own supplies... [68]

The majority of the emigrants pushed on to Ft. Walla Walla in a few days, according to Burnett, arriving about October 16. At this point, the Oregon Emigrating Company disbanded some securing boats to descend the Columbia, while many others made their way on to The Dalles, where they took the river to finish the trip to Fort Vancouver.

The Applegate brothers, along with several other families, chose to leave their stock and wagons in the charge of the Hudson's Bay Company at the fort and go on by boat. Jesse offered to sell his cattle to Archibald McKinley, chief trader for the Hudson's Bay Company at Walla Walla, but McKinley was reluctant to buy them, knowing they were worth three or four times the Spanish cattle that Jesse would get in return when he reached Fort Vancouver. In the end, however, Jesse did sign a contract to sell his cattle. The brothers then secured logs from the masses of driftwood along the banks of the Columbia and used tools they had brought across the trail to hew out several boats. In due time Indian guides were hired, families and all the supplies from the wagons were loaded into the hand-crafted boats, and finally the last leg of the journey was begun. [69]

John Charles Fremont, United States government surveyor was at Walla Walla at the time and noted:

> ...a considerable body of the emigrants, under the direction of Mr. Applegate, a man of considerable resolution and energy, had nearly completed the building of a number of Mackinaw boats, in which they proposed to continue their further voyage down the Columbia. [70]

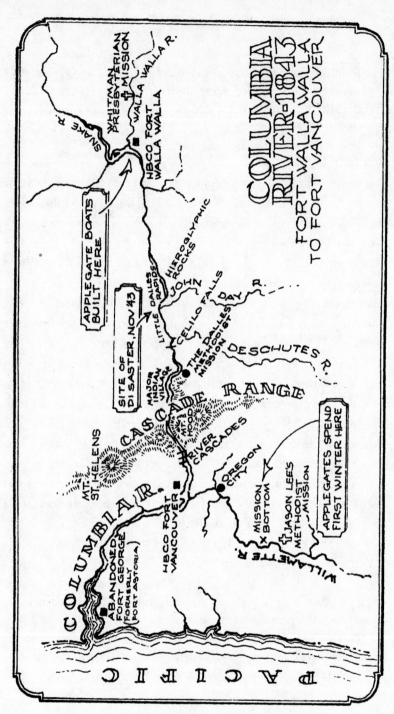

Down the Columbia–map drawn by Rosemary Spires

Jesse A. Applegate, Lindsay's son, describes their fateful trip down the Columbia:

I well remember our start down the river, and how I enjoyed riding in the boat, the movement of which was like a grape vine swing. Shoving out from the Walla Walla canoe landing about the first of November, our little fleet of boats began the voyage down the "Great River of the West." Whirlpools looking like deep basins in the river, the lapping, splashing and rolling of the waves, crested with foam sometimes when the wind was strong, alarmed me for a day or two on the start.

But I soon recovered from this childish fear, and as I learned that the motion of the boat became more lively and gyratory, rocking from side to side, leaping from wave to wave, dashing the spray into our faces when we were in rough water, the sound of rapids and the sight of white caps and foam ahead occasioned only pleasant anticipation. Often when the current was strong the men would rest on their oars and allow the boats to be swept along by the current...

I had not heard anyone complain of hardships or express fear of hardships or dangers to be encountered, and for my part I had come to feel as safe on the water as on land...

We had an Indian pilot, probably selected by McKinley at Fort Walla Walla, although I do not positively remember noticing the pilot before we entered the rapids we were now approaching. At the head of those rapids the river bears from a west course a little northerly, making a gradual curve. As we approached this bend I could hear the sound of the rapids, and presently the boat began to rise and fall and rock side to side. When we began to make the turn I could see breakers ahead extending in broken lines across the river, and the boat begun to sweep along at a rapid rate. The pilot squatted low in the bow. An old, red handkerchief was tied around his head, and his long, black hair hung down his back.

There were now breakers on the right and on the left, and occasionally foam-crested waves swept across our bows. The motion of the boat had never been so excitingly delightful before—it was an exaggeration of the cradle and grape vine swing combined. I began to think this was no ordinary rapid, but felt reassured when I noticed that the older people sat quietly in their places and betrayed no sign of fear…

Our boat was about 20 yards from the right hand shore, when looking across the river I saw a smaller boat about opposite to us near the south bank. The persons in the boat were Alexander McClellan, a man about 70 years old [the old friend who had saved Jesse A's. life when he was just a baby]; William Parker, probably twenty-one, and William Doke, about the same age; and three boys: Elisha Applegate, aged about eleven, and Warren and Edward Applegate, each about nine years old.

The boat now near the south shore, it would seem, should have followed our boat, as the pilot was with us, and this was a dangerous part of the river. But there was little time to consider mistakes or to be troubled about what might be the consequences, for presently there was a wail of anguish, a shriek, and a scene of confusion in our boat that no language can describe. The boat we were watching disappeared and we saw the men and boys struggling in the water.

Father and Uncle Jesse, seeing their children drowning were seized with frenzy, and dropping their oars, sprang from their seats and were about to make a desperate attempt to swim to them. But mother and Aunt Cynthia, in voices that were distinctly heard above the roar of the rushing water, by commands and entreaties brought them to a realization of our own perilous situation, and the madness of trying to reach the other side of the river by swimming.

This was 67 years ago, and yet the words of the frantic appeal of the women, which saved our boat and two families from speedy and certain destruction are fresh in my memory—"Men, don't quit your oars! If you do, we'll all be lost."[71]

William Doke (Doaks) could not swim, but managed to grab hold of a featherbed that carried him safely to the foot of the rapids. Parker,

Doke, and Elisha managed to make it to safety. Warren was never seen after the boat went under. The old man, McClellan, was seen with young Edward on two oars trying to reach the point of land where Parker had ended up, but before they could reach their goal, they were swept under projecting cliffs and never seen again. This tragic event would leave a lasting effect on Jesse and Lindsay Applegate; they vowed that once their families were settled in Oregon, they would find another way into Oregon so that other families could avoid their tragedy. John Charles Fremont and his government surveying party were on the east bank of the river and witnessed this horrific event, but were powerless to offer any assistance.

The day of the accident, November 6, 1843, was a day none of them would ever forget. Jesse's oldest son, Edward Bates Applegate, named for his friend and teacher in St. Louis, and Warren Applegate, Lindsay's second son, were gone, and hearts were broken. Jesse had already lost one son to fire and now one to the river, and for years after he could be heard to say mournfully: "By the elements of fire and water have I lost the pledges of my gratitude for my early bene-factors; and this I regard as a bad omen upon my life. I should never have started in the first place. I had everything with which to be satisfied, I was the protector of my family. I should have thought of them."[72] Somehow, however, the little party had to find the courage to persevere for the sake of the living. William D. Lyman describes their continued journey in "The Columbia River":

"From the Cascades to Vancouver, the company suffered more than in all the rest of their journey. The Fall rains were at hand and it poured with unremitting energy."

The trip had been long and hard. Peter Burnett sums it up well:

It was one of the most conclusive tests of character, and the very best school in which to study human nature. Before the trip terminated, people acted upon their genuine principles, and threw off all disguises. It was not that the trip was beset with very great perils, for we had no war with the Indians, and no stock stolen by them. But there were ten thousand little vexations continually recurring, which could not be foreseen before they occurred, not fully remembered when past, but keenly felt while passing. At one time an ox would be missing, at another time a mule, and then a struggle for the best encampment, and for a supply of wood and water; and, in these struggles, the worst traits for human nature were displayed, and there was no remedy but patient endurance.[73]

Lindsay Applegate gave his own summary of the experience:

Our immigration of 1843, being the largest that had ever crossed the plains, our progress was necessarily slow, having to hunt out passes for our wagons over rivers, creeks, deep gullies, digging down banks where nothing but a pack trail had been before, cutting our way through the dense forests before we could reach the valley of the Columbia, and then it appeared as though our greatest troubles had begun; for here we had to encounter cataracts and falls of the Columbia and the broad and lofty Cascades, with their heavy forests.[74]

Jesse later shared his perspective on the journey to a British officer, Lt. Peel; he recounts the conversation in his "Views of Oregon History":

Lt. Peel came across from Puget Sound where his vessel was lying, visited Vancouver, Oregon City, and the Willamette Valley, and stopped one or two nights with me. He was greatly interested and could hardly believe that the men would under-take and carry out such a journey without assistance, and sup-posed the Govmt. would at least have sent an officer to com-mand each party. I told him he was somewhat mistaken in the character of the people. They were probably brave enough but would never submit to discipline as soldiers. If the President himself had started across the plains to command a company, the first time he should choose a bad camp or in any other way offend them, they would turn him out and elect some one among themselves that would suit them better.[75]

At the end of the long overland journey, Jesse had earned the respect and lifelong friendship of most of those who traveled with him across the Oregon Trail. His accurate knowledge of the difficulties to be encountered, his resourcefulness and courage in meeting each new challenge, and his kind and helpful spirit helped to make the journey not just possible, but bearable for those he led west. However, on a personal level, the price seemed almost too much to bear.

The Promised Land

Robert Shortess, the young man who had worked at Lindsay Applegate's grist mill in Missouri and then gone west in the spring of 1839, met Jesse's group below Cascade Falls with two hundred pounds of flour and other much-needed provisions which the seventy-one hungry souls consumed before they even reached Vancouver. It should have been a joyous time, for at long last, the 2,100-mile, five-and-a-half-month journey was over,[76] but the hearts of all in the party were as heavy and dark as the unceasing rain that fell on them as they drifted down the river to Vancouver. Dr. John McLoughlin, the chief factor for the Hudson's Bay Company, met the destitute pioneers at Ft. Vancouver. Nineveh Ford, a member of the company, praises the kindness of Dr. McLoughlin: "We needed supplies and he gave us all the supplies we asked for. If we had money to pay for it he accepted it, and if we had not we got it without a word. He was very generous and kind; and from my acquaintance afterwards, in all my life I never have seen a man who was more noble and more generous and high minded in my judgment than Dr. McLoughlin."[77]

Peter Burnett, in his "Recollections of an Old Pioneer," describes McLoughlin as "a man of superior ability, just in all his dealings and a faithful Christian ... His views and acts were formed upon the model of the Christian gentleman."

Another example of Dr. McLoughlin's character can be seen in his treatment of Jesse Applegate. When he learned of the deal that Jesse had made with the Hudson's Bay factor at Fort Walla Walla to exchange his cattle for the inferior Spanish stock of the Willamette Valley, McLoughlin would not agree to the arrangement. Claiming that Applegate had made a bargain to his injury, McLoughlin directed that Jesse's cattle be returned free of cost as soon as they could be brought downstream. When in fact the cattle were returned the next spring, however, less than half the herd remained. [78] A number of the cattle had died in the ensuing winter and many more had been consumed by those in need of food.

Jesse had left Missouri vowing to "remove the Hudson Bay Company from the country." However, McLoughlin's kindness changed Jesse's mind and led to a lifelong friendship. This relationship would prove useful to McLoughlin and the Hudson's Bay Company when Jesse worked with the legislative committee in '45.

Frederick Holman, in his book *Dr. John McLoughlin- The Father of Oregon*, quotes from a letter from Jesse to McLoughlin that clearly shows Jesse's feelings toward his friend and benefactor:

> I came to this country in the fall of 1843, and from that time forward I can safely testify that your conduct has been most generous and philanthropic, not only to the immigrants from the United States, but to all requiring your assistance, whether native or foreigners. I can also say that you have greatly encouraged and given much assistance in settling and developing the resources of the country, but I have by no means considered your motives for doing so political, or that your charitable acts were intended to advance the interest of any particular nation, but that you acted in the one case simply

from a sense of Christian duty and humanity, and in the other from a natural desire to be useful in your day and generation.[79]

The Applegates soon moved on, perhaps with the guidance of Shortess, up the Willamette River, ending up at the old Methodist mission settlement about ten miles above Salem on the Willamette River. It had been raining for twenty days when they entered the old deserted buildings on December 1, 1843. It must have seemed like heaven to Melinda Applegate, Charles' wife, who gave birth six days later to a baby boy, and to Cynthia, who would deliver her seventh child two short months later. Years later Lindsay would write, "Oh how we could have enjoyed our hospitable shelter if we could have looked around the family circle and beheld [all] the bright faces that accompanied us on our toilsome journey."[80]

The conditions for the Applegate families were dismal during that first winter. The family often went hungry, as game was scarce and poor. An Indian who came to the Applegates to beg was so moved by the poverty he saw that he divided his scant supply of dried venison with the hungry children.[81] Peter Burnett describes the hardships all the settlers faced:

> We were a small, thinly settled community. Poor and isolated from the civilized world. By the time we reached the distant shores of the Pacific, after a slow wearisome journey of about two thousand miles, our little means were exhausted, and we had to begin life anew, in a new country... For the first two years after our arrival, the great difficulty was to procure provisions. The population being so much increased by each succeeding fall's immigration, provisions were necessarily scarce.[82]

At the request and expense of John McLoughlin, Jesse Applegate and Lansford Hastings took on the job of surveying the town plat for Oregon City in the winter of 1843.[83] Applegate spent much of that winter laying out the town, the job being his only hope of providing for his hungry family.

The three Applegate brothers remained at the old mission until after the harvest of 1844. Sometime in late December of 1843, Jesse had gone west to the Willamette River at the eastern base of the coast range and staked a claim on Salt Creek, where he began to cut logs and prepare them for building houses for the families.

New Beginnings

The settlement in Salt Creek Valley was about three miles north of what is now the city of Dallas in Polk County. The brothers took up three adjoining sections in September of 1844 and began the laborious job of establishing farms on untamed land with few of the necessary tools for the job.

The Applegate brothers were luckier than most because Charles, a blacksmith, could fashion the many tools they needed, and Lindsay was a skilled carpenter. They needed to build houses and barns before winter, fence in their fields, and build replacements for the wagons they had left in Walla Walla: when the brothers returned to retrieve their cattle and wagons, all they found of their wagons was four rear wheels. Once again, their trust in others to manage their property had been abused.

Once Jesse had retrieved what cattle remained and the families began to improve their claims on Salt Creek, their fortunes quickly began to turn around. The 1844 tax rolls list Jesse Applegate as the sixth wealthiest man in Oregon, with property valued at $3,830, the bulk of that property his cattle.[84] However, wealth mattered little when there were no goods available. The families learned to make do: men resorted to buckskin clothing; the women used the canvas from the wagon covers to make outerwear for their families and patched their tattered dresses until new material could be obtained. Farm tools, kitchen implements, and furniture consisted of what the settlers had managed to bring from the states or were hand made at home. As the journal *The Overland Monthly* put it, "The word primeval was found to exist here more completely than the pilgrims found it in the Atlantic shore. Oregon pioneers were further removed from life and the world than were they who landed from the Mayflower."[85]

Perhaps, however, this difficult situation was not all bad, as Peter Burnett points out in his "Recollections of an Old Pioneer:" "I never saw so fine a population, as a whole community, as I saw in Oregon most of the time I was there. They were all honest, because there was nothing to steal; they were all sober, because there was no liquor to drink; there were no misers, because there was no money to hoard, and they were all industrious because it was work or starve."

The situation continued to improve for the settlers, however, and in 1846, Jesse proudly describes (in a letter to his brother Lisbon in Missouri) the little farm he has built, "Nature favored me considerably in enclosing my farm by fencing in two lines both added together being less than 1 ½ miles in length and joining to two small creeks which unite my claim. I have enclosed 5 or 6 hundred acres, which including a living brook and a fine pasture is of the greatest benefit to me, as I am able to keep up my team of oxen & horses & have fine fat calves."[86]

The brothers had done so well, in fact, that Jesse encourages Lisbon later in the letter to join them in Oregon: "But I know that the disadvantage under which we labor in this country cannot be understood by the people of the U.S. And the immense advantages to be gained here by your children will be so powerful an inducement with you that you and Betsy will sacrifice your own ease for their benefit."[87]

But financial clouds still hung over Jesse, and he fretted over the loss of his Missouri property, for which his neighbor never paid him. In October 1847, Jesse laments the loss and what it means to his life in Oregon: "Could I have received the money from Missouri that I have every reason to rely on, I might have considered myself comfortably settled in this country. I have a superior claim with buildings when furnished sufficiently roomy and fine for a farmer's residence, about 80 acres of land in cultivation, and a portion of 500 acres enclosed. I have beside a saw and grist mill which I built this summer, good machines of my own construction."[88]

Jesse did not spend his early Oregon years simply working to build up his claim; he worked just as hard to build up the government and infrastructure of his new home. This work, however, did not have the most auspicious start, but was very typical for Jesse's work in public service: he put his uncompromising personal standards before the majority opinion, the conventional wisdom, and even his own self-interest. In 1844, when the provisional government of Oregon offered to appoint him as its engineer, he declared himself willing to do the work as a public service, but refused an official appointment from a government he considered illegal: the United States government was the only legitimate power in his eyes. He emphasizes this in a note to the committee, "I have only to say that I am a citizen and reside in Territory claimed by the United States and can officially acknowledge the existence of no government within the limits of said Territory."[89]

This refusal did not keep Jesse out of Oregon politics. On the contrary, by the summer of 1845, he would find himself dedicating a large portion of his time and talents to reorganizing and strengthening the existing government of Oregon. Samuel Frear comments in his thesis on Jesse Applegate, "It was never a happy relationship, however, and Applegate as long as he lived could be counted on to denounce government actions, berate politicians, and raise his voice—often alone—in protest. But he could not divorce himself from politics and for 40 years he was a powerful influence in Oregon."[90]

Jesse the Lawgiver

Before examining Jesse's part in reorganizing the provisional government of Oregon in the summer of 1845, it is important to understand how the government in Oregon was established.

America's interest in Oregon began to grow after Captain Robert Gray sailed into the mouth of the Columbia River in May of 1792. The information he carried back to the states piqued President Jefferson's interest and, in 1803, Lewis and Clark set out to explore the vast Louisiana Purchase all the way to the Pacific coast.

The next noteworthy player on the Oregon stage was John Jacob Astor, who had quickly accumulated a fortune in the fur trade. When Lewis and Clark returned with their stories of the Oregon country, he decided he would claim the Columbia by sending a ship around the horn and another party overland. Wilson P. Hunt, who would later be one of Jesse's Missouri mentors, led the overland party. The Astor Company soon established a fur trade in the region they called Astoria and laid claim to the Columbia for the Americans. Soon thereafter, news came that Britain and the United States were at war (the War of 1812) and that a British warship was on its way to capture Astoria. The Americans quickly struck a deal with the Northwest Fur Company and sold their interest to the British, destroying Astor's dreams of a line of forts across the continent.[91]

The United States and Great Britain signed a treaty at the end of the War of 1812, giving the Americans all the rights they had claimed before the war in the Northwest. However, political control was not given to either the United States or the British; the area was considered to be under "joint occupation." Since Astor had withdrawn from the area, the Hudson's Bay Company, with Dr. McLoughlin as the local governor, became the dominant player along the Columbia.

Over the next twenty years, a few mountain men and retired Hudson's Bay Company employs began to take up residence in Oregon. In 1834, Jason Lee came to establish a mission in the Willamette Valley. Soon several more missionary groups would join Lee, including Marcus Whitman's group. Many of the missionaries were highly educated men uncomfortable with the idea of living outside the protection of any government. They therefore began a plan to establish and lead American control over the area. By 1838 the Methodist missionaries had a justice and a constable who dispensed justice over the Indian and American subjects within their organization in accordance with American practices.[92] In 1838, the missionaries also petitioned the U.S. government to extend its authority over the Oregon country,[93] but the United States turned a deaf ear to these voices from the wilderness, in part because of the constraints of the Joint Occupation Treaty with Great Britain.

The settlers began to organize in earnest when, in February 1841, a prominent Oregon settler by the name of Ewing Young died. Mr. Young, the wealthiest man in the settlement, owned a sawmill, numerous cattle, and large land holdings. As he had no known heir (some time later, a son did file a claim against the estate) and there was no civil government to handle the disposal of his assets, many of the settlers decided to rectify the situation. At a meeting soon after Young's funeral, they agreed that an impartial settlement of Young's affairs was necessary to prevent widespread conflict. To this end, a probate court was formed, and Doctor Ira Babcock was elected supreme court judge.

As more settlers came into the territory, the need for government grew. One of the concerns for those already in Oregon was the land bill of 1841, promising free land to new settlers. The established settlers were concerned about the legal standing of their property, which they held on an informal basis.

The formation of an American government in Oregon did not go without a hitch. For one thing, the Hudson's Bay Company opposed this new development, fearing that it might be to their detriment. Dr. McLouglin knew, in fact, that he had enemies among the settlers and that many of the emigrants were suspicious of the company. He therefore recruited the French Canadians who had settled in the French Prairie area to oppose the effort to form an American territorial government.

To circumvent this opposition, the Americans used a little subterfuge. Meetings were called, ostensibly to discuss the danger of wolves, cougars, and bears killing the settlers' stock. At these "wolf meetings," bounties were in fact set on the wild animals, but then the real, tumultuous discussions began: committees were eventually named to draft a form of organic law for the Oregon territory, and a date was set to reconvene.[94]

On May 2, 1843, the settlers met at Champoeg, halfway between Lee's Mission and Oregon City. There were 102 settlers present; 52 of them French Canadians who had instructions from the Hudson's Bay Company to do all in their power to obstruct the organization of an independent government. After much heated debate, a vote was called, with the majority in favor of organizing a provisional government. The exact vote count is still open to some debate. The official record states that the motion carried by a "large margin," but this may have been exaggerated to impress Congress, which received a report on the proceedings. William Gray, in his history, states that the vote was fifty-two to fifty, while Robert Newell, who was present, says that a majority of five was in favor.

A legislative committee of nine men was created and given instructions to draft a constitution and file a report by July 5, 1843, at which time a general mass meeting was held for the report to be read out. This document, called the Organic Act, was based on the statutes of Iowa and the Northwest Ordinance of 1787. The original organic law of the Provisional Government was in fact compiled and written by the Applegates' friend Robert Shortess.[95] Jesse Applegate's comment on the resulting government:

> By making its basis the "Ordinance" of 1787, "passed by Congress for the government of the Territories North of the river Ohio" besides its other excellent provisions was intended to settle the question of Slavery West of the Rocky Mountains as it has in the North Western States East of them. By vesting the Legislature and Executive powers in simple Committees, was to avoid as far as possible even the appearance of an independent and permanent Government... No American better deserves favorable mention in the early history of Oregon than the conceiver of this scheme of Government- Robert Shortess.[96]

Jesse, in a letter to Lisbon, compared favorably the government formed at Champoeg to the Roman Republic, with its three-man executive committee equal to the Roman consuls, the nine-man legislative committee comparable to the tribunes, and the annual elections similar to the assemblies of the people. The tribunes had only to consider what laws were necessary each year and then submit them to the people for approval. Jesse then concluded, however, that the 1843 government was inadequate because it did not specify when or where the legislative committee was to meet or what they were to do when they did meet.[97]

The new government established religious liberty and trial by jury, encouraged education, and prohibited slavery, although the right to vote was limited to white males. The law that held the most interest for the settlers was the land law, which limited a land claim to 640 acres; the claimant had six months to improve the claim and must then live on the claim to hold it. Most important, provisions were made for registering land claims with the recorder of the territory.

There were no taxes levied: the government was to be supported by subscription or voluntary contribution. Jesse comments on this some twenty years later in a letter to Judge Deady, "the constitution of 1843 was good enough as to principle, but a treasury supported by voluntary contributions is soon empty, and men no more than frogs will long revere a king that has no power to enforce obedience."[98]

The new government had by no means smooth sailing from the outset. Heavily influenced by the missionaries, the provisional government had granted the Methodist and Catholic Churches the exceptional right to hold a six-mile square tract of land. This caused much bitterness among the other settlers. Moreover, McLoughlin and the Hudson's Bay Company, as well as the French-Canadian settlers, saw the new government as an American organization with no jurisdiction over them. Without their support or the resolution of conflicting interest, the fledgling government had little hope of stability.

The great migration of 1843 doubled the American influence in Oregon and brought several able men onto the political scene. In the next election, the pioneers took control of the fledgling government and proceeded at once to reorganize the government. Peter Burnett was one who took the lead in the 1844 reorganization of the struggling government. The three-headed executive was abolished and a governor put in its place. A thirteen-member legislature was created, and the judiciary was reformed. In addition, the land law was reformed so that the two townships were removed from the mission's control. One resolution, however, caused great alarm among the patriotic Americans in Oregon; this resolution limited the jurisdiction of the provisional government to the south side of the Columbia River.

Most of these changes were needed, and would have benefited the people, but they were never put to a popular vote. This infuriated Jesse Applegate, who strongly felt that the people should have a voice in their government. It was his opinion that this circumvention of democracy caused the government to fall into "universal ridicule and contempt." Years later, Jesse reflects, "When these nine men proceeded to abolish a Government by which alone they had been raised above the level of private citizens, and proceeded to erect a new one, without so much as saying 'by your leave' to the people, they committed a high political crime. That might have brought the most serious disasters upon the colony."[99]

In a letter to his brother Lisbon, Jesse mocks the 1844 assembly: "The legislature contained many aspiring spirits. Of course, the fabric under which they met did not suit gentlemen of such high political pretensions. Without even examining the tattered bits of paper which they had sworn to support or consulting the people, they went to work upon a Constitution to suit themselves."[100]

In June of 1845, Jesse would have the opportunity to express his views on this issue and several others when he was elected as a delegate from Yamhill County to the legislative committee. Jesse explains that when the legislative committee of '44 met he felt his "large and helpless family needed his service, the colony did not. But when the Legislature of 1844 overturned the Government of 1843, established by the people and left nothing in its place the people would respect, rather than see the Country involved in anarchy and internecine war I thought it my duty to do what I could to prevent these evils."[101]

Creating the Organic Law

A special committee consisting of Henry Lee, Newell, Robert Smith, McClure, and Jesse Applegate was appointed and charged with the duty of writing an organic law. The purpose of the committee was to create a workable government and write a constitution and a code of law. Carey states in his *History of Oregon*, "The election of 1845 is noteworthy for several reasons and the first of these is it introduced Jesse Applegate as a member of the legislature." Jesse was also appointed to three standing committees: road and highway, Indian affairs, and ways and means.

Jesse strongly felt that the government could not function without some cooperation from the British. Although most of his fellow Americans disagreed, feeling that overtures to the Hudson's Bay Company were a lost cause, Jesse went personally to McLoughlin to explain the situation. He pointed out that there were many prejudiced Americans who might be inclined to attack Hudson's Bay's interests, but that if they were part of the government, they could petition that government for protection. Jesse used letters and private interviews to ask if the company would be willing to become a party to the articles of compact by paying taxes. The Hudson's Bay Company agreed to the taxes if it were only on goods sold to the American settlers.[102] Schafer writes, "McLoughlin at first rejected the idea of British subjects becoming parties to an American government; but Applegate had prepared the way for union so skillfully, he urged his reasons with such convincing force, and was so fair in his treatment of the company's interests, his personality commanded such unlimited respect, that gradually every obstacle was removed."[103]

When a formal invitation from the committee came, McLoughlin and Douglas agreed, "to become parties to articles of compact." McLoughlin paid a price for this agreement; within six months he was demoted to associate chief factor. Shortly thereafter, he retired and moved to Oregon City; in due time he became an American citizen.

Applegate entered the session with a complete program of reform that he was able to carry out to the letter. "My intention was to reassert the right of the United States to the whole of Oregon, which the legislature of 1844 had limited to the south bank of the Columbia— and to secure the peace of the country by binding the whole white population in a compact to maintain it."[104] In a letter written October

13, 1867, to Elwood Evans, Jesse explained that one of the purposes of the agreement, which also guaranteed the Hudson's Bay Company the peaceful possession of its posts and farms, was to leave the land as yet unoccupied by the company open to settlement.

He also had hope of "restoring the Oregon Constitution to its original simplicity." His first act to this end was to address what he saw as a legal point that prevented him and members of the Hudson's Bay Company from taking the oath of allegiance to this government. The new oath of allegiance stressed the supremacy of the national governments, making it possible for the Hudson's Bay Company men to take part in the Oregon government without compromising their loyalty to Great Britain. The oath reads, "I do solemnly swear that I will support the organic laws of the provisional government of Oregon so far as said organic laws are consistent with my duties as a citizen of the United States, or a subject of Great Britain, and faithfully demean myself in office, so help me God."[105]

At a meeting of the Legislative Committee on August 14, 1845, Jesse introduced the following resolution:

> Resolved-that whereas the adoption of the amended Organic Law, by the people of Oregon, was an act of necessity rather than of choice and was intended to give to the people the protection which, of right should be extended to them by their government; and not as an act of defiance or disregard of the authority or laws of the United States...[106]

From the opening oath to the closing memorial and petition to Congress, Jesse's literary style, unequalled by that of any of his contemporaries, is easily recognizable in the revised organic law. Historian J. Henry Brown writes, "His Spartan simplicity and fidelity to trust which distinguished him among his fellow colonists is stamped upon the legislative proceedings."[107] One must assume that Jesse's association with the great lawyer, Edward Bates, helped qualify him for this service to Oregon. It is clear from the body of his work that his mind was sharp and his conclusions were accurate.

Part of the revised organic law was to divide the government into three distinct branches: legislative, judicial, and executive. The second article defined the powers and duties of each branch of government. The executive power was invested in a single person elected by the people. Jesse also made some other needed changes to the law: he revised the land law so that no distinction of color, nationality, age, or sex was made as long as each settler met all other stipulations of the land law.[108] An income tax of one-eighth of one percent was also enacted to replace the subscription scheme of 1843, which had proven to be less than successful.

Jesse also ensured that the portion of the Ordinance of 1787 dealing with slavery was included in the new organic law. His hope was that this would end the question of slavery for Oregon; however, it was only the beginning of a long battle. In his "Views of Oregon History," Jesse argues that there was a political purpose not comprehended by the mass of American settlers in basing the government upon the Ordinance of 1787—that purpose being to settle the slavery question west of the Rocky Mountains as the ordinance had settled it in the northwestern states to the east of them.[109]

He included an article guaranteeing the encouragement of morality and knowledge, the maintenance of schools, and the exercise of good faith and justice to the Indians, using the language of the Ordinance of 1787.[110] Jesse held a firm belief that education of the masses "was an indispensable requisite to the permanence of free government and individual virtue."[111]

Another issue important to Jesse was the judicial system. In a letter to Nesmith he declared, "I hold the doctrine to be beyond controversy that an independent and enlightened Judiciary is the greatest safeguard to the liberties of the people."[112]

This conviction is shown in Article II, Section 8 of the 1845 Organic Law:

The supreme court shall have power to decide upon and annul any laws contrary to the provisions of these articles of compact, and whenever called upon by the House of Representatives, the supreme judge shall give his opinion, touching the validity of any pending measure... Sec 2 The Judge of the Supreme Court: at the close of each session of the House of Representatives is hereby required to examine carefully the Laws passed at said session and shall have the power to annul by the publication of his decision directed to the inferior Courts all such Laws or parts of Law, as are in his opinion, in violation of the articles of Compact... [113]

Jesse served on a special committee that drafted a memorial and petition to Congress setting forth the "conditions, relations, and wants of this country." He drafted the final document, which can be seen today, in his unique handwriting, in the state archives.

Your memorializes and petitioners, the representatives of people of Oregon for themselves, and in behalf of the citizens of the United States residing in this territory, would respectfully submit to the consideration of your honorable body some of the grievances under which we labor, and pray your favorable consideration of our petition for their remedies.

Without dilating upon the great importance of this territory as an appendage of the Federal Union, or consuming your valuable time in repeating the oft repeated account of our agricultural and commercial advantages, we would, with due diffidence, submit to your serious consideration our peculiar difficulties as occupants of this territory. As, by treaty stipulations between the Government of the United States and Great Britain, this territory has become a kind of neutral ground, in the occupancy of which the citizens of the United States and the subjects of Great Britain have equal rights, and, as your memorializes humbly conceive, ought to have equal protection; such being the fact, the population of the territory, though promiscuously interspersed, is composed of the subjects of a crown and the citizens of a republic, between whom no common bond of union exists…

To prevent a calamity so much to be dreaded, the well-disposed inhabitants of this Territory have found it absolutely necessary to establish a provisional and temporary Government, embracing all free male citizens; and whose executive, legislative, and judicial powers should be equal to all exigencies that may rise among themselves, not provided for by the Government to which they owe allegiance. And we are most happy to inform your honorable body, that, with but few individual exceptions, the utmost harmony and good will had been the result of this, as we conceive, wise and judicious measures; and the British subjects and Americans citizens vie with each other in their obedience and respect to the laws, and in promoting the common good and general welfare of Oregon.[114]

Years later, in a letter to Joseph Lane he admits, "I have some reason to be vain of my success in drawing up [the] memorial." In 1846, Jesse expresses a similar sentiment in a letter to his brother Lisbon.

The petition also asked for defense, help with dealing with the Indians, a territorial government, land donations, mail service, protection for the emigrants coming each year, and help with an emergency fund. When Senator Thomas Hart Benton presented the memorial to Congress, he made the following comment: "The petition is set forth in strong and respectful language…was drawn up in a manner creditable to the body which it was presented, to the talents by which it was dictated…the best instrument of its kind I have seen during the 25 years in service to this body."[115]

On July 2, the revised organic law was presented to the House for approval. Once it had been accepted, Jesse introduced what to him was the most important part of the process, a bill requiring a referendum on the organic law. Another important part of this session was the redrawing of the geographical limits of the provisional government of 1844 so that the provisional government would govern over the whole of Oregon to endure until superseded by the government of the U.S.

The organic law was to be presented to the citizens in a special election on July 26. The law was presented in the referendum "as a true copy of the original organic laws of Oregon, without alteration or amendment and a copy of said organic laws, revised and amended be submitted to the people of Oregon at the several precincts herein mentioned, for them to declare which shall in future govern the territory." Since there were no printing presses in Oregon, Applegate made manuscript copies of both the original organic laws and the amended laws; a copy of each was available at each polling place to be read before the people voted.[116] The amended organic law was approved by a large majority of the people and served as the basis of the Oregon provisional government until a territorial government was organized under the United States. Stephen J. Chadwick, in his address to the Oregon Pioneer Association in June of 1874 states: "The majority was not nearly as large as it would have been but for the fact that many voted against the proposed changes because the Hudson's Bay Company's foreign born followers were allowed to exercise at the polls the same right which American citizens enjoyed."

However, J. A. Hussey, in his "Champoeg: Place of Transition," argues that "These two important actions of 1845—the adoption of the Organic Law of 1845 and the agreement with the Hudson's Bay Company—are held by at least one historian to mark the fifth and final step in the organization of a truly effective provisional government in Oregon."[117]

Once the new organic laws were approved, the legislators met again on August 11 for a second session. Jesse wanted to define clearly the legislature's duties, resolving that "the people of Oregon are not, in the opinion of this house, morally or legally bound by any acts of the officers, or agent of the people, not expressly authorized or sanctioned by the instrument, in virtue of which they had their official existence." In addition, he further resolves "That this house can not assume, on behalf of the people, the payment of any debt, or the refunding of any funds borrowed, or otherwise unlawfully contracted or obtained, without first obtaining the consent of the people."[118] Both of these resolutions passed, but not without opposition led by W.H. Gray, who argued that the resolutions would destroy the confidence of the people in their legislatures.[119] Jesse's resolution seems to be one of the clearest and earliest acknowledgments of the principle of referendum in Oregon.[120]

Judge William Strong, in an address given at the 1879 Oregon Pioneer Society, praises the early government: "Oregon owes by far the most of its prosperity and rapid progress to the early formation of the Provisional Government, the wise laws which were enacted, and the inflexible justice with which they were administered." Several historians add that the government that came out of the legislative session of 1845 "is the crowning glory of the Oregon pioneers."

Applegate's sway with his fellow legislators can be illustrated by a most unusual event. On August 11, Jesse rushed into the House and asked that the rules be suspended so that he could introduce a bill to prevent dueling. The bill was presented, read, and read once more, all within half an hour, before being sent to the Governor and signed into law within an hour. Explanations of the particular haste of this legislation abound. Gray, in his *History of Oregon*, asserts that it was to prevent a young man by the name of Holderness from challenging Dr. Elijah White to a duel. Jesse took exception to Gray's assumption and wrote him a letter expressing his displeasure at the insinuation that he had forced the bill through to cover up White's cowardice: "Almost everyone at Oregon City (if you did not), knew that the parties to the duel were S. M. Holderness and J.C. Campbell, both young men of promise—a woman, not Dr. White, was the cause of the quarrel."[121]

Schafer, in his essay "Jesse Applegate, Pioneer and State Builder," states, "Applegate's right to be honored as the true founder of Oregon's pioneer government is, by the present generation, commonly ignored. In the beginning it was not so. Oregonians of that day gladly acknowledged him as the sage and law-giver of the colony." It is remarkable that out of all the antagonism, jealousies, and mutual distrust a spirit of compromise and conciliation allowed these early Oregon residents—British, French, Canadians, and Americans—to come together and form a sound, workable government "having for its object the protection of life and property." That Jesse's brilliant mind and force of character played a large part in these events cannot be questioned by impartial readers of this history. Historian F.F. Victor wrote, "The leading spirit in the legislature of 1845 was undoubtedly Mr. Applegate. The Spartan simplicity and fidelity to trust which distinguished him among his fellow colonists is stamped upon their proceedings. His literary style, unequaled by that of any of his contemporaries, is easily recognized in the revised code."[122]

The 1845 legislative session ended on August 20, with plans to reconvene in December for its third session. Jesse returned to his farm along the Salt Creek and soon sent a letter of resignation to the Governor with no explanation. However, in a letter to his brother he does give a reason, "As I thought three sessions with only one election was rather too much, I resigned at the end of the second." He then goes on to give his view of politics in Oregon: "I expect to have nothing further to do with Oregon Politicks. I am disgusted already with the ignorance of some, the prejudice of others, and the want of independence and the demagoguism of any body of men who seek rather to do that which is popular rather than that which is right."[123]

Jesse probably thought this was the end of his political career, and he never took as active a role again, but he would serve in lesser roles several more times during the next forty years. He did run unsuccessfully for the United States Senate in 1876, defeated by Governor La Fayette Grover by a vote of forty-eight to thirty-three. His political contributions are aptly summarized by W.C. Woodward: "Sufficient has been said to indicate the high order of political ability of these pioneer state builders. A few rose in ability to the position of real statesman whose resourcefulness and qualities of mind and heart would have made them marked men anywhere. Such was Jesse Applegate."[124]

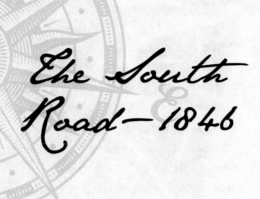

The South Road—1846

In 1844, James Polk was elected president on the slogan "54–40 or fight" (although he later settled for the forty-ninth parallel.) Determined to once and for all settle the "Oregon question," he declared in his inaugural address of 1845 that it was his duty "to assert and maintain, by all constitutional means, the right of the United States to that portion of our territory which lies beyond the Rocky Mountains."

Out in Oregon the Americans and British were living in uneasy harmony under the provisional government, since both groups were well aware that the boundary question had not been settled. The British Government had sent Lieutenant William Peel and Captain Parke to spy on the situation and had also sent a ship-of-war, *H.M.S. Modeste*, to lie at anchor in the mouth of the Columbia River. Jesse explains the tense situation to his brother Lisbon: "News from the U.S. are eagerly sought for in this country, we are in a feverish state of excitement in regard to the Oregon Bill—If the people here were to decide the question every American and many of the British would oppose any part of the Territory being surrendered to G.B. and if the Columbia is made the line a majority of the people will leave the country, the exclusive navigation of the Columbia is of as much importance to Oregon as the exclusive navigation of the Mississippi is to the western States."

Jesse went on to state that because of the memories of the British as an enemy from the French and Indian War and the Revolutionary War, many settlers "believe in case of War between the two countries that they will heretofore set the tomahawk and scalping knife of the savages to work upon the defenseless families."[125]

The political question loomed large in the minds of the Americans in the Oregon country. Jesse knew from personal observation how easy it would be for the enemy to block the Americans through the Cascades and along the Columbia. A southern route into Oregon that was not under the control of the British was sorely needed.

Jesse and Lindsay Applegate also held a deep personal conviction, impressed upon them by their family's tragic journey down the Columbia, that an easier route must be found, one that did not require new settlers to endure the same extreme difficulty and suffering they had endured in 1843. More lives had been lost to the river in 1844, and in 1845, an entire family drowned on the Columbia, so the Applegate brothers were not the only ones who felt the need for a route that avoided that treacherous river. Lindsay explains the Applegate brothers' feelings about the river route: "Under these sad reflections, we resolved if we remained in the country to find a better way for others who might wish to emigrate, as soon as we could possibly afford the time."[126]

The desire for a safer trail led Stephen Meek in 1845 to lead some two hundred wagons on to a new cut-off. Meek's cut-off was an effort to avoid the Columbia River and rumored Indian harassment along the Oregon Trial. The new route was represented as being 200 miles shorter than the old Oregon Trail. Meek and those following him headed west from Fort Boise crossing the Malheur River (near Vale) across Oregon's high desert and central Cascade Range headed to The Dalles. At one point the group split but eventually reunited near present day Madras. There was a long stretch where they found little water; what water they found was in stagnant pools, unfit for use for animals or humans. Disease spread rapidly among the emigrants and many emigrants died from typhoid fever.

Eventually ten men rode off towards The Dalles seeking help for the stranded emigrants. After a ten day ride, they arrived in The Dalles so exhausted they could not dismount without assistance. Moses 'Black' Harris led a relief party out to look for the 'lost company.'[127] Two months after they turned on to Meek's cut-off, the last of the wagons rolled into The Dalles. Twenty-four deaths can be documented for this 'cut-off,' and another twenty died from typhoid or exhaustion after they arrived at The Dalles.

Samuel Parker an emigrant of 1845 described the trail. "Tuck what is called Meek's Cutoff...a bad cutoff for all that tuck it...I will just say, pen and tong will both fall short when they go to tell the suffering the company went through."

Samuel Barlow was two weeks ahead of Meek and on September 24, 1845, Barlow left The Dalles with seven wagons, determined to make his way over or around Mt. Hood. Joel Palmer soon joined him with an additional twenty-three wagons. They traveled southwest over rolling hills towards Five Mile Creek. Barlow had no concept of the cavernous ravines or steep ascents his little company would need to cross as they tried to find a way around the south side of Mt. Hood. The rain and snow of winter caught them before they could hack a road through the wilderness. In desperation they decided to leave the wagons with a guard and to place the women and children on horses and lead them to the settlement. It was a race against the weather and a growing lack of food. Two men went ahead looking for provisions and were able to make it into Oregon City and then back into the mountains with supplies before the women and children died from exposure or starvation. The emigrants reached Oregon City late in December of 1845.

Barlow applied to the Territorial Legislators for funds to help build a road across the Cascades and in the spring of 1846 he took forty men into the mountains to build his new road. It was agreed that it would be a toll road with a charge of five dollars per wagon and ten cents per head of livestock.[128]

By the spring of 1846, George Abernethy, Oregon's provisional governor, was lobbying for an exploring party to locate a southern route into Oregon. A public meeting was held on March 14, 1846 in Salem for the purpose of securing a volunteer exploring party. The meeting was publicized in the *Oregon Spectator* on March 19, 1846:

> To the Editor of the Oregon Spectator:
> Sir—I am requested to forward to you for publication the proceedings of a public meeting, which was held at Salem mills On Saturday the 14th inst.—said meeting being convened for the purpose of devising means to explore and open a wagon road from the waters of the upper Willamette to Snake river…The following persons were selected as said committee, viz.: John B. McClane, Thos. Holt, Jas. P. Martin, J W. Boyle, Shaw, and Moses Harris. The aforesaid committee were instructed to circulate the subscription as extensively as possible, and to call a meeting of the subscribers whenever they shall judge proper; also, to inquire who are willing to go on the expedition, and are competent to go as pilots, and to report the result of their inquiries to the aforesaid meeting, which is to convene at the call of said committee.
> J.M. Garrison, Ch'mn.
> JNO. B. McClane, Sec'y

Levi Scott would comment years later that the provisional government had "no revenue, nor any means to do anything towards making a road across the mountains, and the settlers, although possessed of incomparable pluck and energy, had scarcely anything to contribute towards such an enterprise."[129]

On May 15, a group of men under the leadership of General Cornelius Gilliam and including Levi Scott, William Parker (Cynthia Applegate's brother,) John Owens, Bennett Osborn, David Goff, Ben Burch, Robert Smith, John Scott (Levi's son,) William Sportsman, Samuel Goodhue, Jack Jones and Moses "Black" Harris set out in search of a southern route.

The explorers traveled southward up the Willamette Valley along the river and then up the North Fork of the Willamette to the foothills of the Calapooya Mountains hoping to find a pass across the mountains. When they did not find the pass, they crossed to the east side of the Willamette River, where the Middle Fork and Coast Fork meet.[130]

General Gilliam left the group and returned home shortly after they came upon an Indian trail crossing the Calapooya Mountains into the Umpqua Valley. Levi Scott writes in his autobiography about Gilliam's leaving: "We had no guide nor leader, and our party was without any organization. In starting out we had overlooked the important principal that an organized plan, with a head and leader is essential to the success of almost every undertaking."[131]

A few days later, three more of the group grew discouraged, abandoned the enterprise, and headed towards home. The rest of the explorers went on for two more days, reaching a spot close to the present-day town of Oakland. Here they realized they did not have enough men to complete the expedition and decided to return home with the hope of recruiting more volunteers.

Levi Scott let it be known that if a new company could be raised, he would join the expedition, and would keep his outfit in readiness to be prepared to go at a moment's notice.[132]

The following editorial in the *Oregon Spectator* of June 25, 1846 clearly shows the citizens' concern about this endeavor:

Whilst on the one hand we learn with regret, that the company of road hunters which started from Polk County, has returned unsuccessful and discouraged; in the other part, we are cheered with the intelligence that another party from Champoeg County is forming and will soon be prepared to start, under the command of an able and experienced pilot.

When all are impressed with the conviction, strengthened in many instances by painful experience, of the vast importance of obtaining an easy and safe road to the Willamette Valley, by a southern route and thus avoiding the numerous and heart-breaking difficulties of the Columbia, it will afford us no small gratification, to be able to give the names of the patriotic little band, who inspired by the safety and welfare of this country, engage in the arduous and praise-worthy undertaking; that the hopes and wishes of the community will be with them there is no doubt...that they will richly deserve our praise and gratitude, no one will for a moment question,...as well as to testify, that those who render valuable services to the state, when she needs it, shall not labor without reward.[133]

A Second Attempt

Jesse and Lindsay Applegate decided that it was now time to step forward and join the road-hunting expedition, but first they had to arrange for the care of their young families during their four-to-five-month absence. It was decided that older brother Charles would remain behind, shouldering the responsibility for the three farms, three wives, and the twenty-four children of the Applegate clan. Years later Charles would say that his was the hardest job.

The new road-hunting crew consisted of fifteen men, eleven of whom had been on the first exploring party and were eager to try again. Levi Scott states that when he came back from the first exploration, he took up his claim and gave it his full attention and energy until "early June when Jesse Applegate, having raised another company to prosecute further the enterprise which had occupied the other company during a portion of the month of May, came to my place and requested me to join the expedition."[134]

Jesse Applegate was elected captain of the new company and Levi Scott and David Goff took on the role of lieutenants as the party neared the Tule Lake country in Northern California. Levi's son, John Scott, was one of the members along with William Parker, Jesse's brother-in-law. Other members were Lindsay Applegate, John Jones, Robert Smith, John Owens, William Sportsman, Samuel Goodhue, Bennett Osborne, Benjamin F. Burch, Henry Boygus (or Bogus) and Moses "Black" Harris. Each man had his own packhorse and saddle horse, making thirty animals to care for and guard every night.[135]

Before the new company started on their journey, they obtained all the information they could from the Hudson's Bay Company and acquired a map drawn by Peter Skene Ogden in 1826–27 that proved to be quite accurate whenever the party was in territory over which Ogden had actually traveled.[136] Jesse also consulted John C. Fremont's journal from his Topographical Expedition through Oregon in the winter of 1843 and learned that a straight line between a point slightly south of the head of the Rogue River Valley and a point on Bear River in extreme southwestern Wyoming approximated the forty-second parallel. The road explorers' intention was to intercept the 1846 Oregon Trail emigrants at this point on the Bear River. This line now forms the southern boundaries of Oregon and Idaho.

Jesse had made his living as a surveyor and spent much of his youth surveying the wilderness of Missouri. Family tradition has always said that Jesse owned a Burt's Solar compass and that he had it with him on this expedition. Some recently discovered letters between Oregon's first Surveyor General, John Preston, and Jesse indicate that Jesse did not own a Burt's Solar Compass until September of 1851, so he could not have had it with him in 1846. In a letter of June 4, 1851, Jesse declares his desire to buy a solar compass from John Preston, "If one of them is yet to be disposed of I should feel it as a great favor if I am allowed to be the purchaser. The solar compass is not an instrument that I have ever seen-but if as I understand it in part removes the difficulty of local attraction; there is no country where it will be more in request than in this."[137] Years later when Jesse lost most all of his worldly possessions to the state of Oregon, his compass was one of the few things that he was able to keep.

There is some conflict as to the date they left: Lindsay puts it on June 20, while Scott and Jesse say it was June 22. They started from La Creole (Rickreall) near Dallas. The *Oregon Spectator* reports on July 4, 1846: "The party left the Rickreall on the 22nt. In fine spirits and high hopes of bringing the next emigration in at the head of the Willamette valley. They left with a firm determination never to retrace their steps—never to abandon the noble and philanthropic enterprise, until they shall have found a good wagon road, if such a thing be possible."[138]

The new road company, officially named the South Road Expedition, adopted a unique governing strategy called "Committee-of-the-Whole." Lindsay Applegate in his reminiscences writes, "The party was governed in all its proceedings by a majority vote of its members." Even though Jesse was named captain and felt the burden of leadership, he followed the wishes of the Committee-of-the-Whole.[139]

As they were preparing to leave, Lindsay Applegate states clearly the reason the volunteers were going on such a dangerous journey: "It was important to have a way by which we could leave the country without running the gauntlet of the Hudson's Bay Co.'s forts and falling prey to Indians which were under British influence."[140]

The road company headed south on the old Hudson's Bay Company trail, crossing the Calapooya Mountains into the Umpqua Valley, where they picked up the Old California Trail, the route that had been traveled by the trappers and cattlemen who had traveled between Sacramento and the Willamette Valley. This path ran north to south between the Cascade Mountains and the Coast Range. Levi Scott gives the following description of the Umpqua Valley: "We were delighted with the Umpqua valley. The air was soft and balmy; the water plenty, clear and pure, and the grass was fine. There was plenty of timber, fir, pine, red-oak, alder, laurel, yew, balm, myrtle, white oak, etc."[141]

The road company crossed over the low hills to the North Fork of the Umpqua River, and as they approached the Umpqua Mountains, they met a group of emigrants fleeing from California. Among the group were a Mr. Hess and his son-in-law, who were driving a small herd of cattle and Mexican horses north to the settlements. Rogue Indians had killed one of their cows along a small stream, now known as Cow Creek, on the south side of the mountain. Hess told the explorers that it was impossible to build a road across the mountain ahead of them; it could scarcely be crossed with horses.[142]

It would not be the mountain ahead of them that became famous, but the creek that cut a rugged swath through the canyon floor. That canyon became known as Canyon Creek, and would become infamous for the danger and hardship it would cause the emigrants who would traverse it the winter of 1846. The mountains of the coast range of western Oregon are often very rugged and sharp as they shoot up from the deep canyon floors and are covered with dense vegetation. The pioneers had learned to go up and over most of them, but this mountain presented a barrier that could only be crossed by using the crooked canyon creek bed.

Lindsay Applegate describes the journey through the canyon:

> We entered the canyon, followed up the little stream that runs through the defile for four or five miles, crossing the creek a great many times, but the canyon becoming more obstructed with brush and fallen timber, the little trail we were following turned up the side of the ridge where the woods were more open, and wound its way to the top of the mountain. It then bore south along a narrow back-bone of the mountain, the dense thickets and the rocks on either side affording splendid opportunities for ambush...

On the morning of the 26th [28th?] we divided our forces, part going back to explore the canyon … The exploring party went back to where we left the canyon on the little trail the day before, and returning through the canyon, came into camp after night, reporting that wagons could be taken through.[143]

Levi Scott says of the canyon:

The Canyon was very bushy, so much so that we were frequently compelled to clamber over masses of vine-maple and other bushes which grew so densely that a man could not crawl through among them. And there were great quantities of logs and boulders choking up the pass, which should have to be removed in opening a road … That evening we returned to camp … We made our report to the rest of the company, and all of us together gravely and carefully discussed the feasibility of making a wagon road through the canyon … We had no difficulty in arriving at the conclusion that it could be done.[144]

View of the Pacific Highway south of Canyonville. Descending into Canyon Creek Canyon, Circa 1925. (Courtesy of Douglas County Museum.)

After leaving Canyon Creek, the explorers moved south through the range of hills south of Wolf Creek and crossed a little creek that has been known as Grave Creek ever since Martha Leland Crowley, a member of the company of 1846, died nearby. They then moved over Sexton Mountain and down into the Rogue River Valley.

Indians helped them cross the Rogue River at an area that later became known as Vannoy Ferry. Lindsay Applegate, in his reminiscences of 1846, describes the Rogue Valley: "On the morning of June 29th, we passed over the low range of hills, from the summit of which we had a splendid view of the Rogue River valley. It seemed like a great meadow, interspersed with groves of oaks which appeared like vast orchards. All day long we traveled over rich black soil covered with rank grass, clover, and pea vine."

The party of road hunters proceeded across the valley, and near the present-day site of Ashland they caught up with a party of French-Canadians on their way to California. These men advised the road hunters that there was a way into the Cascade Mountains by turning east and going up a creek now known as Emigrant Creek.[145]

It is at this point that the road-hunters began to explore a completely new trail into Oregon over the Green Springs mountain pass of the Cascades.

Once the explorers reached the Klamath River valley, they crossed the river below present-day Klamath Falls and traveled along lower Klamath Lake, crossing into what is today California. They then turned northeast in the direction of Tule Lake, where they encountered rough lava ridges and soon stumbled upon a river with very high banks and water too deep to permit crossing. Lindsay Applegate describes this area:

> After spending a couple of hours in this splendid pasture, we re-packed and started on our way towards the timbered butte, but had not proceeded more than a mile before we came suddenly upon quite a large stream [Lost River] coming into the

lake. We found the stream near the lake very deep, with almost perpendicular banks, so that we are compelled to turn northward up the river. Before we proceeded very far we discovered an Indian crouching under the bank, and surrounding him, make him come out. By signs, we indicated to him that we wanted to cross the river. By marking on his legs and pointing up the river, he gave us to understand that there was a place above where we could easily cross. Motioning to him to advance, he led the way up the river about a mile and pointed out a place where an immense rock crossed the river. The sheet of water running over the rock was about fifteen inches deep, while the principal part of the river seemed to flow under. This was the famous Stone Bridge on Lost River, so often mentioned after this by travelers.[146]

This ford of the Lost River saved the immigrants many miles of travel and contributed to the eventual success of the Applegate Trail.

After crossing the stone bridge, the road party worked their way eastward through rock-strewn country that was very hard on the horses. They were headed to a green spot at the foot of the hills on the far side of the valley. Levi Scott continues the story:

> There was an extensive level plain lying before us in the direction we desired to go. We could see a green looking spot at the foot of the hills on the farther side of this sandy, sage-plain, which we supposed to be rendered verdant by grass and willows, which we thought indicated plenty of water and a good place to camp. We discussed the matter thoroughly, and all agreed that this green patch should be our next camping place...We found the place to be a grove of juniper trees, growing on a dry, sand tract of land without so much as a suggestion of water anywhere...This was a sore disappointment to us after having toiled so far over the dry, hot sand during the afternoon.
>
> We could not think of camping here on the dry, barren sand, so we turned to the south along the foot of the hills, and after traveling three or four miles further, were compelled to

camp in a dry gulch without having a drop of water. Many of the men, inconsiderately, vented their disappointment in bitter curses and complaints against the Captain for leading us into such a place.[147]

Scott then points out that all the road-hunting party was just as responsible as Captain Applegate: after all, they had all viewed the "green spot" from across the valley in the morning and agreed it was a good place to head towards with the idea of camping.

Early the next morning they started out again and soon came to an excellent spring. The men who had complained so bitterly the night before seemed to forget and forgive once they had found water, but Jesse was deeply wounded and felt unjustly accused. After breakfast that morning he said, "Now boys, I want you to choose another leader, if you wish to have any leader, at all, for I will have nothing more to do with the control of this crowd."[148]

Surprised by Jesse's reaction to their complaints, the men insisted that they did not want any other leader. In the end, the conflict was settled by electing David Goff and Levi Scott to share the daily responsibilities as lieutenants to Captain Applegate. Both Goff and Scott were some fifteen years older than Jesse and were well respected for their sound judgment and good sense.

They continued east, making their way around the end of a shallow lake now known as Goose Lake, climbed a ridge, and entered into a valley they named Surprise Valley because of their surprise in finding plenty of water and grass there.[149] Some thirty miles east of Surprise Valley, the explorers came to High Rock Canyon. Levi Scott describes it as one of the most remarkable places he had ever seen:

> We go down this creek, which sinks in the sand a little way from its source, but the gorge deepens as we advance, till we find ourselves in a deep canyon about one hundred yards wide, almost as level as a pavement, and strewn with the skulls and immense horns of the mountain sheep along the dry bed of

a small branch winding through it…A perpendicular wall of lava rises up on either side two or three hundred feet high. We traveled some ten or twelve miles through this wonderful place.

High Rock Canyon

From here, the road party pushed on to the Black Rock Mountain, where they found many hot and cold springs. One large spring of boiling water irrigated a large meadow full of tall grass, a spot that would be a welcome resting place for weary travelers over the new road.

Big Boiling Springs at Black Rock

The landscape to the east of Black Rock is extremely flat and a barren desert. Scott says in his remembrances that they feared a lack of water and did not know which direction to go across this barren country. The whole company, with Captain Applegate abstaining, voted to turn south in hopes of hitting Mary's (Humboldt) River, but then Applegate, unhappy with this decision, announced that he would head east with anyone who volunteered to go with him. The company now split: nine going south, six going east with Captain Applegate.[150] Lindsay describes what Jesse's group encountered on their eastward journey:

> Our wish was to continue our course eastward but the country, as far as we could see in that direction was a barren plain, we concluded to follow the granite ledge, which extended in a southeasterly direction. We then begin to see smoke off to the south and turn toward it hoping to find water. The smoke, as we afterwards learned, was caused by the burning of peat beds along the Humboldt river, the stream we were now wishing to find, though we had no correct idea of the distance we would have to travel in order to reach it, nor of the difficulties to be encountered.[151]

Lindsay writes that on the morning of July 17 (probably the nineteenth,) as they were riding along in desperate need of water, they saw a horseman approaching and discovered it to be John Jones, one of the party who had gone south with Scott. One of Jones' horses had wandered off the night before, and in following its tracks, he had located water. Jones led the weary, bedraggled group on to the water and thus probably saved their lives. The dehydration and prolonged exposure to the sun during their desert journey would have long-term effects on Jesse and several others of the group.

Jesse reached the Humboldt River and the California Trail on July 20, 1846.

Levi Scott's autobiography says: "About seven o'clock in the morning, near the middle [of] July 1846 we reached the Humboldt River. It was very deep, sluggish stream where we struck it...We struck the river but a short distance from the Lake, or Sink."[152] Scott's and Jesse's groups reunited along the Humboldt River, about ten miles southwest of present-day Lovelock, Nevada.[153]

Jesse Applegate was not a traditionally religious man, but his writings do show he had a deep faith in God. Scott shares in his remembrance that when the group came back together, Jesse went off by himself, wrapped himself in a blanket, and lay down in the shade of some sagebrush. After some time, he came back to the group and proposed that the group should all get together, kneel down, and give thanks to God for their deliverance from the desert. But there was so little religious sentiment among the group of sunbrowned men that there was no second to the motion.[154]

Once they left the last water hole beyond the Black Rock, they all felt they had traveled too far south. The road explorers now turned east and worked their way up the river for three days. At this point, they could see a ridge to the west with a pass through it that they thought might lead them more directly back to the Black Rock. Levi Scott and William Parker were sent to explore the pass to the west and in fact, found water about fifteen miles out. They were then able to go on to Rabbit Hole Springs (the last water hole beyond the Black Rock) within a day's journey. With this discovery, the new road became a reality; the exploring was over. Applegate and his party had succeeded in finding a route across the wilderness from the Oregon settlement with camping spots and water at a reasonable distance apart.[155]

The Rush to Use the New Trail

Now that the course of the road had been charted, the road needed to be improved. However, the expedition was running low on supplies; they also calculated that they would need about thirty strong men to help open the new road for wagon traffic. The company agreed that if sufficient men were not secured, no one was to be encouraged to use the new road.[156] Jesse Applegate, Moses Harris, Henry Bogus, David Goff, and John Owens left for Fort Hall to secure supplies for the destitute road explorers and possibly to turn some of the '46 emigrants onto the new road. The rest of the expedition stayed behind to recoup their animals and begin work on the new road.[157] Levi Scott, with David Goff as his aide, was appointed to guide any emigrants who might come over the new road to the Willamette Valley.[158]

Edwin Bryant, in his book *California*, describes his meeting with the Applegate party:

> At Mary's (Humboldt) river, Nevada, met the Applegate party with pleasure and parted with regret. I could but admire the public spirit and enterprise of the small band of men to whom we had to say good-bye. Whatever has been accomplished has been the bold daring of our frontiersmen and pioneers. To whom we are indebted for the good, well beaten and plain trail to the Pacific. Let us honor those to whom honor is due…A singularity of the incident was that, after having traveled across a desert by a new route some three or four hundred miles, we should have met them just at the moment when they were passing the point of our junction with the old trail. Had we been ten minutes later, we should not have seen them.[159]

Somewhere along the trail, as Applegate and his four companions headed to Fort Hall, they met William E. Taylor on his way to California. Taylor recorded in his diary: "met Black harris and applegate who had been to view a new Road to Oregon and designed meeting the emigrants to turn them into it."[160]

At that meeting with Taylor on the California road, Henry Boygus heard that Captain Grant's son was going east. Boygus wanted to return to Missouri and thought he could do it with Grant's son's party, so he took off at once to catch up with them. He was never heard from again.

Also at this meeting, Moses Harris learned that his friend from his mountain man days, Medders Vanderpool, was leading a wagon train down the Snake River ahead of them. Harris and David Goff hurried ahead to meet Vanderpool and were successful in directing them to the new road. In addition, as Jesse continued toward Fort Hall, he met Virgil Pringle's twenty-one-wagon train and turned them toward the new road.[161]

Jesse Applegate arrived at Fort Hall on August 8. He described his situation to his brother Lisbon on August 9.

Dear Brother,

I arrived here yesterday alone and on foot from the Willamette Valley at the head of a party to meet the emigration. We left our homes on Willamette the 22d June last to explore a Southern route into that valley from the U.S.— After much labor and suffering we succeeded in our object tho it occupied us so long that a part of the emigrants had passed our place of intersection with the old road before we could possible reach it.

The new route follows the California road about 350 miles from here, it then leaves Ogdens or Marys river and enters Oregon by the way of the Clamet Lakes, [sic] Rogue river, Umpqua and the head of the Willamette Valley—it shortens the road—avoids the dangers of Snake & Columbia rivers and passes of the Cascade Mts.—there is almost every place plenty of grass and water & every wagon ox or cow may enter Oregon.

I would give you a more lengthy description of this road if I had time or opportunity but I cannot escape the importunities of the emigrants who are pursing me into every room of the fort and besieging me with endless questions on all possible subjects—so much am I confused that I scarce know what I have written or wish to write—Suffice to say we fully succeeded in our object tho not a man of us had ever been in the country before—

I met Larkin Stanley going to California & Oregon who told me you were coming to Oregon next year, if it is so I am glad to hear it—and gladder still that I have assisted in finding a new route. I would write and wish to write much to you but at present I have no opportunity the emigrants will give no peace ... Jesse Applegate[162]

Jesse did write a second letter to his brother the next day, August 10:

Tell Betsy and the boys that upon the new road ... they will see some of the greatest wonders of nature. So truly wonderful is some parts of the road that I am unequal to the task of giving you a description. The immense masses of mountains covered in eternal snows, the black smoke of volcanoes, the boiling springs, and deep and dark passes among the Mountains into which the sun never shines, and the high plains over which we pass, where frost falls and ice freezes every night. It is worth a year's travel to see these wonders of nature, to say nothing on the immense number and variety of wild animals to be seen upon the road. In haste,
Jesse Applegate
P.S. Tomorrow I start homeward ... [163]

Jesse also wrote an open letter to future Oregon emigrants and mailed it to the *Western Expositor* in Independence, Missouri:

Fort Hall, August 10, 1846
Gentlemen:
The undersigned are happy to inform you that a southern route to the Willamette has just been explored, and a portion of the emigrants of the present year are now on the road. Owing to the unavoidable delay, the exploring party did not arrive at the fork of the road until some of the front companies of emigrants were passed, perhaps eighty or one hundred wagons.

The new route follows the road to California about 320 miles from this place, and enters the Oregon Territory by the way of the Clamet [sic] Lake, passes through the splendid valley of the Rogue and Umpqua rivers, and enters the valley of the Willamette near its south eastern extremity.

The advantage gained to the emigrants by this route is of greatest importance-the distance is considerably shortened, the grass and water plenty, the sterile regions and dangerous crossings of the Snake and Columbia Rivers avoided as well as the Cascade Mountain—he may reach his place of destination with his wagons and property in time to build a cabin and sow wheat before the rainy season. This road had been explored, and will be opened at the expense of the citizens of Oregon, and nothing whatever is demanded of the emigrants.... [Would not be a toll road]

Editors of Missouri, Illinois, and Iowa, friendly to the prosperity of Oregon will please insert the foregoing communication.

Jesse Applegate.[164]

In his book *The Plains Across,* John D. Unruh Jr. explains Jesse's role in the new road: "In early August, the contingent of Oregon boosters at Fort Hall was bolstered by the arrival of Jesse Applegate and several members of his exploring party direct from the Willamette Valley over a southerly trail they had just blazed. Applegate's open letter to the emigrants, his effective proselytizing at the fort, and the promise of exploring party personnel as guides for the remainder of the journey were enough to turn many over-landers previously committed to California toward Oregon—and Applegate's new trail."[165]

The new trail sounded promising to many of the emigrants: Unruh states in *The Plains Across* that approximately five hundred emigrants turned onto the new trail in 1846. Buena Cobb Stone in her article "Southern Route into Oregon" in the June 1946 *Oregon Historical Quarterly* writes that about 100 wagons turned on to the new road. Helfrich's "Applegate Trail" says that ninety to one hundred wagons used the new trail in 1846.

Now Jesse Applegate could truly claim the title of "pioneer," for he had led men into unexplored regions to find a new, and he hoped safer, route into Oregon. This selfless act should have earned him, and those brave men with him, the status of western Daniel Boones. However, we will see that they were repaid by many with only scorn.

Homeward Bound

On Tuesday, August 11, Jesse hurried back to his small band of explorers with the much-needed supplies, and on his way, continued to show emigrants to the new road. On August 13, somewhere near Raft River, Jesse met the Dunbar Wagon Train, whose members included Mr. and Mrs. Jesse Quinn Thornton, the James Smith family, and the Rev. J. A. Cornwall family.[166] Jesse not only convinced them to try the new road to Oregon but also added two young men to the road building crew: William Kirquendall and Charles Putnam.[167]

While on the Oregon Trail, the Thorntons had been traveling with the Donner family. They had camped together on Little Sandy before reaching Fort Bridger,[168] where the Donners were persuaded to take Hastings Cut-Off, with famously tragic results. Knowing the fate of the Donner Party, Thornton might have felt himself fortunate to have instead taken the Applegate Trail, but we will see that is not his response.

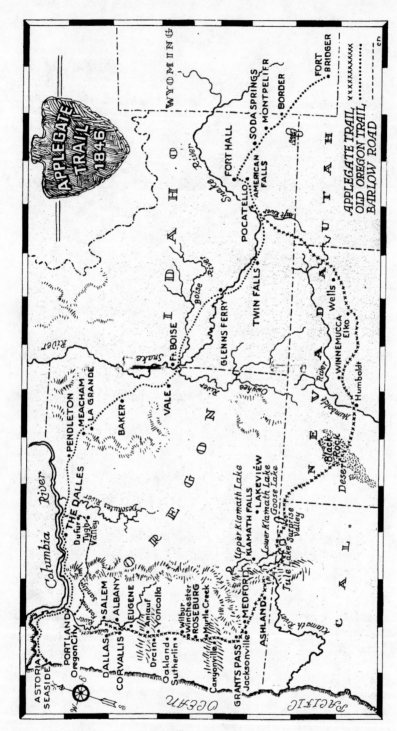

Applegate Trail; 1846

Thornton and Virgil Pringle kept diaries of their overland journeys. Pringle's diary, a daily account from Missouri to Oregon, is a valuable resource to all students of the pioneer experience and the Applegate Trail. Thornton kept a daily journal up to August 21, but claimed to have lost the subsequent pages somewhere in the Rogue Valley. He later wrote a "remembrance" of that time, but this document is flawed by the confusion about dates and places as well as by some exaggerated accounts.

Jesse Applegate met the road exploration crew somewhere near the Thousand Spring Valley, and a new company of road workers was formed. The road crew included all the original outward-bound explorers except for Henry Boygus, Levi Scott, and David Goff, along with several new volunteers recruited from the various trains coming down the trail toward the new cut-off. Lindsay Applegate later remembered the number in the road crew to be twenty to twenty-one.[169] However, Joseph Burke, a young British botanist who had joined the road crew, stated in a letter dated October 17, 1846 that there were twenty-four men in the road crew. In either case, they did not have the thirty men that they had all agreed would be needed to cut the trail ahead of the wagons. In fact, Harris, Goff, and Jesse had failed to heed their own advice by guiding wagons onto the new road without having the thirty men needed to clear it. This decision would have some unfortunate consequences.

The road workers turned onto the new southern route, or Applegate Trail, on September 6, 1846.[170] Before they started out ahead of the wagons to improve the road, Jesse gave some very sound advice to the emigrants; information he had learned from his experience as the leader of the "cow column" of 1843. His first piece of advice was that they should do nothing that would delay them, but keep moving! Secondly, he warned the emigrants that they should travel in companies of no less than twenty wagons each, so that they could protect themselves from possible attacks from local Indians.[171] As Jesse himself had forgotten his own advice about the number of men needed for the road clearing, the emigrants chose to ignore his advice, again with unfortunate consequences.

Although Burke states in his letter that there were twenty-four men in the road crew, Dever Helfrich in his *Klamath Echoes* articles on the Applegate Trail documents that seven of the twenty-four dropped out before the road crew had crossed the Devil's Garden area west of Goose Lake.

At Goff's Spring, now known as Pot Hole Spring, near Clear Lake, Jesse Applegate decided he could best serve the emigrants by returning to the valley and securing supplies to send back to the train, as it was late in the season and evident that supplies were running low. He blazed a tree and left a note buried among the roots informing Scott of his decision.[172] It is unclear what the note said, but there is reason to believe that Lindsay Applegate was left in charge of the road crew. Joseph Burke states in a letter to his patron in England that appeared in the *Spectator,* that he, John Jones, and Jesse arrived back at Jesse's home near the Rickreall River on September 26.

Scott, after finding the note, paused for two days to refresh the teams and "to give me an opportunity to go forward and examine the country and select the best way for the road." He felt that Applegate's road party had "pushed on, doing but little to aid those behind them." Scott also complained of how little work had been done to clear the heavy forest of the Siskiyou Mountains. The road party had blazed (marked trees) the trail, but had done little to clear the roadway.[173]

Jesse set about securing supplies to send back to the beleaguered emigrants as soon as he arrived home. Among the supplies were cattle from the Applegates' own herds. Jesse sent Asa Williams and William Kirquendall down the trail with a small herd of cattle to help replenish the emigrants' stock. John Jones and Tom Smith were also soon on their way back down the trail with what food could be gathered from the settlement's slim supplies. Jesse had intended to return with the relief party, but Cynthia was less than a month from delivering her eighth child. It had been a very difficult pregnancy and it was decided that since he had pressing responsibilities at home, someone else could take the relief supplies back down the trail.[174] Among the fifteen men who had set out to explore a new way into Oregon, only Jesse and Lindsay had young families at home. Scott and Goff had grown children, and the remaining young men were all bachelors.

Lindsay Applegate describes the work crew's job:

> No circumstance worthy of mention occurred on the monotonous march back from Black Rock to the timbered region of the Cascade chain; then our labors became quite arduous. Every day we kept guard over the horses while we worked the road, and at night we dared not cease our vigilance for the Indians continually hovered about us, seeking for advantage. By the time we had worked our way through the mountains to the Rogue river valley, and then through the Grave Creek Hills and Umpqua chain, we were thoroughly worn out...Road working, hunting, and guard duty had taxed our strength greatly, and on our arrival in the Umpqua valley, knowing that the greatest difficulties in the way of immigrants had been removed, we decided to proceed at once to our home in the Willamette...having been absent three months and thirteen days. During all this time our friends had heard nothing from us, and realizing the dangerous character of our expedition, many believed in the news which some time before reached them, that we had all been murdered by the Indians.
>
> As soon as we could possible make arrangement, we sent out a party with oxen and horses to meet the immigrants and aid them in reaching the Willamette settlement. For this assistance we made no demand, nor did we tax them for the use of the road, as was alleged by parties inimical to our enterprise. It had been the distinct understanding that the road should be free, and the consciousness of having opened a better means of access to the country than was afforded by the expensive and dangerous route down the Columbia, which we had tried to our sorrow, would be *ample* compensation for all our labors and hardships in opening the South road.[175]

Many find this description of the work done by the road crew very unsatisfactory; as it gives no real detail of the work done on the road, or indication of the time spent. However, to this date, it is the only description of the road crew's work that has been located.

First Use of the Trail: Real and Perceived Difficulties

There are several excellent books documenting the journey of the 1846 emigrants across the new southern route into Oregon, the Applegate Trail, so we will only examine the journey in enough detail to understand the controversy that was to follow. One problem that arose for the emigrants was difficulties with Indians, who shot poisoned arrows at them and stole their cattle. Since the emigrants, against Jesse's advice, were travelling in small companies, they did not have the numerical strength to intimidate the Indians, and the small road crew could be of little assistance.[176] Levi Scott would later comment that some of the emigrants seemed to think that he was under obligation to furnish them a good, easy road with plenty of grass and water. "These demands were extravagant and foolish, for they knew as well as I did that there was no road at all till we should make it." [177]

Wagons going into High Rock Canyon

When they finally reached the foot of the Cascade Mountains, many of the emigrants, instead of letting nothing delay them, rested for several days before beginning the laborious climb up the mountains. The slope was so steep that it took three to four yoke of oxen to take each wagon to the top; Thornton would later claim that it took as many as twenty-three yoke of oxen for a single wagon. Because the wagons were so scattered, it took three weeks to bring all of them across the mountains, and the length of time combined with the arduous climb meant that many, Thornton among them, lost live-stock and were forced to abandon wagons and equipment. Bitter at his loss, Thornton blamed Jesse Applegate personally for this loss and took it upon himself to record problems that might discredit the road and the road builders. As the emigrants continued on their difficult journey, food grew scarce and winter drew near.[178] Once they were across the mountains they might have thought that the worst was behind them, but in reality, the portion of the trail that would cause the most grief was still to come.

Miss Martha Leland Crowley, a popular young lady aged four-teen, died October 18, 1846, as the wagons were coming down Sexton Mountain into the little valley that is now known as Sunny Valley. The next morning the wagons moved about a mile to Grave Creek, where the emigrants spent the day giving Martha a proper burial.

Levi Scott describes the next few days:

> It was about twenty-five miles to Cow Creek, but the road lay through very rough timbered hills, and it took us three days of hard labor to reach that creek…The next day we moved up the creek, only about eight miles, and camped to give the cattle a chance to graze, and the men an opportunity to rest a little.
>
> The next morning, when we were about ready to start, Jack Jones and Tom Smith of Oregon City, came into our camp. Jones had gone into the Willamette Valley with Captain Applegate, and now in company with Smith had returned to meet us with a few beef cattle. They came to our camp just as

we were about ready to start. The people were anxious to hear anything from the place of their destination.[179]

Smith described the supposedly insurmountable difficulties of the canyon before them in such graphic detail that the emigrants were completely demoralized, bordering on despair. Scott could not get the emigrants to move until three o'clock in the afternoon and then they only moved about two miles.

The relief party moved on and met Thornton on the south side of the Rogue River, near present day Grants Pass. Jones sold two steers and some flour to Thornton and moved on down the trail looking for other stragglers. Thornton records in his journal:

> Sabbath. We met Messrs. Brown, Allen and Jones and some two or three other persons. The first two had come out to the wilderness for the purpose of meeting their friends in the company of Messrs. Brown and Allen [Seniors], who have already been mentioned as having retreated back in haste, to Ogden's river, when they at length became convinced of Applegate's want of veracity respecting the road....Mr. Jones, knowing that the emigrants would be in great danger of perishing for the want of food, had gone forward into the settlements for beef-cattle, with which to meet them.[He had gone forward with Jesse and in all probability the beef was from Jesse's herd] He had left some with the forward company, and had now brought two to us.

Meanwhile, Scott was trying to move the lead group forward, and the next day they finally moved on to the dreaded canyon:

> and I must say dreadful canyon, where we really could go no further without first having made a road through this formidable gorge. I spent two days in a fruitless endeavor to get a party to go with me, on foot, through the canyon. No one would go. Finally I emphatically called the company to attention, and told them that I was going through the next

morning...If no one would go with me, nor make any effort to get through the mountain, I should go home, I said: "I will not stay, idly, here and see you all perish, because you will not put fourth an effort to help yourself...I shall start into the canyon in the morning. Will you go with me?"[180]

Scott and four men ended up going into the canyon the next morning, and they struggled through the worst ten miles of road he had ever seen.[181] However, it was concluded that if all available men were willing to work at making a trail through the canyon, it could be done in a few days. Indeed, the road exploration crew had all agreed on the outward-bound journey that it was possible to build a road through Canyon Creek canyon. Scott explains the difficulties:

> There was a swift, rocky creek running through the canyon which was a serious difficulty that we could neither remedy nor avoid. In many places it was shut in between high, perpendicular walls of rock, where there was no other possible place for the road except in the channel of the stream, sometimes for a distance of fifty yards to a furlong in a place. The bed of the creek was, in many of these places, a slick, smooth rock, pitching down at a steep angle, or with an equally steep dip to one side, over which the wagon must be steadied, and let down with ropes.
>
> There were several short bends in these narrow places which were very difficult to get through, and in some of them, large boulders blocked up the channel, where the strait was narrow and the bluffs abrupt, so that a wagon could not by any means pass around them...In such places we were compelled to throw in logs and brush with earth and stone to fill and bridge over the boulders.[182]

The road they had just created required that the creek stay low so that all the logs and boulders would stay in place and allow the emigrants to slowly work their way across the improvised path. The uniqueness of this mountain was described in the Way Bill, printed in the *Oregon Spectator*: "You go over other mountains, this you go through."[183]

The way bill in the *Spectator* has always been attributed to Jesse Applegate, but a letter recently discovered in the Abernethy manuscript file at the Oregon Historical Society sheds some new light on the matter. The letter is from Jesse Applegate to George Abernethy, dated March 20, 1848:

> Before leaving for the Umpqua Capt Scott left with me a way bill of the road as it now stands which with some advice and illustrations drawn from my journal of 1846 I herewith enclose to you to be used as you think proper...If the state of the upper country should continue as at present and you should advise immigrants to travel the South road, the way bill will be envaluable [sic]information to give them." [184]

The way bill was printed in the *Oregon Spectator* on April 6, 1848 with the reference that it had been received from Jesse Applegate. Taking the new information into account, it seems reasonable to draw the conclusion that Jesse wrote the advice to the emigrants that appears at the front of the document and perhaps the summary at the end, but Levi Scott wrote the day-to-day descriptions and millage quotes of the often quoted "way bill."

Finally, on the morning of October 26 the wagons started into Canyon Creek Canyon, but on the twenty-seventh it began to rain; the rain would not stop for at least a week. Weather records show that there was a series of severe storms from Vancouver to the Sacramento Valley during this time period. One of these storms turned to snow on October 28 in the Sierra Nevada Mountains, stranding the ninety wagons of the George Donner party. Trapped on the mountain, the Donner Party would lose twenty-two emigrants to starvation; another fourteen died trying to make their way over the mountain to the Sacramento Valley.

Virgil Pringle had faithfully written in his journal every day from the start of his trip, but the trials of the canyon caused him to stop writing for ten days. Finally, on November 1, 1846, he records the difficulties of the journey: "We started through on Monday morning and reached the opposite plain on Friday night after a series of breakdowns, hardships, and being constantly wet. Laboring hard and very little to eat. The provisions being exhausted in the whole company. We ate our last the evening we got through. The wet season commenced the second day after we started through the mountains [October 27] and continued to the first of November, which was a partially fair day. The distance through: 16 miles."[185]

The Pringle family and those in the forward group made it through the canyon in five days, but those who followed would suffer more and more with each passing day. The small, swift creek had now turned into a raging river. The logs and boulders placed by Levi Scott and his road crew had long since washed away. Now the emigrants were forced to wade in the streambed, sometimes in water to their waist or chest. There was no escape from the freezing cold water they waded in or the never-ending rain pounding them from above.

Wagons going into Canyon Creek Canyon using the flooded river bed as their road

Cornwall and his family lost so much to the canyon that they built a small cabin near present day Oakland and spent the winter there, going on to the Willamette Valley in the spring. He writes the following description of the canyon from his little cabin that winter:

This Canin[sic] is a very narrow passage through the mountain, along a branch or ravine; having perpendicular rocks on each side for a considerable distance, and a miserably rough craggy bottom. It presents 15 to 18 miles of road that would be pronounced altogether impassible by any other than an Oregon teamster, who had already driven between 2 and 3,000 miles,—and the truth is, it proved so to about one-half of our wagons.

The emigrants were divided into 3 companies of about equal number, who traveled 7 or 8 days in advance of each other. The first succeeded in passing the Canin after a great deal of labor and fatigue, with the loss of some of their wagons, and a great many oxen. I was in the second company, and as we could not pass the Canin so well in a crowd, I set out with two other wagons a day or two in advance of the rest and Proceeded only about 3 miles the first day; which was considered a very good day's travel. The rain commenced the first night, and after laboring hard for 3 days longer, I succeeded in accomplishing only 6 or 7 miles further; in all but a little over one-half of the distance through the Canin. On that fatal spot, I lost 8 yoke of oxen, about half of my loose cattle and a good young mare, which rendered me incapable of removing from the encampment for about 10 days…

But to return to my companions. The most of them entered the Canin, proceeded about one-third distance, left their wagons, and were reduced to the necessity of packing upon their backs their clothes, bedding and other light articles out of the Canin, A distance of 10 or 12 miles… Now their sufferings were to their height. For all who were able to walk, men, women, and children wading the Canin which was considerably swollen by the recent rain and melting snow on the mountains. The water was almost as cold as ice. To see delicate females, old and young, who had been tenderly raised, wading the water almost to the waist, and small children to the arm pits, presents a spectacle of distress and suffering, which beggars description.[186]

Jesse Quinn Thornton and his wife Nancy were among the last group of emigrants to arrive at the canyon and start through. His journal indicates it was November 4, a week behind the Pringles, a week in which it had rained hard every day, "I had little remaining, save our buffalo robes, blankets, arms, ammunition, watch, and the most valuable of our wardrobe—and fearing that we would yet lose the most of this, Mrs. Thornton selected the more expensive articles of clothing, and I packed them into two sacks. I succeeded in hiring a man too carry these upon his horse. We finally determined that, on the morning of this day, we would make an effort to pass the mountain."[187] It is unclear from Thornton's journal how long it took them to get through the canyon, but the following entry shows they were through the canyon by November 14.

Most historians feel Thornton's dates are off by about a week, probably closer to November 20:

> On the following morning, both being very weak and hungry, Mrs. Thornton and myself strolled along down the river bank, with the hope of seeing something that I might shoot for food. I suddenly saw persons approaching from the direction of the settlements. I recognized Mr. Kirquendall, who together with some others had come with flour and fat beeves. They came to camp, where the animals were slaughtered on Friday, November 14, when I obtained eighteen pounds of flour, twenty pounds of beef, and one pound of tallow, at a price which, although very high, would not cause a starving man a pause.[188]

All who passed through the canyon on those terrible rain-filled days of 1846 lost most of their earthly possessions. There was not a single family that did not suffer a fearful loss in that canyon. There were deaths in the canyon, as there had been all along the trail. Mrs. Calvin Crowley gave birth to a baby in the driving rain; she and the baby died before night's end. Alonzo Wood, son of J.D. Wood, had been ill for weeks and he died during their trek through the canyon. Mr. Wood, who was bringing honeybees to Oregon, lost his hives to the raging water. The Smith Company was several days behind the lead wagons and when they reached the entrance of the canyon, a discussion arose about abandoning the wagons. William Smith, the leader of the Smith Company, was adamant that they should not leave the wagons behind. He gathered the group around a large fire and began to argue his point; suddenly he fell to his knees and, crying out, "Lord have mercy upon me," collapsed and died. At least two other deaths took place in the canyon that year, one a young girl by the name of Lettie, who had been ill for some time. Most of the families who came through that canyon, however, were able to overcome their losses and go on to productive lives in Oregon.

Virgil Pringle and one other family were the first to reach the Willamette Valley from the south on November 22, 1846. Pringle's journal records the event nonchalantly: "Help finish and complete the pass of the mountains and camp 2 miles from the foot in the Willamette Valley. My wagon and one other the first that entered the valley. All in good health and well pleased with the appearance of the Country."[189] Soon after this diary entry, Virgil Pringle left his family and rode ahead looking for badly needed supplies.

Orus Brown, who had arrived in the settlements by the northern route, heard of the plight of those coming by the southern route and started out to look for his mother and sister. Tabitha Brown, Virgil Pringle's mother-in-law, was Orus Brown's mother and Pherne Brown Pringle was his sister.

> Tabitha Brown...our scanty provisions were all gone. We were in a state of starvation...We had all retired to rest in

our tents, hoping to forget our troubles until daylight should remind us again of our sad fate. In the gloomy stillness of the night, footsteps of horses were heard rushing toward our tents. Directly a haloo! It was the well-known voices of Orus Brown and Virgil Pringle. Who can realize the joy?

Scott, feeling that his job was done, records in his remembrances: "I performed the duty I had assumed, and had led the immigration into the Great Valley at the head of the Willamette River, and most likely, by the best way for a road that could be found. I felt sure that a little time and labor would make this a good road, and the principal route of travel to the Willamette."[190] Scott's prediction has proven to be right on the mark. Interstate 5, the major North/South highway in Oregon, follows very closely the road that the small band of explorers laid out in the summer of 1846.

Reactions to the Southern Route

Jesse Q. Thornton and his wife Nancy arrived in the vicinity of Corvallis at the home of a Mr. Lewis on Tuesday, November 29. He records in his remembrances "where a little milk and butter having been added to our rapidly increasing luxuries we regarded ourselves as having renewed cause to be grateful." They soon moved on to a claim in Yamhill County, later Polk County, that he called Forest Grove, the site of the present-day town of Albany.[191]

Safe from the toils of the journey, Thornton quickly forgot his "renewed cause to be grateful" and soon began criticizing the southern route in the *Oregon Spectator*, beginning a lifelong tirade against Jesse Applegate, blaming him for all his hardships and personal inconveniences along the trail, and never acknowledging that his own inadequacies might have caused most of his problems. He never admitted, for example, that his party might never have arrived at all had it not been for the relief supplies that were sent back to the emigrants by the Applegates and many other concerned citizens.

Thornton's own journal indicates that he took advantage of those supplies at least twice.

Thornton and his wife had health problems on the trip to Oregon and it was only through the kindness of their fellow travelers that they got through at all.[192] Thornton was an asthmatic and all who knew him declared he suffered from a well-developed case of hypochondria. A cash-strapped Thornton had started west in a partnership with James Goode, with Goode furnishing the wagon. They had not been on the road long, however, when a dispute erupted as to who owned the wagon and team. A wagon train court was convened, and after much haggling the wagon and team was given to Thornton because he had a wife and Goode was single. Now Thornton had to drive his own wagon. At first, Thornton refused to do such physical labor; after all, he felt that as a gentleman, he was precluded from doing such a lowly thing.

Bancroft describes Thornton's shortcomings in his *History of Oregon*:

> At Green River, Thornton began to take care of his own team for the first time and experienced much difficulty from not knowing how to yoke or drive oxen, only succeeded by the assistance of the charitable Mr. Kirquendall and others who pitied his infirmities. From information obtained from his own journal, it is evident that Thornton loitered by the way, and from comparing his estimates of distance with others, that he (Thornton) has nearly doubled the length of the worst portions of the road. The whole distance to Oregon City was really 980 miles from Fort Hall, whereas Thornton makes it 1,280.

The Scott/Applegate way bill recorded the distance to the beginning of the Willamette Valley as 860 miles. Virgil Pringle's diary shows the distance as about 940 miles to the Willamette Valley, and modern mapping indicates that Pringle's mileage is very close to being accurate.

Thomas Holt, an emigrant of 1844, was one of the settlers who organized a relief party to go to the aid of the incoming destitute emigrants. He did not have family or friends among the emigrants but felt compelled to do all he could to aid in helping them arrive at journeys end. Holt had been a member of a committee formed in Salem in February of 1846 for the purpose of raising funds for a road exploration endeavor, and to indentify those who would be willing to go on this road-hunting expedition as competent guides. Holt, however, was not one of the men who accompanied Applegate on the road-hunting expedition.

Holt kept a journal of his rescue effort, and he recorded that he met the first wagon on December 5, "a Mr. Goff bringing in Mrs. Newton." On December 8, he recorded that they overtook Capt. Campbell, Mr. Goodman, Mr. Jenkins and Mr. Harris with 25 horses and some provisions. "They were all headed to the canyon [Canyon Creek] with relief supplies." On December 6, near present-day Corvallis, Holt met, "five families with their wagons here, and one family packing." Holt indicates that he reached the last of the stranded emigrants of the South Road on December 17 near today's city of Roseburg.[193]

In March of 1847 Holt appealed to the subscribers to the *Oregon Spectator* to help with paying the $426.37 cost of the relief supplies. He felt for the cost to be "wholly defrayed by persons in as indigent circumstances as we are in, will be felt considerably."[194]

The 1846 pioneers' daily struggles helped open the new South Road, and if they had been able to follow the road they left behind, they would have, in all probability, arrived in the Willamette Valley in late October or early November. They would have been well beyond "the dreadful canyon" before the terrible storm of '46 and at journey's end before they all began to run out of supplies.[195] Though the road exploration crew set out with noble intentions and created a route that has proved to be reliable, a series of circumstances—a rush to use the road before it was properly cleared and marked, the emigrant's leisurely pace and refusal to travel in groups large enough to discourage the Indians, and the unexpectedly severe weather—all collided to make the 1846 crossing less successful than the road crew had envisioned.

Heroes or Villains?

The Southern Oregon Road Exploration party was organized as a public service to find a way into the valley that avoided not only British-controlled forts but also the treacherous Columbia River. The local newspaper, *Oregon Spectator*, had carried articles concerning the preparations for the expedition and hailed the road crew as heroes. The following article appeared in the paper after the return of the expedition: "The public mind has been happily put at rest, in relation to the welfare of Captain Jesse Applegate and party...he has succeeded in covering a most admirable road for the emigration enterprise, and on the part of Captain Applegate we hope he will be rewarded accordingly."[196]

However, Jesse Quinn Thornton was determined that Jesse Applegate receives an entirely different reward. A Virginia-born lawyer educated in London and a friend of Horace Greeley and Stephen A. Douglas, Thornton quickly made the acquaintance of several very influential fellow Methodists like George Abernethy, the territorial governor. Only six weeks after arriving in Oregon, Thornton was appointed Supreme Court justice of the Oregon

Territory by his new friend Abernethy. This was seen by many as a way to strengthen Methodist influence, which had reigned supreme in early Oregon politics.[197] This new position certainly gave Thornton a bully pulpit both in Oregon and on the national stage. He went to Washington, D.C. in 1848 representing the Oregon Territory and used the opportunity to repeat his tirade against the south road and Jesse Applegate.

Thornton lays out a detailed complaint against Jesse Applegate and the South Road in an opinion piece in the *Spectator* of March 4, 1847, of which the following is an excerpt:

> 3rd that those who have arrived in the settlements have "ARRIVED SAFELY." This also is incorrect, if anything is meant by the expression "arrived safely' beyond the simple announcement of the fact that many immigrants, after traveling a country dangerous in consequence of the hostility of the savages, have at length arrived in a very enfeebled condition to which they had been reduced by hunger, cold and nakedness. In addition to this, it may be affirmed, that almost every man, (perhaps indeed, every one) who came to Oregon by the southern route is, in a pecuniary point of view, ruined by so doing. Do men arrive "safely" lose their wagons, teams, tents and clothing and who freeze their feet, and come in looking like famished wolves?
>
> 4th That the accounts of the conditions of the immigrants "have been exaggerated." To exaggerate this account, it is feared, would be a difficult task. It is probably one which could be accomplished by those only who are the sources of your information … And I must be permitted to say, that had I been instrumental in placing a multitude of men, women, and children in such a situation, I would have eaten my bread in bitterness until I rescued them, instead of attempting to amuse the public mind either by speculations with regard to the practicability of some other route, or by wickedly attempting to produce the impression that accounts of the conditions

of the immigrants "HAVE BEEN EXAGGERATED." I say "wickedly" because I believe that, had not some influenced by improper motives, succeeded to some extent, in producing this impression on all the immigrants would by this time have been in the valley.[198]

In his book *Oregon and California*, written about a year after this article, Thornton describes his first impressions of Jesse Applegate. It seems inconceivable that Thornton would choose to follow Applegate onto the South Road if these were indeed his thoughts at the time.

> In the forenoon one Jesse Applegate came into camp, informed the company that himself and Colonel Nat. Ford had united together for the purpose of organizing a company of road-hunters; and that as a result, himself, Major David Goff, a brother-in-law of Col Nat. Ford, Major Moses Harris, and Captain Scott, had led out a party of road-hunters from the Willamette Valley, for the purpose of exploring a new route, which should be both better and nearer than the old one to Oregon. I never could learn how it was that Applegate obtained the title of "captain," unless it was in some such way as that to which I once knew a "major" resort for the purpose of obtaining a supply of linen. *Captain* comes from the Latin *capat*, a head. But Captain Applegate has not enough head to make it appropriate to bestow upon him so great a title for the sake of a head which is not sufficiently large to be taken for the primitive of such a derivative.[199]

Bancroft/Victor critiques Thornton's book:

> These two volumes could well have been contained in one by the omission of the author's narrative of the incidents of the immigration, which reveal a narrowness of judgment and bitterness of spirit seldom associated with those mental en-

dowments of which Mr. Thornton gives evidence in his writings … As this was written after he had been a year in Oregon and learned the high character of the men who composed the expedition … the vituperative censure indulged in by Mr. Thornton, is, to say the least, in bad taste.[200]

The pages of the *Spectator* began to burn with angry rhetoric from both sides of the South Road issue. The anti-south road group lived in the north end of the valley, many of them connected to the Methodist mission, and they stood to lose heavily in trade and community development if each year's new wave of emigrants came in from the south. This group declared the new route far more dangerous than the well-established Columbia River road and went so far as to declare that the men who opened the new road did so from purely selfish motives,[201] having seemingly forgotten the original motivation for the south road, the fear of war with the British. However, by the time this debate was raging, the border dispute between the United States and Great Britain had been settled in favor of the United States, and so the need for a new route had lost its urgency.

There were many complaints made about the South Road that could have been made of the entire Oregon Trail. Thornton speaks of every ox that died along the way as a sacrifice to the misrepresentation of the Applegate party, though many oxen had died long before he reached Fort Hall and had contact with Jesse. Nevertheless, Thornton chose to refer to the road crew and Jesse in particular as "outlaws and banditti."

Jesse Q. Thornton was the most vocal of the new road's critics but certainly not the only one. Tabitha Brown, mother-in-law to Virgil Pringle, a prominent and well-respected citizen, certainly felt that the promise of the south road had not been kept. She tells the story of her 1846 cross-country journey at the age of sixty-six not to the newspaper, but in a letter to her brother and sister in August 1854:

The novelty of our journey, with a few exceptions was pleasing and prosperous until after we passed Fort Hall, then we were within 800 miles of Oregon City. If we had kept the old road down the Columbia River—but three or four trains of emigrants were decoyed off by a rascally fellow who came out from the settlement in Oregon, assuring us that he had found a near cut-off; that if we would follow him we would be in the settlement long before those who had gone down the Columbia. This was August. The idea of shortening a long journey caused us to yield to his advice. Our suffering from that time no tongue can tell. (He left a pilot with us who proved to be an excellent man otherwise we never would have seen Oregon.) He said he would clear the road before us; that we should have no trouble in rolling our wagons after him; and left us to the depredations of Indians, wild beasts, and starvation—but God was with us. We had sixty miles desert without grass or water, mountains to climb, cattle giving out, wagons breaking, emigrants sick and dying hostile Indians to guard against by night and by day to keep from being killed, or having or horses and cattle arrowed or stolen.—passed the Umpqua mountains (twelve miles through) I rode through in three days at the risk of my life, having lost my wagon, and all I had but the horse I was on.[202]

The Applegates and the South Road had their supporters too, and they firmly maintained that the road crew had set out to explore a new road for nothing but pure patriotic motives; none of them ever gained financially for their dangerous labor on behalf of the community.

Even the editor of the *Spectator* was caught in the crossfire. Moses Harris, one of the members of the original exploring party, sent a blistering letter dated November 26, 1846 to the editor:

Let me tell you, Mr. Editor, the company to which I am proud to belong, did not leave their homes to ride a few days up the Willamette river and return with a false report to the people: they went seriously determined to find a road, if one was to be found; they went actuated by the purest motives, and in the spirit of patriotism and philanthropy, and they were more than successful. They have explored and opened a wagon road to the western valley of Oregon which may be traveled at any time and at all seasons, by a shorter and in all respects better route than any heretofore known...And lastly, by their own unassisted means, they have succeeded in establishing a connecting link between the waters of Oregon, and those of the great interior basin of California, before unknown, and which one of the ablest explorers (Fremont) in the service of the United States attempted, without success. Such, Mr. Editor, are the achievements of the exploring party, which envy and cupidity would render nugatory.[203]

A letter written to the editor under the name David Goff, (probably written by his son-in-law, James Nesmith,) responds to one of Thornton's letters with a strong defense of the new road and notes, "the most bitter and false attacks upon myself and my associates who were employed last season in exploring the southern route to Oregon." Goff then describes Thornton as a man whose "conduct had made him so odious that the company with whom he traveled would scarcely have raised a hand to defend his life or dig a hole to hide him when dead." Goff (Nesmith) then goes on to say "that the quibble, subterfuge, and falsehood which might pass unnoticed in the pettifogger becomes conspicuous in the judge, and his present elevation, like the monkey on the pole, only shows the plainer that the robe of ermine but half conceals the dog."[204]

Thornton replied in a similar tone that Goff could not write his own name, let alone the letter. He then assailed the editor for allowing the press of Oregon to sink to the lowest scurrility and personal abuse, and for permitting his paper to be filled with epithets more suitable to a London fish market.[205] The editor replied to Thornton that he thought both he and the paper would survive the attacks.

By the beginning of the summer of 1847, the debate raging in the paper had grown so heated that James Nesmith, champion of the Applegate faction, came to Oregon City vowing to kill Thornton. Nesmith challenged Thornton to a duel, but Thornton refused to accept any communication from Nesmith, thus technically avoiding the issue. Nesmith then sought his due by posting a handbill all around the Willamette Valley, which reads:

TO THE WORLD!! J. Quinn Thornton, having resorted to low, cowardly and dishonorable means, for the purpose of injuring my character and standing and having refused honorable satisfaction, which I have demanded, I avail myself of this opportunity of publishing him to the world as a reclaimed liar, an infamous scoundrel, a black hearted villain, an arrant coward, a worthless vagabond and an imported miscreant, a disgrace to the profession and a dishonor to his country.
JAMES W. NESMITH
Oregon City June 7, 1847

To the World-Broadside

Thornton must have had some redeeming qualities because he became Dr. McLoughlin's lawyer and remained in that capacity until McLoughlin's death; Jesse always said that Dr. McLoughlin was one of the noblest men he ever had the privilege to know.

Jesse Applegate endured the public slander from Thornton with calm detachment. Family history holds that he forbade the matter to be discussed at home, and no one ever saw him reading any of the newspaper accounts, though it was his habit to read every word of the paper and often responded to an article with a letter to the editor. However, he allowed himself to give vent on the issue to his brother Lisbon:

> Unfortunately for the present emigration the emigrants who traveled the Southern route to Oregon did badly. For want of energy and diligence in traveling they were caught by the rains which were of unusual severity at the Umpqua Mountains about 75 miles from the Willamette Valley. Being out of bread and much discouraged many of the families abandoned their wagons and much of their property and were packed into the settlements. The merchants of Oregon City, a chartered company which has a toll gate in the Cascade Mountains, and the major part of the old settlers, being interested in the profits arising from the old road down the Columbia, eagerly seized upon the circumstance to denounce the newly discovered route, and of course the men who had found and recommended it. As our whole party with I think few exceptions undertook the hazardous duty of discovering a better route from the purest spirit of philanthropy having no pecuniary views whatever, you may imagine our feelings when for our exertions for the general good instead of thanks of our fellow citizens, we were assailed from all sides with abuse, and slander the most injurious. By exercising my patience and summoning all my fortitude to my aid, I steadily maintained my position, and defended the *road* without noticing private slanders. In a series of articles signed Z, I reviewed the dif-

ficulties encountered by the several emigrations in reaching this country and closed by showing plainly the advantages of the Southern route over any heretofore known.[206]

Jesse wrote a series of four letters to the *Oregon Spectator* titled "The Road to Oregon." The first one was published on January 21, 1847 and the last April 16, 1847. He signed them 'Z,' never identifying the author as Jesse Applegate. The first letter began:

From the great length of the journey from the United States to the Willamette Valley, the many rivers to cross and mountains to climb, it is but reasonable to suppose that emigrants would meet with many accidents, and suffer many losses in its accomplishment. To lessen these casualties to those who follow them, should therefore be the wish, as it is the interest of every citizen of the valley.

To show the necessity of improvements upon the route, and the means adopted to effect them, I shall briefly refer to the time and manner in which the three preceding emigrations have accomplished the journey; as the latter part of the road is much the most difficult, as well as most susceptible of improvement, all improvement worthy of notice, have been made or attempted west of the Rocky mountains.

Jesse described the journey of 1843:

When we consider the scarcity of grass and water along most of the route, the dangerous crossings of the Snake river, and the making of the road for so great a distance, over wide plains of sage and sand, most impassible mountains, that they arrived on the Columbia at all, is a proof of energy and perseverance not often equaled by those who have followed them.

The obstacles so formidable had not been surmounted without much labor and loss, both of life and property; yet, though so near the end of their journey, they experienced by far, more losses, hardships and suffering in descending from the Dalles to the Willamette, than all the rest of the journey...

The letter proceeds to document the emigration of 1844:

> The emigrants of 1844 fared even worse than those of the preceding year; arriving late in the season, when by reason of the snow, the trail by Mount Hood was thought to be impassable; the greater part of their worn down animals were swum to the north side of the Columbia, which is nearly a mile wide, driven down on that side and re-crossed in boats at Vancouver; a rout of great danger, fatigue and exposure to the owners, and in which more than half the animals were lost... Most of the citizens having experienced these calamities, and seeing their friends arrive in this distant country, shorn of the means of their comfort, or of becoming useful citizens; a desire to remedy these evils became universal.

The letter then describes several attempts to find a new route from far Eastern Oregon to the Willamette Valley by crossing the high desert into the Cascade Mountains and ends with the following:

> The failure of Dr. White's enterprise left the large emigration of 1845, to find their way into the Willamette valley by the usual means; the supply of boats being wholly inadequate to their speedy conveyance down the Columbia, and the stock of provisions failing at The Dalles, famine and a malignant disease at the same time raging amongst them, a scene of human misery ensued which scarcely has a parallel in history—the loss of life and property was enormous... the year of 1846 is not more an epoch to be remembered in the history of Oregon for the quiet settlement of the boundary, than for the arrival of emigrants from the United States with their wagons, at both ends of the Willamette Valley.

The second letter written by Z was published in the *Oregon Spectator* on February 4, 1847:

> To avoid the danger and heavy expense of descending the Columbia by water, a party of the emigrants of 1845, under the direction of Samuel K. Barlow, undertook to open a road for their wagons along the southern trail. (Around Mt. Hood.)
>
> They succeeded in penetrating the mountains to within a few miles of the main ridge, but the increasing snow, and the scarcity of pasturage and provisions forced them to leave their wagons and hasten with their animals to the valley. To encourage Mr. Barlow to complete his road, as it would be of great benefit to future emigrants, a considerable sum was raised by subscription for the benefit, and the privilege granted him by the Legislature to collect a toll of $5 on each wagon, and 10 cents a head for horses and cattle that passed his road…

The *Oregon Spectator* of March 18, 1847, carried the third letter written by Z. In this letter Jesse gives a lengthy description of the South Road:

> On the road in the valleys, it is only necessary to state that the grass is every where plenty, and water at convenient distances-the road crosses a few hills in the different valleys, and some rocky country in the valley of the Sacramento; with these exceptions, it is over firm, level plains-the streams are crossed at good rocky fords, and at the proper season are, from their size, of little impediment. The mountains require a more particular description.
>
> The ridge dividing the water of the Willamette and Umpqua rivers, is called the Calapooia mountains: it is narrow and of no great height, and may be crossed in many places; the wagon road crosses it by ridge way about 10 miles in length from prairie to prairie, and is not complained of by the immigrants…

The Umpqua mountains divides the waters of Rogue river and Umpqua and is much more formidable than the Calapooia, being a much higher, rockier ridge, and over it, it is impracticable to make a wagon road.

The road passes through a chasm which cuts the mountain from side to side to its very base. As this pass has been a place of much disaster in some of the immigrations, and is of itself a natural curiosity. A pool of water about 15 feet in diameter, occupies the dividing ground between waters of the Rogue river and Umpqua; there is from the east to the west about 30 yards of level land between the mountains which rises abruptly to the height of about 1500 feet-the descent each way from the point is very gentle-that to the south in about three miles there is sufficient space of level ground, and but little work required to make a good road; but below this, the stream increasing in size by the entrance of effluents, and the mountains closing in upon it, the road must descend in its rocky bed, made more difficult by some large stones and short falls…The party employed in opening the road being in want of the necessary tools and scarce of provisions, were unable to make this road properly, and attempted only to make this road passable with as little labor as possible. On the level ground it is made crooked in going around logs and trees, and the banks at the crossing of the creek are left too steep, and at that part of the pass properly known as the kanyon (sic), the road is taken along the side of the hill so steep as to require the greatest care to prevent wagons from upsetting. The difficulties of the road were much increased by the rains commencing about the time the first wagons were left on the south side of the mountain, there owners thinking it impossible to take them through the pass.

The fourth letter form Z was printed on April 16, 1847, and the letter ends with this critique of the southern route by Jesse. "Though the southern route to Oregon, so far as traveling is concerned, is much superior to the northern route, yet under present circumstances, I should hesitate to advise immigrants to travel it, particularly if their destination be to the northern portion of the territory." Jesse was concerned about the Indians along the southern route harassing the emigrants.

Years later, Jesse states in a letter to Bancroft: "The cause of loss and suffering to Emigrants to California and Oregon in the year of 1846 was that a very dry summer which much diminished the supply of grass and water on the plains was (as is nearly always the case) followed by an unusually early wet, and inclement, winter." In this same letter, Jesse takes exception to a statement that Bancroft's colleague Mrs. Victor had made about the south road in her book *River of the West*, namely that "The first emigrants who got through into the valley sent relief to those behind." Jesse gives this correction: "It was the explorers assisted by other benevolent citizens who hastened to their relief taking with them provisions, horses and oxen, and never left them until every man, woman, and child, (except a family that of its own choice stopped in the Umpqua Valley) were safe in the settlements."

In the spring of 1847, Levi Scott traveled over the southern route once more to meet incoming emigrants and led about eighty wagons back down the trail. They arrived in the valley in good time and good condition on October 24, 1847, three days before the rains had started at Canyon Creek in 1846. Shortly after their arrival, Jesse Applegate sent the following letter to the *Spectator:*

Polk County, Oregon, Nov. 2, 1847
Dear Sir—I am happy to inform you of the safe arrival, In the Willamette Valley, of Capt. L. Scott and party, by the southern route...Capt. Scott, who has by no means lost his character for perseverance, has considerably improved many places in the road, both in the ground and in lessening the distance.

The immigrants also deserve praise for their readiness and alacrity in assisting him in his efforts for their benefit...Much honor is due the immigrants who followed Capt. Scott over the southern route, for they have done much for the future prosperity of this country. By their energy and perseverance, they have redeemed the character of a road ... [207]

A look at the diaries of two travelers along the Oregon Trail and south road from 1847 might provide a valid comparison of the two routes. Peter W. Crawford and Lester Hulin traveled together across the Oregon Trail until they split at Raft River. Crawford, who continued on the old Oregon Trail, wrote a very detailed description of his journey down the Snake River, on to the Columbia, and down the Columbia gorge. He arrived at Switzer's Landing on the Columbia, across from Fort Vancouver, on November 26, 1847.[208] His diary describes long stretches with little food or water for the animals. Lester Hulin, on the other hand, traveled the south road and arrived in the southern end of the Willamette Valley on November 2, 1847, and at Skinner's Cabin on November 4, twenty-two days before those who traveled the Columbia River route reached their destination at Switzer's landing.[209]

A similar account of the success of the new route is given by Charles Putnam, who praises the Applegate Trail to his parents in a letter of January 28, 1848:

> Mr. Applegate is the gentleman who discovered the southern road to this country, which is by far the best if not the nearest to Oregon that has yet been made. The companies that came the southern road last fall all arrived in the valley without sustaining any loss of consequence, and made the trip in much quicker time than those who came the northern route, and their cattle looked fine, while those who came the northern route lost a great many of their cattle and what few they brought through with them looked very poor ... I have mentioned the road to this country for the purpose of laying before you their true condition and to let you know the character of the man and the motives that induced him to open the road ... Instead of receiving thanks from his fellow

citizens many enemies were created who slandered him on all occasions, charging him with sinister motives... But this was not the case, for he gave a number of young men outfits to start the trip with him and also made himself responsible to those who worked the road, and also sent provisions to the immigrants at his own expense.

Perhaps the best vindication for the southern route was that on December 20, 1847, the Provisional Legislature passed the Act to Improve the Southern Route to Oregon. The act's preamble states, "Whereas the Southern Route from the United States to Oregon has the present season proved a safe and easy road for immigrants to this country" and contrasts it with the "unsafe and perilous Columbia River route."[210] The Legislature proposed that the southern route be a toll road just like the new Barlow Road around Mt. Hood, but Levi Scott and the Applegate brothers were adamantly opposed to this idea. Scott found the idea of taxing the immigrants for the privilege of entering Oregon *odious.*"

Though the Applegate party's choice of route appeared to have been validated by the legislature, many more contemporaries would weigh in on the southern road controversy. S. A. Clark tries for a balanced view in his *Pioneer History of Oregon*, "Having in later years known intimately both Applegate and Thornton, I found much good in the last and much excellence in the first. It is only possible to reconcile the differences between them by recognizing the varied features of weak human nature, of the two of the southern route, Jesse Applegate was capable of the greatest and truest nobility of character. He seems not to have appreciated the dangers and difficulties."[211]

Peter Burnett defends Jesse Applegate more strongly:

In the summer and early fall of 1846 Jesse Applegate, at his own expense as I understood, opened a new wagon road into the Willamette Valley at its southern end. He met the emigrants at Fort Hall and induced a portion of them to come by that route. They suffered great hardships before they reached the end of the journey. This was caused mainly by their own mistakes. Though he was much censured by many of them, he was not to blame. He had performed one of the most noble and generous acts, and deserved praise rather than censure. I traveled with him across the plains in 1843, and I can testify that he was a noble, intellectual, and generous man; and his character was so perfect as to bear any and all tests, under any and all circumstances.[212]

Levi Scott's assessment of Jesse and the events of 1846:

His sanguine temperament certainly led him to risk a little too much, but most of the harsh abuse that was heaped upon him, for turning the emigrants in this direction was unjust to him."

Finally, John Minto, one of Oregon's foremost citizens and a man who knew Jesse well, praises the Applegate exploring party:

For their effort to find a new way into western Oregon, which British power could not control, not one of them ever received pay in any shape for the time, labor and personal cost given to it. The Applegate families in particular gave to the enterprise more value in property and time than any three families, who took the way into Oregon lost.[213]

Jesse Applegate and his crew had given up almost five months of their lives and with it the opportunity to tend to their farms, families, and businesses. They had exposed themselves to danger and the elements only to find themselves exposed to harsh criticism.

The Whitman Massacre – Cayuse War

Even as late as December 1847, the controversy over the southern route continued, and the newspapers continued to carry defamations of Jesse's name. Even Governor Abernethy had taken Jesse Quinn Thornton's side during the controversy, openly denouncing the southern route and all connected to it. Abernethy had handbills sent to Fort Hall in the spring of 1847, warning that year's emigrants not to take the "damnable" southern road. At first, his wrath had been directed almost exclusively towards Jesse Applegate, but in time, even Levi Scott became a target of his wrath. However, tragic events would soon force Abernethy to reconsider his relationship with the "uncouth independent" and Levi Scott.

This tragedy began, as is often the case, with good intentions and misunderstandings. In 1836, Dr. Marcus Whitman, Rev. Henry

Spalding, and their wives, Narcissa Whitman and Eliza Spalding, had crossed the Rockies and come into the Oregon Country as some of the first white settlers. The Whitmans settled at Waiilatpu, near Fort Walla Walla, and began mission work with the Cayuse Indians. From 1843 on, each fall the Cayuse watched as the white-topped covered wagons rolled down the slopes of the Blue Mountains into the valley of the Umatilla, their ancestral lands. As they saw each new wave of "Bostons" come into the land, trampling their crops, running off the game, and bringing sickness from the East, the Cayuse began to feel that both races could not live in harmony.

The Cayuse began to suspect that Whitman's missionary activities were nothing more than a front for white domination over their land. A Delaware Indian named Tom Hill who had come to live among them warned them that the whites would take their land just as they had taken his ancestral lands in the East years before.[214] These suspicions caused tensions to grow between Whitman and the Indians at the mission.

The deadly measles had arrived in the Umatilla Valley early in the summer of 1847. A trading party of Cayuse and Walla Walla Indians went south to Sutter's Fort looking to revenge the death of the Walla Walla Chief's son who had been killed by one of Sutter's employees. They also planned to do some trading and acquire slaves. They did do some trading, but also came home with the measles. The Indians lacked any natural resistance to the measles and died by scores. Thirty members of the trading party died before they reached home and it then spread rapidly through the Indian communities. Dr. Whitman tried to stop the spread and moved among them giving what help and comfort he could, but still they died. Joe Lewis, an eastern half-breed, began to circulate the rumor that Whitman was not treating them, but poisoning them.[215] When the chiefs gathered to discuss the situation, the half-breeds whispered, "Dr. Whitman has done this. He has brought poison from the States to kill you all, that he may take your lands." Although Dr. Whitman had been warned of these rumors by his faithful Stickus, he refused to desert his post.[216]

On the afternoon of November 29, 1847, the Indians attacked the mission and killed Dr. Whitman and his wife Narcissa, along with twelve others, John and Frank Sager among them. Fifty-four women and children were taken captive and held for ransom, including the daughter of Joe Meek and the remaining Sager children. The seven Sager children had been orphaned when their parents died as they were coming west to Oregon. The Whitmans adopted the orphaned children.

Word of the horrific event was carried down the Columbia to Fort Vancouver, headquarters of the Hudson's Bay Company. James Douglas, the company's chief factor, at once sent word to Oregon City and the territorial governor. He then sent Peter Skene Ogden, his most influential employee, to rescue the captives. Ogden was able to ransom the captives for a small quantity of blankets, cotton shirts, rifles, and tobacco. There is no evidence that the Hudson's Bay Company ever billed the American settlers for the ransom, or that the Americans ever offered to repay them. Jesse Applegate praised the much-maligned company for its actions in a letter to S.F. Chadwick on November 8, 1877: "For this great service no pay was asked of Government or people, nor would it have been received if offered, and the act stands today, as on the day of performance, one of pure mercy and philanthropy, that money could neither hire nor reward."

Call to War

Governor Abernethy received the message from Douglas on December 7. The following day he shared the terrible news of the massacre with the provisional government's legislature, which was meeting for its annual session. Immediately upon hearing this news, James Nesmith was on his feet calling for fifty riflemen to be equipped and sent at once to protect the mission at The Dalles, the closest mission station up the Columbia.

The territorial government was ready and willing to send an "army" against the enemy, but in truth, they had no organized militia and no funds to finance one. Shannon Applegate points out, "The unhappy fact was that there were, on the verge of the continent, fewer than two thousand American settlers whose existence their national government had not yet seen fit formally to acknowledge and whose temporary governing body had less than fifty dollars in its coffers."[217] The exact amount was in fact $43.72.[218] Even so, within twenty-four hours a band of fifty men under the command of Captain Henry Lee was on its way to The Dalles, charged to wait there until reinforcements could be sent.[219]

On December 10, 1847, the Provisional Government passed an act authorizing the governor to raise a regiment of five hundred volunteer riflemen to pursue and bring to justice any Indian who had aided in the Whitman massacre. On Christmas Day in Oregon City, five hundred men gathered ready and willing to ride into battle to avenge their friend Dr. Whitman.[220]The women of Oregon City baked and sewed, and out of bits of red flannel, blue overalls, and white muslin, women like Lucy, Cynthia, and Betsy Applegate made a flag for the First Oregon Regiment. Farmers came hurrying through the woods with beans, bacon, lead, and blankets—whatever could be spared to outfit the little army.[221] John Minto and his new bride owned only three blankets, but they gladly gave one to a neighbor who had volunteered for the citizen's army. Over at the Applegates,' nothing was spared that could help in the war effort: even the children's toy cannon was melted down and turned into bullets for the percussion rifles.

In his *History of Oregon*, Bancroft states that Jesse Applegate, on hearing the news of the massacre, suggested to the legislature that a message be sent to Washington urging the United States government to assume control of the situation and send military reinforcements.[222] This suggestion was adopted on December 10, and all the evidence indicates that Jesse, in fact, wrote the communication to Washington. Schafer states in his paper on Applegate, "It is in my estimation, one of the finest papers ever produced west of the Rocky Mountains." The following excerpt illustrates its literary merit:

> Having called upon the government so often in vain, we have almost despaired of receiving its protection, yet we trust that our present situation when fully laid before you, will at once satisfy your honorable body of the necessity of extending the strong arm of guardianship and protection over the distant but beautiful portion of the United States' domain. Our relations with the proud and powerful tribes of Indians residing east of the Cascade Mountains, hitherto uniformly amicable and pacific, have recently assumed quite a different character. They shouted the warwhoop and crimsoned their tomahawks in the blood of our citizens…To repel the attacks of so formidable a foe and protect our families and property from violence and rapine, will require more strength than we possess…We have the right to expect your aid, and you are in justice bound to extend…Our love for the free and noble institutions under which it was our fortune to be born and nurtured remains unabated. In short we are Americans still, residing in country which the government of the United States has the sole and acknowledge right of sovereignty; and under such circumstances we have the right to claim the benefit of its laws and protection.

The messenger chosen to proceed to the United States was Joe Meek, whose years as a mountain man in the Rockies suited him for this dangerous midwinter journey. Governor Abernethy requested that Meek go east by way of California so that he might seek aid from Governor Mason, and through him, request that the commander of the United States Navy in the Pacific at Yerba Buena, California, send a war ship north to the Columbia River to help supply arms and ammunition. Meek replied that any man who felt compelled to push over the Siskiyou in January would find himself stopped dead in his tracks; half dead if he was lucky.[223] On January 4, carrying the official papers of the Oregon legislature and bearing dispatches from the governor to the president, Meek went east to The Dalles planning to retrace the Oregon Trail back to the States. Meek remained at The Dalles until March, three months after the massacre. He was then escorted by a company of one hundred men as far as the Blue Mountains. From there he and eight other men continued eastward with the official papers pleading Oregon's desperate need of protection.[224]

At the same time the memorial was approved, a commission of three was appointed and entrusted with the task of securing funds to finance what was now called the Cayuse War. The newly formed loan commission consisted of three of the most able men of the community: Jesse Applegate, A.L. Lovejoy, and George L. Curry. These three immediately appealed to the three sources that they felt could help them raise the funds necessary to send their little army into battle: the Hudson's Bay Company; the Reverend William Roberts, superintendent of the Methodist mission in Oregon; and the merchants and citizens of Oregon. Jesse was appointed chair of the commission because of his friendship with the Hudson's Bay Company officials and the hope that friendship would help secure the needed supplies. The following letter of December 17 shows the desperate situation that faced Oregon and the loan commission:

> Gentlemen;—You are aware that the undersigned have been charged by the legislature of our provisional government with the difficult duty of obtaining the necessary means to arm, equip, and support in the field a force sufficient to obtain full satisfaction of the Cayuse Indians, for the late massacre at Waiilatpu, and to protect the white population of our common country from further aggression.

In furtherance of this object they have deemed it their duty to make immediate application to the merchants and citizens of the country from further aggression.

Though clothed with the power to pledge, to the fullest extent, the faith and means of the present government of Oregon, they do not consider this pledge the only security to those who, in this distressing emergency, may extend to the people of this country the means of protection and redress.

Without claiming any special authority from the government of the United States to contract a debt to be liquidated by that power, yet from all precedents of like character in the history of our country, the undersigned feel confident that the United States government will regard the murder of the late Dr. Whitman and his lady, as a national wrong, and will fully justify the people of Oregon in taking active measures to obtain redress for the outrage, and for their protection from further aggressions.

The right of self-defense is tacitly acknowledged to every body politic in the confederacy which we claim to belong, and in every case similar to our own, within our knowledge, the general government has promptly assumed the payment of all liabilities growing out of the measure taken by the constituted authorities, to protect the lives and property of those who reside within in the limits of their districts.

If the citizens of the States and territories, east of the Rocky mountains, are justified in promptly acting in such emergency, who are under the immediate protection of the general government, there appears no room for doubt that the lawful acts of the Oregon government will receive a like approval.

Though the Indians of the Columbia have committed a great outrage upon our fellow citizens passing through their country, and residing among them, and their punishment for these murders may, and ought to be, a prime object with every citizen of Oregon, yet as that duty more particularly devolves upon the government of the United States, and admits to delay, we do not make this the strongest ground upon which to found our earnest appeal to you for pecuniary assistance.

It is a fact well known to every person acquainted with the Indian character, that by passing silently over their repeated thefts, robberies, and murder of our fellow-citizens, they have been emboldened to the commission of the appalling massacre at Waiilatpu. They call us women, destitute of the hearts and courage of men, and if we allow this wholesale murder to pass by as former aggressions, who can tell how long either life or Property will be secure in any part of this country, or what moment the Willamette will be the scene of blood and carnage.

The officers of our provisional government have nobly performed their duty. None can doubt the readiness of the patriotic sons of the west to offer their personal services in defense of a cause so righteous. So now rest with you, gentlemen, to say whether our rights and our fire-sides shall be defended, or not.

Hoping that none will be found to falter in so high and Sacred a duty, we beg leave, gentlemen, to subscribe ourselves.

Your servants and fellow-citizens,

Jesse Applegate

A. L. Lovejoy

Geo. L. Curry[225]

Commissioners

The only storehouse that had sufficient quantities of the supplies that were needed was the Hudson's Bay Company at Fort Vancouver, so this letter was sent at once to Douglas. The chief factor had no authority to deal in public security and so at first refused the commission's request for supplies to outfit the troops.[226] However, Douglas did agree to accept the personal security of Governor Abernethy and two of the commissioners, Jesse Applegate and A. L. Lovejoy, and so the supplies necessary to equip Lee's rifle company were secured.

On December 24, the commissioners made a progress report to the legislative assembly, detailing their personal pledges to the Hudson's Bay Company that had allowed the first regiment of Oregon riflemen to be outfitted for battle. They had also secured an additional loan of some $1600 from Oregon merchants and the promise of $1000 from the Methodist mission.[227] The revenue raised by the commission was far less than hoped for, but feeling their work was accomplished, they resigned.

Jesse realized that the failure of the commission to garner more funding would put those in the field at a great disadvantage. He addresses the issues of the campaign in a letter to Captain Lee on April 16:

> I take this opportunity to speak three words to you. I find some of the friends of the former commander will do everything they can to injure you. *Never mind them.* If you can bring the Indians to an engagement, and make a short campaign, you will not only serve your country in the best possible manner, but place yourself beyond the reach of envy. To enable you to do this I would make almost any sacrifice. I found Fulkerson had got but one beef to feed you up, and you know Palmer had no other resource for it. I have sent fifteen beeves, and will give the last hoof I have rather than your movements should be crippled for want of means. I found no money at home, nor could get any at O'Neil's.... It is needless to say I wish you success.[228]

Since hard cash was scarce in Oregon, other means of raising the revenue had to be accommodated. Scrip, wheat, and merchants' orders became the chief medium of exchange. Some farmers whose granaries were better filled than others gave wheat to the cause. In February of 1848, Jesse Applegate furnished 187 and a half bushels to the army.[229] The following excerpt from a letter written by Jesse in April of 1848 gives us some insight to his spirit of community:

> Dear Sir: I have just had an interview with Mr. Fulkerson who informs me that you have become distrustful of the policy of the wheat loan, and have instructed him to cease operation in that matter whenever he had raised an amount sufficient to secure to me payment for the beef cattle he purchased of me for

the use of the army. As I do not wish that you assume responsibilities on my account that you deem unsafe, I have taken this
opportunity to inform you that unless the plan of taking wheat
notes is made a general practice, I do not wish any notes taken
up for my exclusive benefit... For my part I would not touch a
note obtained from my neighbor for my exclusive benefit, and
at the expense of the disgrace of a friend.

I am myself in favor of raising a revenue by direct taxa-
tion, as I consider that method as the only fair and equitable
plan of distributing the burden of this unlucky war among
the people who are equally interested in its maintenance...

Sincerely your well-wisher, Jesse Applegate[230]

Jesse Applegate had given freely of his time to the loan commission,
his money to the impoverished government, and his wheat and cattle for the war effort, but he would be called upon to give even more.

Mission Impossible?

On the twenty-seventh of January, Governor Abernethy wrote to
Jesse requesting that he raise a small company of men to carry a
dispatch to the military governor of California. Having failed with
his request to Joe Meek, he now sought the help of the "uncouth
independent" in this important mission to secure troops to aid in
the war effort.[231]

"Meek is still at The Dalles, and does not intend going to
California...I immediately proposed you as the man...and
[you] can at the same time render essential service to this
country by informing the proper authorities of California of
our situation. I see nothing in the way to prevent your immediate departure...I would like to see you before your start, but
this would be wasting time. This package contains letters and
papers for Commodore Shubrick and Governor Mason."[232]

Meek had said the mission was impossible; Jesse believed a man who exercised self-discipline could accomplish virtually anything.

According to Scott, Jesse declined to lead such an expedition but agreed to go along as a private citizen under the leadership of Scott, who comments, "I was glad to have Captain Applegate accept the place of Orderly Sergeant in my little company, which he, with unassuming patriotism generously did."[233] Applegate was given the official dispatches to carry south and Scott took charge of the patrol that went along to protect the governor's messenger.

After receiving thirty pounds of flour, twenty pounds of bacon, and five pounds of lead, plus one box of caps each, Scott, two of his sons, Jesse, John Minto, and ten other men started on their journey south on the morning of February 5. They had no tents and were forced to deal with the weather as best they could.[234] Minto shares that the men both in camp and on the trail pressed Uncle Jesse (Applegate) to share his acquired knowledge. "Around the evening camp-fire we listened to the sage utterances of our chief, whose discourses on political and natural science was a valued entertainment…Whenever we could ride in groups there would be a part of us around Uncle Jesse plying him with questions.…We were in messes of 8 each and this gave me the great pleasure of standing guard with Mr. Applegate. He was animated by a noble ambition to give high service and was a great help to others in that respect."[235]

The men pushed south through blinding rain and snow until they reached the northern slopes of the Siskiyou Mountains. They made no attempt to take the mountains at the California Trail but bore eastward to the very head of the valley, following the road Applegate and Scott had brought the emigrants over in 1846. Scott describes the dire situation: "Before reaching this point we had not encountered snow more than eighteen inches deep, but here we found if from three feet to five feet deep, with a hard, cutting crust, which was not thick enough to bear the weight of a man, much less that of a horse."[236]

The company of men tried to push on but soon found the labor too great for the animals; they realized that all would die if they continued to press on. The meadow where the forlorn little group camped for the night was covered with snow; the horses had now been without food for two days. Given these conditions, the men decided to give up and return home, proclaiming that old Joe Meek had been right, that the journey was impossible in the dead of winter.

Jesse, however, was not ready to call it quits. He retreated off to one side and sat down on a log, defeat and despair showing on his face. Minto went to him and said, "Mr. Applegate, I see you are much cast down. But surely the people of the Willamette do not expect the impossible of us. This is no fault of yours."[237] Jesse replied that he felt this endeavor so important that if only one man would agree to go on with him he would make the effort to get through on snowshoes. "If but one of us got through the result would justify the effort." Years later Jesse stated, "To give up the expedition and return without further effort was not to be thought of." John Minto and six other men volunteered to go on the next day, but Levi Scott had grave doubts about this scheme and was unwilling to take the responsibility for having encouraged it.[238]

The next morning, Jesse and seven others of the company fashioned crude snowshoes from willows they found along the creek bed, hoisted fifty-pound packs onto their backs, and plowed forward on this desperate mission. They struggled through the snow, slow mile after slow mile, until finally one of the men, who because of his large size was unable to walk atop the snow, became exhausted and begged the others to leave him behind. "They refused to leave him, and all turned back, abandoning the project altogether."[239] Shannon Applegate reports, "This failure hit Jesse hard; failure was then, and would always be, even more difficult for him to endure than criticism. They took only what they still had the strength to carry and limped north."[240]

As the weary, discouraged company limped north, they came to the infamous Canyon Creek where the wreckage of the 1846 emigrant's wagons plainly told the story of their suffering. As the company cleared the north end of the canyon, they fired a shot and to their surprise heard a reply from a mile or so ahead; they had caught up with Scott and his group.

A few more days brought the men to the little valley that Jesse had admired two years before while exploring the southern route. Since the rain forced them a little farther west than before, Jesse would get his first glimpse of the little round mountain he would come to call Mount Yoncalla. As he looked out over the land, he reflected that the journey had not been a complete failure after all; he had found "home." He vowed to return to build the house he had promised Cynthia so many years ago in St. Louis.

The bedraggled band of men, having been gone about thirty days, returned to the settlement, disappointed that they had not succeeded in the mission entrusted to them by Governor Abernethy, but rejoicing that they were all alive and had given it a valiant effort.

Meanwhile, the army of volunteers under the command of Colonel Gilliam had been so successful in their campaign against the Indians up the Columbia that by spring all fear of a widespread war in the Willamette had vanished. While the murderers had not been apprehended, the tribe had been so decimated that they could not fight on; the other tribes of the area chose to stay out of the battle. Eventually five Cayuse men were turned over to the Territorial Government. After a lengthy trial in which they were found guilty, the newly appointed Territorial Marshal, Joe Meek, carried out the sentence of hanging on June 3, 1850.

Before this was to happen, however, Joe Meek would reach Washington with his pouch of official papers from Oregon, including Jesse Applegate's communication. At long last, Congress was shocked into action and on August 14, 1848, a bill was passed creating the Oregon Territory. It would be five long months, however, before the news reached Oregon City.

The decisive actions of that little isolated Oregon community of 1847 are instructive to this day. A crisis arose; they assessed the need, raised an army, and with very limited resources, found creative ways to finance the outfitting of that army. Without delay, they sent the citizen soldiers against the enemy; the Indians would interpret any delay as weakness. To wait for the federal government to send help would have spelled almost certain disaster for the Oregon community. In fact, when the federal government finally sent a regiment of mounted riflemen in the fall of 1849, the war was already over.

The Applegate Trail proved its usefulness once again in this case: it was used to send a supply of fresh beef to Fort Hall to meet the new Oregon Rifle Regiment. It was a well-known fact that cattle driven along the original Oregon Trail by the Snake River route would have arrived mere walking skeletons, but the cattle driven over the Applegate Trail arrived fat and tasty due to the abundant pasture of the southern route.[241]

1849 — A Year of Change

The settlers in Oregon had yet to recover from the crisis of the Cayuse War when events elsewhere swept them into an even more exciting drama: gold was discovered in California. Since the news of the event was able to reach Oregon well ahead of the rest of the country, there was considerable movement south to the gold fields. Peter Burnett resigned as chief justice of Oregon, gathered fifty wagons and a hundred and fifty men, and "Burnett's ragged regiment" was soon on its way south. Within days, two-thirds of the able-bodied male population in the territory, including Lindsay Applegate, joined them on their way to California. Jesse remained at home; he and his wife would find other ways to "mine" the gold rush.

With so many of the men gone to the gold fields, the 1848 session of the Oregon Legislature was cancelled. Only thirteen of the twenty-two members showed up for the December fifth session, and five of those came only under duress from the sergeant-of-arms. The legislature adjourned until February of 1849 so that a special election could be held.[242]

Jesse Applegate was one of the men elected in the special election, filling the vacated seat of J.W. Nesmith as Polk County's representative. At the opening of the session, Governor Abernathy informed the new legislators that the officers needed to form a territorial government were en route and would soon arrive.[243]

Jesse assumed his customary leadership role within the first few days of this short session, making the first officially recorded resolution.[244] The primary business of the session concerned the expenses of the Cayuse War, an amendment to the oath of the organic law, and prohibition of the sale of liquor to the Indians.

Jesse served on the House rules committee and currency committee.[245] He helped to write a law that allowed the minting of "heavier money," which was needed because of the influx of gold from the California gold fields. The committee authorized the minting of five and ten dollar coins. In reality, the coins were illegal tender because the United States government did not mint them, but the committee's opinion was that the measure was a "necessity which knows no law," providing a standard medium of exchange. However, once Joseph Lane, the new territorial governor, arrived, one of his first official acts was to stop the minting of the "Beaver coins," and the opening of the U.S. Mint in San Francisco helped eliminate the need for the provisional currency. Lane attempted to collect all the coins, but some refused to give them up because they contained eight percent more gold than their U.S. equivalent.

One of the bills that Jesse introduced was to establish the Klamet (Klamath) Company. This company would have the power to trade with the Indians and purchase land from them. The bill faced strong opposition, however, and Jesse withdrew it from consideration.[246]

The one bill he was successful in sponsoring enshrined his firm belief that government was directly responsible to the people. On his motion it was affirmed that the laws adopted by Oregon were not to be considered as "circumscribing the right of petition, nor should the right of petition be circumscribed."[247]

On the last day of the session, Jesse introduced a bill that would pay the loan commissioners of the Cayuse War, himself included, $800 for their service to the war effort. However, the bill bogged down when some members objected to A.L. Lovejoy's receiving the same amount as the two other members of the commission. The matter was not resolved, and with this the provisional government adjourned.[248] Once again, Jesse's service to the territory had gone unpaid.

At the end of the legislative session, Jesse Applegate's official duties as an elected politician were finished as well.

Applegate's significant work of reorganizing the provisional government in 1845 had stood the test of time by remaining in force until March of 1849, when Oregon became a territory of the United States. Schafer points out that "In all that time it commanded universal respect, secured equal justice, and promoted the prosperity of the colony. The people had gained full control of affairs, and special interest had to comply with laws passed for the general good."[249] Jesse said that because of his efforts: "Both the Methodist mission and the Hudson's Bay Company ceased to be political powers either to be feared or courted in the colony, and to the end of its existence the Provisional government of Oregon attained all the ends of good government."

These early years of active service to Oregon are what would build Jesse's reputation as the "sage of Yoncalla." His name and views on many subjects were known and respected; over the years, he would build on that reputation through hundreds of letters to newspaper editors and other influential people of the territory and beyond. This early reputation is part of what would lead many an influential man to seek his door and his hospitality in the years to come.

With the end of the 1849 legislative session, his mind and heart turned to more personal matters: the little valley down in the Umpqua country.

Yoncalla — Home of My Heart

In the fall of 1849, Uncle Jesse, as he was universally called by this time, gathered up his wife and nine children along with his livestock, consisting of his beef cattle and Cynthia's herd of forty milk cows, and moved from the Willamette Valley across the Calapooya Mountains and down to the lovely little valley in the Umpqua country that he would call Yoncalla for the eagles that soared overhead. This was the valley he had described when he was exploring the southern route as a "beautiful little valley where the grass was good and the ground almost covered with the finest strawberries." Levi Scott, who had already moved to a neighboring valley, described Jesse's valley as a place where "the air was soft and balmy; the water plenty, clear, and pure, and the grass was very fine."

As Jesse prepared to move his family south, his friend Chief Quatlee of the Klickitats tribe decided to accompany him with a number of his warriors dressed in full ceremonial regalia. Chief

Quatlee may have decided to accompany Jesse because his son-in-law, Dick Johnson, and his family were moving with Jesse to Yoncalla or, as some have suggested, to protect him from the "renegade" Indians of the southland who had harassed the travelers of the southern route in 1846. What a sight this must have been: a number of wagons rolling south driven by white men and escorted by a large contingent of Indians dressed in their ceremonial clothes.[250]

Down in the Yoncalla Valley, Jesse laid out his 642-acre donation land claim, the reward promised to all Oregon pioneers (by Thomas Benton and Lewis Linn back in Missouri) and finally approved by the United States Congress in 1850.[251] A drawing of Jesse's claim looks like an asymmetrical arrow.

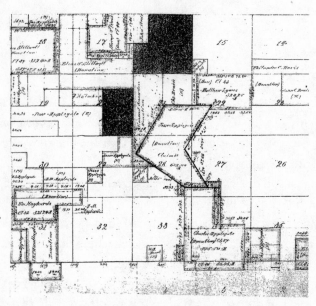

Jesse's donation claim map-1850

Over the years, many have attributed that shape to Jesse's eccentric personality, but when the claim map is compared to the topographical map of the area, it is clear that Jesse, ever the skilled surveyor, laid out his claim to take full advantage of the valley floor. Almost all of the 642 original acres lay on the fertile, treeless valley floor. Soon he would add a forty-acre plot to the southwest that included the little knoll where the family cemetery would eventually be established. Jesse explains to his friend, Archibald McKinlay, "I like this farm better than any I ever had; I love its mild and gentle climate, its picturesque hills with their oaken groves and grassy intervals."[252] Unlike most of the settlers, Jesse bought his land from the local Indians, establishing a lifelong friendship with Chief Halo and his small band of Indians.[253]

Jesse's brothers, Charles and Lindsay and their families, would soon join him down in the Umpqua country. Jesse, his brothers, and all the early settlers certainly benefited from the passage of the Donation Land Claim Act; but Jesse, with his typically candid, retrospective way of thinking, had some reservations about the law. He believed the requirement of four years' occupancy to perfect claims would slow growth by delaying the ability to subdivide the land and build towns, forcing the population to spread out and making it difficult to establish and support viable schools. He also felt that the Donation Land Claim Act encouraged only farmers to come into the territory, while a growing, thriving community needed merchants, professional men, and mechanics.[254] A century later, authors Johansen and Gates drew a very similar conclusion in *Empire of the Columbia*, maintaining that the Donation Land Claim Act "impeded the growth of towns, and the diversification of occupation, industry, and crops."

The area was still a wilderness when Jesse moved his family to the Umpqua. His first task was to use his hand tools to build a large, sturdy two-room log cabin. The logs for the cabin were hewn until they were almost smooth, giving the appearance of planed logs. They were perfectly square and fit together so well that, according to Sallie Long, "a mouse could find no room to creep between them." The house was low: a single story with a fireplace on each end. There were two large rooms, about twenty feet square with a door in the middle connecting the rooms, called "your Mamma's house" and the "other house." The "other house" was used as a bunkhouse for hired hands as well as lodging for male travelers. All travelers who came looking for shelter were fed and housed free of charge. On each side of the house was a long room under a shed roof. The room on the backside of the house was used as a milk room, eating room, and storehouse. After Cynthia had secured a cook stove, the room became the kitchen. The shed room at the front of the house was the bedroom for the girls and any female guest who might need shelter. This room lay along the center of the house, allowing room for a porch on each end. The door from the girls' room opened onto what was known as "Mamma's porch." The family would remain in this house for almost ten years before Jesse finally built his grand house, a kind of latter-day Shirley or Westover.

Next, Jesse put his hand and back to the task of turning wilderness into productive farmland:

> He was very methodical and particular about all the work done on the farm. All fences were laid off with the compass in perfectly straight lines. There were no projecting corners, no slovenly panels. All ditches were made in the same way. The little brooks which from time immemorial had curved and twisted here and there about the farm were corrected from their dilatory ways and put into straight ditches, frequently being sent to some destination quite different from their natural one.[255]

Jesse would find the task of establishing a workable farm so far from civilization very demanding and time-consuming: "Having to go 100 miles to mill and still further for supplies other than bread—a young family to care for and protect from Indians, I had little time to bestow on public affairs ... In fact, I was not again as far north as Oregon City for many years."[256]

In May of 1850, Jesse wrote to his friend McKinlay that his family was, "well, and remarkably well contented considering we are so far from an inhabited part of the globe." Cynthia had already begun to make money for her family by making and selling butter and cheese to the miners, securing high prices for her efforts and adding to the family's well-being. Cynthia increasingly found that she needed to take over the day-to-day running of the farm whenever Jesse found tasks that took him far from home for extended periods of time. Her administration and authority were never questioned.

Soon after the Applegates arrived at their new home, they planted an orchard that covered about eight to ten acres. Most of the orchard was apple trees, but there were a few peach and pear trees in the mix. The peaches proved to be good, but the pear trees were improved over the years by grafting on better varieties. Sallie, Jesse's third daughter, describes in an article about her father an incident concerning the apples:

> One fall my father concluded to make cider of these little apples: so a trough was hollowed out of a log and various members of the family were set pounding up apples in this trough. The cheese press utilized to press the fumice [*sic*] but it was laborious work.
>
> One day my Father said to the little old man who was at work with him, "You are a skilled workman Uncle Billy but you can't make a cider mill out of wood and that is all we have." The old man could not endure a challenge. "I think I can make something better than a pig trough," and he pointed disdainfully at the trough where Father was pounding apples. "Well try it, I will have the boys bring any material you want that is available and let us see if you really are a mechanic." My father was delighted with the idea that he had puzzled his ingenious old henchman but he laughed too soon.
>
> Uncle Billy called for some ash timbers of certain sizes, a generous allotment of nails and locked himself into his little workshop. He could not abide any witness of his experiments

but at the end of some days [he] invited "Mister Applegate" very ceremoniously, "bring a bucket of apples and try the new mill."

When my father entered the work shop there stood the mill, hopper, crank and all complete. The grinding was three wooden rollers two small, one large. The apples fell from the hopper between the two little rollers which as well as the large one were driven full of nails, the sharpened ends of which were allowed to project about half an inch from the wood. These were the teeth of the cutters. The mill was a success and was used for years ... Every fall my Father would make several hundred gallons of cider which was preserved at what ever stage of fermentation he wished by a process of which I never learned the secret. These barrels of cider were fine in the hot summer weather and he sent many gallons of it as presents to friends and gave it to every one that cared for such drinks.[257]

Uncle Billy

The Uncle Billy referred to in this story is William Hayhurst, born in Lancastershire, England in 1792. He came to North America in his youth to work for the Hudson's Bay Company, but due to a severe injury that had crushed both feet he was turned out by the company, and by 1845 was destitute. He walked with two canes and appeared to be very feeble. Begging to be allowed to work for food and shelter, he came to Jesse Applegate's gristmill on Salt Creek near Dallas.

Jesse gave Hayhurst a job at the mill and discovered he was a very clever and useful carpenter and millwright. Soon Jesse's children were calling him Uncle Billy; he became so much a part of the family that he moved down to the Umpqua with them. Hayhurst took a land claim out in a little valley that soon became known as Hayhurst Valley. He helped build houses for Jesse and Jesse's daughter Rozelle Putnam, and then turned to improving his own claim by building a small cabin, where he lived for the required four years before selling the land to Jesse for $1000 to be held for Jesse's two oldest sons, Robert and Alexander.[258] Uncle Billy then moved back to live with

"Mister Applegate and the Missus" and spent his time building furniture, cabinets, wooden implements, barrels, churns, and other farm implements like the cider press described above. He took special delight in building things for "Missus Applegate." Cynthia was a small woman, and so he built a special, low rocker for her that no one else was ever allowed to sit in. He also built her a little desk with locks and small cubbyholes for storing her special treasures. One cubbyhole held the little, red, leather-covered Bible that Jesse's mother had given him when he left home, another a little pair of red cloth pants that had been worn by her little Milborn before his death in Missouri, and another a book that her son Edward had written his name in before he was lost to the Columbia River.[259]

Setting up School

One of the first priorities for the Applegates in the Yoncalla valley was to build a schoolhouse for all the children of the valley. Jesse believed that education was "an indispensable requisite to the permanence of free government and individual virtue." Jesse loved to read and could quote long, complicated passages of Shakespeare by memory.[260] Education was very important to all the Applegate brothers, which points up the contradiction of their moving their families far from any established schools. James Applegate, Charles's oldest son, became the first teacher at the new Applegate school, whose curriculum was based on whatever useful books the children could bring to school. The schooling there, however rough and improvised, was sufficient to enable Jesse's three oldest children to attend school at Bethel in Polk County in the early fifties. In 1855, Jesse and Charles Applegate sent an order to Harpers Publishing House in New York for somewhere between one and two thousand books, including all standard works of history, travel, science, math, philosophy, poetry, and fiction, as well as maps and globes. The Applegates also ensured musical education by ordering a number of musical instruments, including a melodeon. The young Applegates now had available to them the resources needed for a broad education.

New Ventures

Life in the Yoncalla Valley settled into a slow ebb and flow; however, Jesse's restless nature soon had him involved with a new venture. In the summer of 1850, the San Francisco firm of Winchester, Payne & Company brought a ship, the *Samuel Roberts*, into the Umpqua River with the purpose of establishing town sites. The company envisioned thriving communities that would supply and exploit the northern California and southern Oregon gold mines. Jesse and Levi Scott were recruited by the Umpqua Town Site and Colonization Company to explore and survey the riverbanks where the towns of Umpqua City, Winchester, Elkton, Scottsburg, and Gardiner would be laid out.[261] Soon Jesse was urging his friend Archibald McKinlay, a merchant in Oregon City, to establish a store in Scottsburg. "I admit I am not an impartial judge when the Umpqua and its destiny are to be decided upon." Jesse then went on to say that because of Scottsburg's proximity to the gold mines, "a rapid increase in population cannot be doubted." Jesse even offered to invest several thousand dollars in the venture if McKinlay would take him up on his offer.[262] A ship from San Francisco soon brought about a hundred prospective settlers back to the area. For a short time, things looked very favorable for the new venture, but then Winchester, Payne & Company went into bankruptcy due to the new Oregon Land Law, which prevented companies and nonresidents from holding land for speculation purposes. The Umpqua Company was then unable to issue patents or convey title to the land it was selling, and thus the fledgling company was doomed. There was a bright side to this failed enterprise, however: Two of the settlers who came in with the company would later become governors of the state of Oregon: Addison C. Gibbs and Stephen F. Chadwick.[263]

A historian of the area describes the boom of the early fifties:

> The Scottsburg of 1852 presented a striking picture. The mines of southern Oregon and northern California demanded trade goods and the Scottsburgers were there to supply them. Hundreds of pack animals jostled each other in the streets, their drivers cursing and shouting as they lashed the packs fast so that they would not be shaken loose on the long trek over the rough mountain trails. Ships nosed in from the sea, bringing clothing, food, and tools for the miners. On their outward trips they carried beef, mutton, hides, and lumber to San Francisco and Portland.[264]

Even though the little town of Scottsburg seemed to flourish at first, by the late fifties, the gold rush in the area had petered out and the town began to fade. Finally, in the winter of 1861–62, a huge flood wiped out much of the town; thirty buildings were swept out to sea, and the town never rebuilt to match its days of glory.

In January of 1851, the legislature created the county of Umpqua, and in April, Jesse Applegate's house in Yoncalla was designated as one of several polling places for the election of officers for the new county. The election was held on the second of June with the following officers elected: J.W. Drew, representative; J.W.P. Huntington, clerk; H. Jacquett, sheriff; A. German, treasurer; A. Pierce, assessor; and three commissioners.[265] Jesse was elected justice of the peace for the newly formed county. The first court session met in 1852 at Jesse's house with the Honorable O.C. Pratt presiding. The most important item before the court was the impaneling of a grand jury, whose members included Lindsay and Charles Applegate along with John Scott and William Hayhurst.[266] The county of Umpqua was destined to exist for only twelve years before it was dissolved in April of 1863; much of it was then incorporated into Douglas County.

By 1851, Jesse was acting as the Umpqua Valley agent for the *Oregon Spectator*, and on March 14, 1851, became the Yoncalla Valley

Postmaster. At first, the mail came by horseback once every two weeks, and the mail route stopped six miles short of Jesse's home. Jesse plays down the long ride in a letter to Bancroft, "...but to hear from the rest of the world I was willing to make the journey to meet the mail." The post office, located in his home, helped to make his home the hub of the little community.[267] Because Jesse's neighbors were making the trek to his door for their mail, he opened a little country store in his home. Jesse had little success in running this mercantile business, not because he was not capable of keeping accurate books, or because he did not know what merchandise was needed, but because he had a soft heart and misplaced his trust, as he so often would: "I sold my goods on credit to those who needed them most, not to those who were able to pay, lost $30,000 and quit the business." Peter Burnett, his old friend from the Oregon Trail, heard this story and commented, "Any one knowing Jesse Applegate as I do would at once recognize the truth of this statement. It was just like the man. His fine intellect and his experience in life said no; but his generous heart said yes; and that kind heart of his overruled his better judgment."[268]

Also, in 1851, Jesse was corresponding with the patent office in Washington D.C. He sent them a lengthy article describing the agriculture scene in the Umpqua.

> But, as a sketch of the agriculture of a "new country" may be useful to the farmers of the old and highly cultivated portion of the Union, the better by contrast to appreciate the blessings they derive from civilization, established communities and the labor of the generations that have preceded them, and also to those who, in disregard of these blessings, desire to make their homes in this far-off country, these remarks are submitted, to be used as you think proper.
>
> ...To a person accustomed to the level or gently undulating surface of the western states, the term valley appears wholly misapplied to the Umpqua country, as the broad plains and gently-swelling hills associated in their minds with that

term are no-where to be seen. The basin, being very much broken (the narrow valleys lying between ranges of high hills) appears, when viewed from the mountains that enclose it, to be merely a mass of hills and mountains, differing from its rim in being of less elevation, bald or timbered with oak, the evergreens only appearing in clumps on the loftiest summits or linking the deep ravines ... There are no lakes nor marshes; the waters of the surrounding mountains rush from their dark chasms in many streams ... and find their way to the ocean.

Of the whole list of vegetable and fruits found in the temperate zone, there is scarcely one that may not here find its favorite soil, and with little attention, be adapted to the climate; and in the vegetable market, having no foreign competition, the farmers have the greatest encouragement to engage.[269]

About this same time, Jesse was also appointed by the territorial government as one of three men to survey a road from the Willamette Valley to the ferry on the Umpqua River, a commission that took him from home for days at a time.[270] Then, in June of 1851, Major Philip Kearny came into the Umpqua Valley leading a regiment of dragoons and a number of wagons to California. He had heard about the "dreaded Canyon" and sought out Jesse Applegate and Levi Scott to help him locate a road that avoided Canyon Creek. He had been led to believe that a road could be built from the Umpqua Valley across the mountains to Table Rock in the Rogue Valley. Applegate, Scott, and Williamson (one of the engineers on the staff) went out to explore the feasibility of such a road but were unable to find a route that was suitable for wagons.[271]

While they were out exploring, Kearny learned of a skirmish between the settlers in the Rogue River Valley and the Rogue Indians. He divided his troops into two equal parties, sending one through the canyon with baggage and supplies, and the other back over the trail Jesse and Scott had just explored, for it was a faster route for men on horseback, although not suitable for wagons.[272] Realizing he would be greatly outnumbered by the Indians, Kearney sent Applegate to the gold mining area of southern Oregon to recruit miners to help in the battle. Jesse was able to convince thirty men to take up arms and return with him to Major Kearney's camp on June twenty-second.[273] Scott notes that "These men were a sort of 'go-as-you-please' body of men, from all quarters, and all occupations, without any recognized leader or organization, and just 'spoiling for a fight' with the Indians."[274]

Captain Stewart of the dragoons was killed when he leaned over an Indian whom he thought was dead. The Indian was not dead and he shot Stewart in the stomach. Stewart lingered most of a day and commented before his death, "It is too bad to have fought half the battles of the Mexican War then to be killed by an Indian." Sallie Applegate Long describes her father's reaction to this incident:

> Captain Stewart was killed on this Rogue River expedition. My father was much touched by the incident. He sat beside the dying man and held his hand until life was gone. Many times after I heard him speak sorrowfully of this young man, talented, educated and so young. They had no choice but to bury him and leave him alone in the wildwood. "Poor boy, poor boy," Father said often in speaking of it. He said the young man asked him to stay by him. "I am not afraid of death, but there is so much that I had hoped to do, but to feel your sympathy, Mr. Applegate gives me fortitude to brave the great unknown."[275]

Within a week the Indians were defeated and the little war was over. Kearney would later issue a report stating that Applegate and the others were "gentlemen of high standing and have rendered me much service, by their courage and coolness before the enemy."[276]

The Shadow of Politics

Several letters appeared in the *Oregon Spectator* in 1851, urging Jesse's election as a delegate to the U.S. Congress. He was praised as "a worthy and meritorious citizen" with an "exalted patriotism and high moral worth."[277] Jesse was touched by his fellow citizens' faith in him, but replied, "While deeply sensible of the honor their preference does me, I wish them distinctly to understand that I have no political aspirations whatever."

Jesse instead urged that Joseph Lane be elected, and this in fact came about. Over the years, Jesse and Lane would exchange many letters and maintain a warm friendship, even after the issue of slavery placed them in politically opposite positions. Samuel Freer explains: "Without Applegate knowing it, Lane was working through President Franklin Pierce to have Jesse appointed surveyor general of Oregon, but powerful railroad interests in Oregon had their own man and Jesse lost out. The benefits of the friendship did not all lie with Jesse, however, since most of his letters kept Lane advised of political sentiments in Oregon, an important service in a day when communications were poor."[278]

John B. Preston was appointed surveyor general of Oregon and Jesse promptly sought the position of a deputy surveyor under Preston. Jesse responds to letter received from Preston:

> In your letter you are kind enough to inform me that *Burt's Solar Compass* must be used by your Deputies, and to enquire whither I am familiar with the use of that instrument—I have never owned nor seen Burt's Solar Compass and of course cannot be familiar with its use, and as I infer from the emphatic manner you mention the subject the possession and familiar use of that instrument are indispensable qualifications for a deputy I at once withdraw my application for employment in your department.
>
> I have executed contracts of surveying in the state of Missouri to the satisfaction of three different surveyors Genl.—but as a plain compass of the Rittenhouse Construction is the only instrument used in the public sur-

veys in that and the adjoining states, I was not aware until recently that a superior instrument had been introduced.[279]

Jesse did buy a Burt's Solar compass in November of 1851 and served an apprenticeship shortly thereafter so that he could meet Mr. Preston's qualifications for being a deputy for the surveyor general of Oregon.[280]

As a delegate to Congress, Lane was successful in acquiring an appropriation for the construction of a military road from Myrtle Creek, near Lane's claim, to the Rogue River Valley. In the summer of 1853, Major Benjamin Alvord, a veteran of the Mexican War, came to explore and determine the best route for the new road. Alvord sought out Jesse for advice and assistance with this endeavor and hired him as guide and surveyor. Jesse sent the following message to Preston: "I have this day received marching orders from Maj. Alvord and will leave tomorrow in obedience there to....As Maj. Alvord merely requires the length of the road and not the elevation and depressions I shall not have with me my theodolite, and cannot therefore ascertain with that degree of exactness you may require for the distance to noted land marks."[281] Alvord was pleased with Jesse's work and recommended him for the next military project.

Political jealousies and a desire to keep all positions in the hands of the ruling Democratic Party machine kept Jesse from being hired for this new military road from Myrtle Creek to Scottsburg. Even so, Alvord encouraged the young man who replaced him to seek out Jesse's assistance.

Yoncalla, Umpqua Co. O.T.
Private & Confidential

Dear Sir,
    The young man appointed by the War Department has been here and located the road from Myrtle Creek to Scottsburg, and let the contracts for its construction. I have

assisted him in his duties, but I assure you had I not felt my service necessary to the public and that I was bound by a promise exacted of me by Maj. Alvord I would not have done so. In fact, as it was I did all I could to get off, particularly after I ascertained Lieut. Withers was an honest man and earnestly determined to do his duty.

I have learned lately that strong interest was made at Washington to prevent me from having anything to do with the road, and after the arrival of Lieut. Withers every art was tried to bias his judgment and excite his prejudices. And failing in this, every bribery was resorted to induce him to favor individuals and misapply the appropriations. He has located the road clearly on the best and shortest route without being at all influenced by the pleasure or displeasure of individuals, and obtained contracts on terms favorable as to place every difficult place on the whole line under contract, and by the first day of June next there will be a better road from Myrtle Creek to Scottsburg than to be found anywhere else in the territory.

I have requested Lieut. Withers to send you a copy of his report sent to the Secretary, in which you will perceive he asks for further appropriations to erect a depot at Scottsburg, bridges across the Umpqua at Winchester and the other two crossings, and to continue the road to Fort Lane, Pitt Valley, and so eastward. What he says in that report in regard to the advantage to result to the War Department from such further improvements, is strictly true, while none better than yourself can see the advantage it will be to Southern Oregon... It is, of course irksome to play second fiddle to some young man whose inexperience in such matters makes a mentor necessary, but I suppose it must continue to be so so long as Whigs are considered "unfit to be trusted with office."[282]

Later, in the same letter, Jesse expresses concern for Lane's political future: "Let me assure you, you have never stood so well nor so deservedly well with the people of Oregon as you do at present, and if you suffer yourself to be victimized by these base interpolators you will be guilty of a betrayal of your duty to your country."[283]

He proceeds to ask Lane to forward him a copy of the petition that was "got-up" to prevent his employment on the military road. With typical Applegate frankness and irony, he finishes the letter: "If you will do this to oblige me, I will not vote for you. That, I expect never to do."

Jesse never received a dime for the assistance to Lieutenant Withers that he gave over a period of several weeks.[284] It is clear to see that even though it rankled him to do so, he had given his word to Major Alvord and valued his good word over his feelings or time. This is a perfect example of Jesse's complex nature: he did a service for someone he respected, sacrificing his financial well-being and self-esteem in so doing, and in the process disregarded the well being of his own family all in the name of 'honor.'

In a letter to Governor Addison Gibbs in January of 1865, Jesse deviates from his normal aversion to asking for a favor:

> Since writing to you John Fullerton called upon me on his way down to see you and Gen. Alvord He said he was going to ask a special service to be ordered East taking his departure from Rogue river valley. This will take him along our southern boundary.
>
> Since my exploration of the country in 1846, I have been exceedingly anxious to go to it again. ... if I could be appointed to locate a road say from Camp Stewart [Medford] Rogue river valley to Fort Boise and a sufficient force furnished to open the road and guard the operator *I had rather have such an appointment that to be Senator or the appointee to any office in the gift of the President* ... If no road is ordered I think it will not require more than three months to make the reconnoisance [sic] from Rogue river valley to Boise. I shall take with me my solar compass or theodolite perhaps both of them, with either I can determine each day at noon my latitude with considerable accuracy, near enough to determine within a mile or

two the State line.... a road of the description I name besides being almost a military necessity, *will be the salvation of the Southern part* of *the State.*[285]

This favor was not granted to Jesse and the road was not built.

Dick Johnson

The Applegates were known for being sympathetic to the Indians and when called on to help with an "Indian problem" always stepped forward to help find a solution. Thus it was that they became involved with the sad fate of the Klickitat Indian family who had followed the Applegates south to the Yoncalla Valley. Dick Johnson had decided that he preferred the certain rewards of farming to the uncertain of the chase and the comfort of a fixed home to the vagrant life of a nomad. Because of this, Dick and his family took up a claim even though, as Native Americans, they had no legal right to own land. The Oregon superintendent of Indian affairs, J. W. P. Huntington, had encouraged them to do so, and Dick Johnson even had a handwritten note giving him possession of the land. This note was as close to a deed as was possible:

> This Indian, Dick Johnson, has taken a claim of land lying a short distance west of the house of Mr. Knowles and wished to live upon it and cultivate it. He has hitherto borne a good character, is disposed to be industrious and wishes to live by farming.
> It is to be hoped that, as the claim contains but little level land and is consequently of little value to a white man, and as Dick has bestowed considerable labor upon it, that the Indian's claim may be respected although he has no *legal right* to it.
> Dick has requested me to give him this paper.
> J. W. Perit Huntington[286]

The Johnson family consisted of Dick, his wife Mary, their two children, his mother Lemyei, his stepfather Mummy, his brother-in-law Klickitat Jim, Jim's wife Eliza, and their child. Sallie Applegate Long describes the Indian women:

> Eliza was clean and neat, in person and in dress. Dick's wife [Mary] was inferior to the others in appearance...Lemyei in spite of her age, was straight, tall and lean, walked with a long strong step, wore always upon her head a little conical shaped basket from below which her long straight hair, mixed with white hung down her back.
>
> They were the friendliest people I ever knew, never obtrusive, never saucy, very industrious, very honest, every promise kept, every debt paid. My father [Jesse Applegate] kept a little store and they bought many things for which they paid promptly—dressed deer skins were legal tender, smoked venison, wild nuts and berries, all members of the family worked.[287]

In the summer of 1858, several white residents of the area decided they wanted the thriving little farm the Indians had hewn out of the wilderness. These families already owned tracts of land in the area of 320 or 640 acres, yet they coveted the fifty acres being farmed by Dick and his family. The whites applied to the Indian agent to have the Indians removed from the land. J.W. Nesmith, the agent who replaced Huntington, was not willing to force the Indians from the land, but did advise them that it would be best to move to the Grand Ronde Reservation in Yamhill Country.

Dick appealed to his old friend Jesse Applegate to help him with the matter. Jesse wrote out a pass for Dick and sent him to Nesmith to plead his case. "The bearer of this (Dick Johnson) is an honest, industrious Indian who has a farm in the Umpqua Valley. He is now on his way to visit the Superintendent of Indian Affairs at Salem on business of his own. He is fully deserving the confidence of the people and recommended to their humanity."[288] Dick carried the pass because without it, he could have been stopped and taken by force to the nearest reservation. Dick did meet with Nesmith and carried the following letter back to Jesse.

> I have to acknowledge the receipt of your letter of the 18th instant by Dick Johnson, and while I can but acknowledge that his case is a peculiarly hard one, I sincerely regret that it is beyond my power to afford him relief...I think General Palmer committed a mistake in encouraging him the idea that he could ever acquire a title to the land.
>
> It is true that if not already claimed by pre-emption, it is with in the power of Congress to make him a donation of the claim—but I think you are too well aware of the delays incident to any such efforts to advise a resort to it—besides, it is a question whether or not individuals have not already acquired rights to the soil which would render any such effort useless.
>
> My advice to Dick is to make the best disposition he can of his improvements, and remove to the Grand Ronde Reservation, here I will give him a piece of land, and see that he is protected and cared for—a military force at hand to enforce the laws and keep white intruders out.
>
> Nesmith[289]

Dick and his family felt they had been given a right to farm the land, and since the government was not willing to compensate them for their improvements on the land, they felt they had no choice but to stay put. They had built two snug log cabins, a stable, a smokehouse, and several other outbuildings. The property was fenced and a small orchard had been planted. The fruit trees were a gift from Jesse Applegate. Jesse contended that Dick's crops of grain and vegetables were on a par with those of his neighbors and his orchards and fields were the neatest and cleanest in the neighborhood.

The eight white men who wanted the land then decided to take matters into their own hands. They went to Dick's farm late on the afternoon of November 28, 1858 and, finding Dick chopping wood in the front yard, they shot the unarmed man; his lifeless body fell across the log he had been chopping. Mummy, his stepfather, heard the shot and ran unarmed into the yard; he, too, was shot. The men then pistol-whipped the women and left them for dead. Struggling to survive, the women made it to the home of a neighbor, who took them in and offered protection. Klikatat Jim, coming upon the scene while the murder was in progress, was shot and wounded. He, however, was armed, and fired on the assassins, who promptly fled.[290]

Jesse sent a very detailed letter to the Indian Department laying out all the events leading up to the murder, the murder itself, and ending: "at the hazard of being identified with 'the sympathizers for the inferior races,' I will venture to remark that under the circumstances which I have herein attempted to faithfully detail, had this killing been done upon any but 'an inferior and proscribed race,' it would have been regarded as a great atrocity in this country."[291] In reality it was a massacre carried about by white men against the Indians.

Five men were brought to trial and were all acquitted because there was no legal witness to the murder: Indians could not testify in court. Three young, white women who had overheard the murder plan were whisked away before the trial; soon two of them were married to two of the men who were on trial.

S. F. Chadwick, the prosecutor, comments in a letter to Jesse: "We can now see what crime will do. One criminal act committed seemingly in the eyes of the criminal justifies all that can possible succeed it. The murder of Dick Johnson and father opened the gate thro' which those girls have passed to their ruin. The murder alluded to has almost and may yet make a suicide of C, and destroy forever the peace, happiness, and respect for that family."[292]

Many of the local residents, shocked by the murders, offered aid and assistance to the survivors. Charles Putnam, Jesse's son-in-law, offered Klickitat Jim eighty acres of land if he would improve it and build a home. Robert Smith, son-in-law to Charles, offered to take in the family and make sure the children received proper schooling. James Miller, brother-in-law to Lindsay and Charles, did take the family in for a short time. Mary Johnson spent several months on the Lindsay Applegate farm, but eventually all the surviving Indians would move from the Yoncalla area.

The Applegates, along with many others in the valley, were galled and disgusted that the son-in-law of one of the murderers moved onto the farm within days of the murders and no one made any effort to remove him.

In 1863, a new superintendent of Indian affairs was appointed, and Jesse urged him to reopen the case now that the law that had prevented the Indian women from testifying in court had been changed: "As the new code now in force in this state removes the disability of Indians to testify—those guilty of that murder might now be tried and punished, if the Indians who witnessed it could be found."

After some time had gone by with no word from the superintendent, he sent another letter addressing the issue: "The people here expect you to do something in the matter and anxiously await your answer. Will you do anything in the matter? If not, say so. If you do nothing, we will try the Superintendent of Indians in Washington. We are determined to be met and elbowed in all public places by men guilty of the highest crime known to the law no longer."[293]

The witnesses were never located, and a second trial was thus never held. Jesse, his brothers, and his neighbors never had the satisfaction they sought on behalf of their Indian friends.

Chief Halo

The local Indians of the Yoncalla area were an offshoot of the great Calappoia tribe of the Umpquas. Some years before the arrival of the pioneers, this little band of Indians broke off from the main body of their people and moved to the northern part of the country to avoid the continual dissention and fighting among their tribe. When the Applegate brothers first arrived in the Yoncalla Valley they were welcomed by Chief Halo and his band of about sixty members.

Charles and Lindsay, like Jesse before them, paid the Indians for their land and built their homes on land that had been claimed by Chief Halo. He accepted the situation and looked to them for protection from other raiding Indians. Halo so admired and trusted the white man he declared his desire to become a "Boston." He was a frequent visitor to the Applegate homes, and when he expressed his desire to have a house like theirs, the Applegate men brought lumber and built him a snug, log cabin. When Halo complained that his white brothers' sheep were eating his pony's pasture, they came and built fences. When Chief Halo expressed a desire to grow wheat for bread, his new white brothers helped him plant a crop and showed him how to harvest it. So they lived in peace for a few years.

Joel Palmer, in March of 1853, was appointed to form and administrate an Indian policy in Oregon. He believed that since the settlers had occupied the valley lands, the only hope of saving the Indians was for the government to provide assistance for them on reservations. The decrease in game and their traditional wild roots along with abuse of the Indians by unprincipled whites was causing unrest among the natives.[294] As an off-shoot of this policy, in the fall of 1855 a government agent arrived in the Yoncalla valley and tried to convince Chief Halo and his tribe they would be better off on a reservation. A great feast was held and the agent explained through an interpreter that on the reservation there would be schools for the children, plenty of food, warm homes, and protection from their enemies. All of the band but Chief Halo agreed to go to the reservation. Chief Halo declared, "I will not go. Shoot. It is good I die here at home. My father died here, his grave is here ... Halo is no coward. I will not go."[295]

Charles and Jesse Applegate stepped forward at this point and assured the old chief and the Indian agent that they were prepared to look after and protect the old chief if he did not wish to leave his home in the valley. The Indian agent was incensed that the settlers would interfere with a government order to remove the Indians and he declared, "You have no right." Jesse informed him that they were well aware of their rights, but the Indians had rights also. Jesse's depth of character permitted him to see the Indians as fellow human beings who were facing the problem of race survival and he felt they were worthy of what protection he and his brothers could offer.[296]

Through the efforts of the Applegates, Halo's family was enabled to take out citizenship, legally adopting the name Fearn, and receiving allotments of land. Chief Halo lived out the rest of his life in his little cabin, daily visiting with his old friend Charles Applegate.[297]

The Sage of Yoncalla

After all these exciting and sometimes distressing events, life in the Yoncalla Valley was settling into a slow, steady rhythm for the Applegates. Houses were built, fields plowed and fenced, and schooling for the children had been addressed. Jesse was making some money selling beef to the northern California market and with his surveying. Cynthia was increasing the family coffers with the cheese and butter she sold to the miners who daily passed her front door. The children were growing and life was good. Jesse began to have a little free time in the winter and summer evenings, which allowed him to take up his pen and become actively engaged in local, territorial, and national affairs. His voluminous correspondence with at least a dozen influential people like General Lane, Judge Deady, Senator Nesmith, A. Bush, and Edward Bates kept him connected with the political scene and gave him a forum for his often unique, well thought-out views. These views were honed by his correspondence and developed over years of studying the public documents outlining the political development of the United States. Years of reading the historians of the time—Gibbon, Hume, Allison, Prescott, Carlyle, and Bancroft—had helped shape his analytical mind. Schafer writes, "His keen analytical mind, tenacious memory, and extraordinary intellectual activity, with the aid of his fine library, made possible to him a degree of learning to which few aside from professional scholars ever attained, earning him the title 'Sage of Yoncalla.'"[298]

Judge Deady was the first to apply the title "Sage of Yoncalla" to Applegate because of the wide range of philosophical speculations on many subjects that Jesse expressed in his letters to Deady and others. Jesse himself did not agree with this title, telling Deady, "I am not, nor do I pretend to be a 'philosopher,' I am only a farmer and rough one at that."[299] Jesse felt that Deady was using the term in contempt; he did not see it as a term of praise. However, most who used the term in reference to Jesse did use it as a term of respect and admiration.

One of the issues Jesse championed through the editorial pages of the *Oregon Spectator* was more self-rule for Oregon. The territories were governed, he maintained, "in almost the precise plan of the British Colonies System resisted by our ancestors in the war of the Revolution, and the right of self government which they so nobly asserted to the world and defended against the whole force of the British Empire has been withheld from the people of their own territories." He deplored that the Federal Government simply sent officers to the territory, not allowing the people a say in who governed them. Here he states his case:

> That the people of the territories have submitted to be deprived totally of their natural rights has perhaps been owing to the fact that by their rapid increase of population they looked forward to a near period when they might recover from it under the forms of State Government...It also appears to me that there being, so far as I know no prescribed mode by

which this transformation is effected the irregular and revolutionary process adopted to attain an object so important (statehood) is rather farcical and ludicrous ... If admitted the "state" is received into the fullness of fraternity, if rejected he shrinks back into an abortion or "State" of nonentity ...

Oregon is capable of self government and self defense we know for she has done both in the days of weakness and infancy—let us ask of our country again to restore us to our birthrights. The privilege of making our own laws and electing our own judges and rulers and to be freed from charlatans and strangers that are neither with us nor of us.[300]

In another letter to A. Bush, editor of the *Oregon Spectator,* Jesse lists several of the problems he felt the territory was laboring under. He strongly felt that the people of the territory should have their political rights restored, allowing them to choose their own officers and to vote for President and Vice President of the United States. Secondly, "That such officers as strictly belong to the Federal Government but the duties of which directly relate to Oregon (such as the U.S. Judicial, Indian, Land, and Revenue department) be filled with resident citizens of Oregon." He also argued that the military stationed in the territory should be made available in the protection and defense of the people of Oregon if needed. "If the military is to answer any useful purpose here it is to protect the country. If the frontiers are menaced or endangered from whom are they to receive official information but from the Executive or Indian Department?" He wanted the military establishment to be subject to rule of local civil government.[301]

Matthew Deady took note of Jesse's suggestions and compliments Jesse on being the first to "advance the doctrine that the Territorial system is not in accordance with the spirit of our institutions." Deady, at Jesse's urging, incorporated the ideas into a memorial that he sent to Congress. Records indicate, however, that Congress did not act upon the memorial.[302]

Jesse did attempt to throw his hat into the political ring in 1854, running as a Whig for county probate judge of Umpqua County. His Democratic opponent, S.F. Chadwick, soundly defeated him. The Democrats considered this a major victory, and the Salem *Oregon Statesman* greeted Jesse's defeat with the headline, "Umpqua County Redeemed Itself!" Chadwick, who would go on to be governor in 1877, promptly let Jesse know that his "invaluable services as Probate Judge are not in demand at this time."[303]

Even though—and perhaps because—Jesse found it difficult to remain excluded from the political arena, he began to form his unique, some would say eccentric, views on the political process. As far back as 1846 Jesse expresses his frustration with the political process to his brother Lisbon:

> I am certain I have no wish to curtail liberties of any class of men or to give any class of men privileges or power denied to the rest of the citizens yet I am far from being a Democrat in the present acceptation of the term...If I were to choose a form of Government I would give the appointment of all legislative officers to the people—but all ministerial officers should be removed as far as possible from all participation in party politics and popular excitements—to execute the law is their duty and they should know no man in the discharge of it.[304]

We see more of Jesse's thoughts concerning politicians in a letter written to Bancroft in 1879, "The mere politician is a gambler on the rights, liberties, and lives of men, and should be held up to the hatred and execration of those of whose rights they make the stepping stones to personal advancement."[305]

In 1855, M. Crawford sent a letter to Jesse urging him to run for office, to which Jesse replies:

I would not if I could obtain an office which I am not qualified to fill, nor do I aspire to or desire any, much less that of delegate to which I have not the smallest pretensions.

So far as party is concerned I am averse to any organization of the kind so far as such organization resembles a corporation for political purpose. It tends to supply in the place of patriotism by a devotion to a party creed, to substitute the most available for the most worthy, and as the most important requisites in an available candidate is skill in intrigue and demagoguism—private worth, the only warrant for public virtue, is too often overlooked, and the elevation of vicious men to high and honorable trusts tends to the introduction of low standards of morals among the people. It tends also to produce that most unprincipled and dangerous class, the office seeker by profession.

These characters are constantly fermenting and aggravating political animosity. They set no higher value on the institution of Government than as affording place and profit, and its offices only as the means of rewarding party service. As wealth and power tend to corrupt the purest human institutions, their effects upon bodies like parties which are in themselves corrupt, soon bring rottenness and decay.

Jesse then proceeds to lambaste the long-dominant Democratic Party:

Their leaders instead of being distinguished by their retiring modesty the inseparable companion of real merit, which waits to be sought by rather than to seek office, exhibit the most disgusting scramble of their party they are practicing to supplant each other those base arts of duplicity and intrigue which has made the epithet "party politician" in my estimation a term synonymous to "liar" "thief" "scoundrel" "ingrate" "hypocrite" "apostate" and every other term of opprobrium in the language. Though for the sake of keeping down party spirit I have thought it right sometimes to vote for those styling themselves "democrats" I have not lately *nor will I again* do a thing so much against my conscience.

Nor am I disposed unconditionally to surrender the keeping of my political opinions to any other party. I consider among the dearest rights of a free man the right to speak, think, and vote according to the dictates of my own judgment, and though my rights may be circumscribed and justice denied me by an intolerant majority, yet I thank God I have never surrendered any of them; nor will I by giving in my adhesion to a party and pledging myself to vote for its nominees thereby becoming bound to support men for high trusts whom I know to be dishonest, faithless to their promise, false to their professions, or traitors to the party whose support they seek.

Jesse also addressed the issue that was dearest to his heart and that would lead him back to the political forum several more times. He attended a Whig party meeting for the first time in 1854, to feel out the extent of slave-holding sentiment. He presented a resolution condemning the Kansas-Nebraska Act and was profoundly disappointed when the resolution was not adopted. Later he was sure this "pussyfooting" by the Whigs on the slave question was what allowed the Democrats to take over Umpqua County in the election of 1854:

But on one subject I entertain serious apprehensions. I have for some time been aware that the slave power was at work among us and rapidly gaining strength. It was for this reason I voted last year and used my little influence to call a convention to form a Constitution while there was yet sufficient of the old spirit of 1845 among us to secure to our children the blessings of a free state.

I am not an abolitionist, for I would by no means interfere with slavery in States where it exists, but its extension to Territories now free and particularly to this one in which I wish to plant my descendants, I will oppose with all my powers to the last.

Whoever is against the *extension of slavery* is of my party; whoever is for it is against me. My platform has but this single plank.[306]

He concludes the letter with a personal appeal to Crawford: "P.S. You and I have made our living by honest labor. We both expect to leave our children in Oregon. One of the worst features of slavery is to degrade labor. If slavery is introduced into Oregon our children must blush for themselves or their fathers; if forced to labor they will be degraded from social equality, and blush for themselves; if rich and slave owners, they will blush to confess that their fathers toiled by the "sweat of his face."[307]

In a letter to A. Bush, Jesse makes a detailed argument about the attempt to spread slavery to the territories:

> To make a long story short, Congress has never established slavery anywhere or permitted it in any territory where it did not exist prior to its session to the Union, and from the time the Union became the possessor and sovereign Territory without the limits of the states in the year 1787 to the promulgation of the Dred Scott decision in 1857—a period of 70 years, the *right* of congress to exercise a sovereignty over the Territories, as absolute as the sovereignty of the states within their own limits *has never been questioned* either by the judicial or any other department of the Government, and if slavery is carried by the force of the Constitution into Territories where it has been prohibited by congress or by the people acting under the authority of Congress, then it is carried by that instrument into every free state admitted into the confederate since the adoption. For the Constitution is the supreme law of the land—the term covering the whole land or any part of it—whether it be a state or Territory.[308]

The Whig party faded into history and was absorbed into the Republican Party. Jesse was associated with the new party from its beginning; in 1857, he helped to claim Umpqua County for the new party. Jesse's strong desire to keep Oregon a free state soon earned him the epithet of "Black Republican." Jesse was not a gifted public speaker and left such exhibitions to others. His influence was through the written word and his interaction within a large circle of personal acquaintances.

The Democratic Party in Oregon held about a three to one majority in the early years of the territory. A bitter dispute between the Democrats and Whigs over where the capital would be located started in 1850, when John Gaines, a Whig, was appointed Governor. The Democrats wanted the capitol in Salem and Gains wanted it left in Oregon City. This bitter dispute over the location of the capital helped consolidate the power of what became known as the "Salem Clique." This small group of influential Democrats took control of the power structure in the territory to build a strong, effective political machine that dominated politics throughout the 1850's and beyond. This group had the power to funnel federal money and appointments, doling out favors for loyalty and punishment for all who opposed their agenda. If one was outside of this clique, their chances of influence on the political stage was limited. Jesse was friends with many of the power players in this group: Asahel Bush, James W. Nesmith, Delazone Smith, and La Fayette Grover, but that friendship did not gain Jesse any favors because he was a strong voice for the opposition party and he was never willing to play the political game of "you scratch my back and I will scratch yours."

Chafing in the Minority

In 1857, Levi Scott and Jesse Applegate were elected as delegates to Oregon's constitutional convention, convened to prepare for statehood. An Umpqua County Democrat charged that Jesse "fixed" the election, employing "duplicity and chicanery, the principal elements that enter into his composition." However, this claim seems unfounded in light of Jesse's past: he was known for his honesty and outspokenness in all matters and when convinced of what was right, "he was as firm as a rock against evil doing." Shortly before the convention met, a letter appeared in the *Salem Statesman* signed by "Douglas" that stated "Old Jesse will be a difficult customer to deal with. If he cannot have everything his own way he will make a fuss, get mad, and leave for he is deficient in the spirit of co-operation and having a somewhat dictatorial temper."

Applegate seems to have confirmed "Douglas's" view of his temper with his comments on the Dred Scott decision: "the American flag should trail in the dust while shackles, chains, and fetters are raised."[309] The Democratic Party was quick to use this statement against Jesse. Just before the constitutional convention, Jesse made a trip to San Francisco on business; while he was gone, a local Democrat noted, "we do not expect to see 'chains and fetters' in place of the flag of our union."[310]

The convention met in Salem from August 17 to September 18, 1857. The sixty delegates' first order of business was to elect Hon. M.P. Deady of Douglas County as president. On August 18, Jesse Applegate introduced a resolution noting that the delegates had been "elected with the express or implied understanding that the question of slavery would be decided only by a vote of the people." He then requested that the matter be resolved, as the "discussion of the subject of slavery by this body is out of place and uncalled for, and only calculated to engender bitter feelings among members of this body … to destroy its harmony."[311]

George H. Williams, a fellow member of the convention, believed that Jesse introduced this resolution because he feared that the Democratic-controlled convention would play a trick on Oregon, as they had in Kansas, in which slavery would be forced on the people of Oregon without their being allowed to vote on the issue. He may also have been alarmed that his old friend Matthew

P. Deady, the most influential pro-slavery man in the Territory, had been elected president of the convention.[312]

The resolution opened a hornet's nest, and the debate raged, keeping the convention in session until late into the night. Most of the debate revolved around the idea that this resolution abridged free speech by gagging the members. Thomas Dryer had very harsh words for Applegate, saying that it was wrong to dodge the "nigger question" and he wanted "every man to show his hand." He then went on to demand, "Is the gentleman from Umpqua (Jesse) afraid to meet his constituency upon this question? Does he wish to shirk off the responsibility of defining his position upon the question of slavery?...Why do you want to choke down discussion? To save time? To save expense? Go home if you are not ready or willing to discuss it."[313] At last, the convention was adjourned for the night, and the next day the resolution was indefinitely postponed.[314]

Jesse believed it was wrong to indulge in prejudice of creed or race. Later he would comment in a letter to Judge Deady concerning the final resolution: "It is hard to realize that men having hearts and consciences, some of them today in the front ranks of the defenders of human rights could be led so far by party prejudice as to put such an article in the frame of a government intended to be free and just."

Jesse, though unhappy, did not in fact "make a fuss, get mad, and leave." Instead, he settled down to business and over the next few days made several proposals. He was appointed to the Committee on Boundaries and on August twenty-first made a report to the convention. [315] He also submitted a bill that would exempt minors from the requirements of military service, and when that was defeated, he proposed that a person not entitled to vote should not be required to perform military duty; this was also defeated. Jesse, undaunted, then submitted a bill that required a majority instead of a plurality of votes to elect the governor. This too was defeated.[316] At this point Jesse felt he was "a fifth wheel to a wagon."

Fellow Umpqua County delegate, Levi Scott, describes Jesse's difficulties at the convention:

> Mr. Applegate and myself were both Whigs, and our party was hopelessly in the minority throughout the territory. The Democrats had the reins, and they proposed to run the machine. Captain Applegate with his great talent and energy of character was regarded as the leader of the Whig party in Oregon. Immediately upon the meeting of the convention, many of the Democratic members seemed to league together to destroy his influence, and if possible, to render him ridiculous, and break him down. They opposed and voted down everything he proposed, regardless of its merit."[317]

Bancroft, years later, would quote LaFayette Grover, a member of the opposing party, concerning Jesse's time at the convention: "Jesse Applegate, one of the most talented men in the country, was snubbed at every turn, until, when the draft of a constitution which he had prepared at home was peremptorily rejected, he deliberately took up his hat and walked out of the court house."[318]

Jesse eventually decided he could do no good in the convention, so on August twenty-eighth, he left the convention and rode the hundred miles back home, urging Scott to do the same. Scott refused and stayed until the end; however, he did vote against the final passage of the constitution.

Before Jesse left the convention, he asked for a leave of absence until the end of the session. The convention refused him because they felt his request was filed in contempt of the convention and its proceedings. Jesse responded that the convention had no power to detain him but that he was asking for a leave because without it, he would be presumed to be in attendance and therefore entitled to the daily pay. Some saw this as manipulation, but Jesse's strong sense of right and wrong made him feel he should not be paid if he were not, in fact, in attendance. His parting comment was surprisingly upbeat:

"I have no doubt there is honesty and talent enough in this body to frame a constitution that will be approved by the people of Oregon without my assistance."[319]

In 1868, Deady wrote to Jesse asking him for a picture to be used in a publication honoring the framers of the 1857 constitution as part of a grand celebration. Jesse responds:

> I believe you have asked me for my picture before. It has never been taken, nor is it likely ever will be ... I have no desire to be remembered as one of the members of the Oregon Constitutional Convention. The state is not indebted to me for any part of it. I refused to sign it, and voted against its adoption ... It is no honor to have belonged to a body, a majority of which contained such sentiments. My name, with my consent, never has been, nor never shall be, placed on that "roll of infamy" ... I believe I am ambitious of distinction, but it must be the genuine article. If by acts, they must be good and great. If by discovery, the thing found or invented must be of some account. Excellence of some kind or other is the only foundation of just or lasting fame. Few, if any, gain fame by seeking it. To such, it is denied, and justly denied ... It would be dishonest for me to seek honor as one of the framers of a Constitution in which I took no part.[320]

Again we see Jesse's strong sense of "truth" trumping his "claim to fame." It would have been easy for Jesse to step on board and become a part of this celebration; the party of opposition was offering the olive branch. Yet Jesse was ever true to his own conscience, if not to his self-interest.

On February 12, 1859, a vote was taken on Oregon's admission to the union as a free state. The House passed the bill by a vote of 114 to 108, and two days later, the president signed the bill.

In an editorial for the *Weekly Oregonian*, Jesse rails against the rush to statehood:

We have no capital buildings, no library, and no visible means to support or sustain a State Government, yet we must do it, and for what? Why, that Jo Lane and Delazone Smith can occupy seats in the U.S. Senate and Mr. L Grover in the House of Representatives of the Congress, and draw from the National Treasury $10,000 a year each.

The majority of the people of Oregon have become the charmed victims of party conjurations and political drugs and have been duped into its support, until at last we have a state—the State of Oregon—comprising about 45,000 inhabitants.

No state, except Oregon, has ever been admitted into the Union without some provision being made, or at least, an evidence of the power and ability to support and sustain itself. But, in this case, the parent Government having neglected its offspring entirely, and required the youngest of the family to protect itself—to go out even to war against a common enemy, and fight its own battles, asking her to fly with her own wings.

It is a little puzzling that Jesse pushed so hard for Oregon to become a territory of the United States and then argued so strongly against how that territory was governed. And, again, as Oregon was on the verge of becoming a state, he was willing to spend his time and energy to help that happen and yet declared he would not vote for statehood. His editorial in the *Oregonian* very clearly outlines his convictions that it was an untimely move.

Republican Leader

With statehood in full swing, political parties began to form in earnest; the Republican state convention met in Salem in the spring of 1859. The party members now acted as part of a political organization rather than as a mere assembly of reform enthusiasts and political doctrinaires. The resolutions adopted, written by such men as J.R. McBride, T.W. Davenport, and Jesse Applegate, were sane, conservative, and even conciliating. The strongest devotion to the

Union was avowed and anything approaching hatred of any part of it was strongly disavowed.[321]

The convention stood squarely against slavery and included in its platform a homestead bill, construction of a Pacific railroad, and the immediate payment of the Oregon Indian War debt. Oregon's Democratic Party split into two fractions: the popular sovereignty "Bush Democrats" behind Steven A. Douglas, and the pro-slavery "Lane Democrats." Rumors circulated that Jesse was bidding for a nomination to the United States Senate and was making a deal with the Lane Democrats to advance his chances. However, Applegate had written to Lane that this idea was "erroneous." In March of 1861, Jesse wrote in the Oregon City *Oregon Argus* that neither faction of the Democrats could expect aid "in their party warfare from the Republicans." Jesse then lambastes the Democrats as the source of corruption, misrule, injustice, and rottenness; "such being the case, I cannot see how it is possible, with any consistency, without violating principles, and forfeiting self-respect, to lend ourselves to the base and dirty purpose of one faction of this corrupt party to overthrow the other." He then declared the Republican Party to be a party of principles, not pride, which would not "sell Republican voters like mercenaries."[322]

In 1860, Joseph Lane was nominated for vice president by the uncompromising slavery wing of the Democratic Party. He came home to Oregon to canvas for votes, believing he could carry the entire coast. Jesse, realizing that the question of slavery and the Union itself were at stake, left his farm in the Umpqua and rode back to the Willamette, where he canvassed for votes for Lincoln; it is said that wherever he halted, he left a Union man.

With the victory of the Republican Party in 1860, Edward Bates, now Lincoln's attorney general, lobbied to have his old friend Jesse Applegate appointed surveyor general of Oregon. Lane had lobbied for Jesse in '49 and now Bates would lobby for his old friend. Jesse realized that political infighting in Oregon would make that appointment impossible, but admits to his friend J.W. Nesmith that he "very foolishly consented" to allow his name to be considered for appointment. Jesse was correct in his assessment of the situation, but in May of 1861, he wrote to Nesmith and Bates thanking them for their support.

As the Civil War loomed on the horizon, Jesse strongly felt the need to unite all parties in support of the Union. He explains his philosophy to Medorum Crawford:

> Such of those issues not already settled by the "unavoidable logic of events" have been thrust aside by a present and all absorbing question which as effectually adjourns all minor disputes as the bursting of a bombshell would the festivities of a ballroom. I am for rallying to the rescue without stopping to enquire who leads the way or follows in the rear. Fortunately the question is a very plain one and the elements so clearly defined and distinct that there is no blending of middle ground for which to stand upon. I shall therefore support a "union ticket straight" I want no "trimmings" forced upon me nor do I wish to force any on others for the sugar of republicans might not suit the palate of some willing to take this thing naked any more that the cream of democrats suits mine ... As to how the union is to be brought about, I can only say that "where there is a will, there is a way.[323]

Jesse felt that the citizens of Oregon allowed the newspapers to lead them away from support for the Union and that led to the following letter written to the Oregonian in October of 1861:

> If you would obtain a correct idea of the universal influence of the press, go among the people at large and behold the thirst for newspaper reading. As you pass along the road in hot summer weather, when the farmer has returned from his work and the doors are thrown open to invite the precious breeze, on the porch or just within you will see the man of the house with his paper, swallowing down the editorial as a more delicious morsel than the vitals preparing for his dinner.

If he is a Democrat of the Jo Lane School, it is the Corvallis Union, the Advertiser or some paper of that character, upon which he feeds; and whatever he finds in its columns, if not there condemned, whether murder, rebellion or treason, it is Democratic and good enough for him.[324]

Jesse continues the letter by saying that nine out of ten Oregonians depend on the paper to tell them what President Lincoln's speech's say, and in the rare case when they do actually read his speech, they will comment, "I commenced to read it but got disgusted with the hell-fired thing. I haven't got time to read such d----d abolition stuff...I think Lincoln's done more to destroy the Union than any other man. I think the abolitionists better mind their own business; and if they don't, I tell you the Southerners will larn um[sic] a lesson." This attitude, by much of the population of Oregon, caused great heart-ache for Jesse; survival of the Union was paramount in his mind.

The Union Party convention assembled in 1862, drafted a platform, and elected candidates who vigorously supported the Union. Not all the candidates were acceptable to Jesse, who declares, "In obedience to a higher law than that of conventions, I shall certainly strike the name of Mr. Gibbs from my ticket."[325] He later admits to Deady, "You are right, I did relent and voted the Union ticket straight. I did it upon neighbor Este's principle. He said—I did not like some of the Union candidates—in fact I hate some of them, but I hate the secessionists worse."[326]

Jesse's Political Philosophy

Jesse's fame as a political philosopher is best illustrated by a series of letters he wrote in the fall of 1865 at the request of Schuyler Colfax, Speaker of the House of Representatives. Colfax and Samuel Bowles, editor of the *Springfield Republican,* paid a visit to Jesse at his Yoncalla home and were so impressed with the wisdom and intellectual ability of this man living in the backwoods of Oregon that Colfax asked Jesse to write his views on Reconstruction. Jesse sent his views to Colfax between November 19 and 29, 1865; they appeared in a series of four letters in the Eugene *Oregon State Journal*.[327] Schafer praises the letters: "They reveal a profound insight into the government system, a steadfast affection for the constitution with its many superlative excellencies, and also—which is a much rarer virtue—a true appreciation of its defects."[328] This insight can be seen in this excerpt:

> The constitution of the United States has been rightly called the greatest monument of human wisdom; it has secured civil and religious rights of self-government to a great nation, and though constrained by the necessity of harmonizing conflicting opinions and reconciling opposite interests, the convention devised machinery to effect the great objects that have stood the test of nearly eighty years—a period in which man has progressed more mentally and physically than in many centuries of any prior epoch. It is therefore no disparagement to the wisdom and patriotism of its immortal framers if, after the people to be governed by the constitution have increased tenfold and spread themselves from ocean to ocean, and the interests it was to foster have grown and diversified in far greater proportions, that under the severe strain of a bloody civil war some parts of its machinery have proved defective and others obsolete by the changes wrought by it...
>
> If the right to choose a form of government was the right of our ancestors, it is ours, and will descend in posterity, and anything we may do to take away that right will be impotent.[329]

Jesse felt that one or both the houses of Congress should act as a committee and report from time to time such amendments as seemed advisable. That recommendation would then be submitted to the people for a vote at the next regular election. This change in the method for amending the constitution was the essence of his first letter.

The third letter dealt with an issue that was near and dear to Jesse's heart: citizenship and suffrage. Jesse felt that the framers of the constitution acted inconsistently when they granted exclusive power to the federal government to determine who should be a citizen of the nation, yet gave the states exclusive power to determine who had the right to vote, the most basic right of citizenship. "Without the power to say who shall wield the sovereignty, the purpose of the constitution, to establish justice and secure liberty, are failures, and the Union itself is a rope of sand." Jesse believed in universal suffrage with some minor restrictions:

> Every member of the commonwealth, no matter of which sex, what color, or where born, if free from the tutelage imposed by the domestic relations should have the right to vote, if morally and mentally qualified to do so ... I say the right, not the privilege, because he, or she, who obeys the laws, pays taxes, or renders bodily service to the government has a right to be heard in its administration. But the American citizen who exercises the elective franchise is clothed with high duties and responsibilities, and the divine injunction that binds him to care for his own household applies with equal force to his duty to his school district, town, county, state, and lastly, to the Union; and though the numbers increase who share his responsibilities as he rises in the political circles that surround him, yet he is as much bound morally, and should be lawfully, to discharge his duties in each relation as if the whole responsibility rested upon him alone. It should be no excuse for non-performance or neglect of public duty because thousands or millions were equally responsible.[330]

It would seem that though the right to vote has expanded, as Jesse urged it should, the attitude of the average citizen toward the responsibility of voting has decreased, not increased since Jesse's time. Perhaps society's lackadaisical attitude to voting would have changed had his next recommendation been taken:

> I should therefore require that the voter be of good moral character, that he clearly understands our system of govern-

ment, and the responsibilities he took upon himself as one of its rulers. I would bind him in an oath of fidelity to it, and to cast his vote in all cases for that man or that measure that he, in his judgment and his conscience, believed would be to promote the public good; and that in casting his vote he would not be influenced by personal friendship, or any advantage to himself individually.

The fourth and final letter dealt with the newly freed slaves and their place in society. He confessed he did not understand God's purpose in dividing mankind into different races, and he understood that each race finds features in others that seem repugnant. "Nevertheless, the negro is still a man and entitled to all the rights of manhood. As a nation we are bound by principles of eternal justice to restore him to *all* the rights we have taken away." He believed that it would be best for both races if the freed slaves lived in separate communities, but "if we retain him among us, for our own good as well as his, we must take him like Onesimus, 'a brother and an equal.' But it is not among the rights he is entitled to that his sons shall marry our daughters, or that our sons shall marry his; a power higher than man's has forbidden such connection, and man must respect His decrees or suffer the penalty."[331] Jesse goes on to declare that the negro of 1865 was intellectually inferior, but it was only a temporary state, "if we remain together, the negro will rise to take part in all states of society, because intellect is not a birthright of any race."

These letters were sent to Colfax and the Thirty-Ninth Congress, and there is some evidence that Congress did read them and even consider the idea of national suffrage. Schafer posits, "Had the committee seen its way clear to recommend it as the Fourteenth Amendment, instead of the non-workable scheme they did propose, it is at least allowable to conjecture that the results would have been beneficial. There would then have been no need of the Fifteenth Amendment, and the problem of the Negro vote would have been settled at the outset on right principles."[332]

Samuel Bowles, traveling with Schuyler Colfax when he came to visit Jesse in 1865, writes the following description of Jesse Applegate in his book *Across the Continent*:

> A man of another description and history is Mr. Jesse Applegate, whose fame as an old pioneer, an honest, intelligent gentleman, incorruptible in thought and act, and the maker of good cider, kept increasing as we neared his home in the Umpqua; and we made bold to stop and tell him we had come to see him and eat our breakfast out of his larder. We did all to our supreme satisfaction, finding a vigorous old man, who has been here twenty-five years, participated largely in the growth and history of the country, and the conversion of its people to the right political principles; clear and strong and original in thought and its expression, with views upon our public affairs worthy the head of our wisest; every way, indeed, such a man as you wonder to find here in the woods, rejoice to find anywhere, and hunger to have in his rightful position, conspicuous in the government. Oregon ought surely to send Jesse Applegate to Washington, and the general testimony is that she would, were he not so implacably hostile to all the helping arts of politicians and place-seekers, which is of course only another reason why she should do what she yet does not.[333]

In 1863, Jesse Applegate was appointed to a joint commission of British and Americans to settle the treaty claims of the Hudson's Bay Company and its subsidiary, Puget Sound Agricultural Company. The Hudson's Bay Company set a price of $3,822,036 for their possessory rights, including Fort Vancouver and the Puget Sound Agricultural farms.

Jesse spent many months gathering information and documents to argue the United States' side of the issue. Three months after the British claim was submitted, Jesse wrote to Oregon's governor claiming that it was "full of misrepresentation if not down right falsehood."[334]

In July of 1866, Jesse was appointed to a board of experts that traveled to Fort Colville, Walla Walla, Vancouver, and Cowlits. They surveyed the existing buildings, and checked the local tax records to determine monetary value. In August, Applegate was called as a witness for a deposition that would be used as evidence for the United States. The Hudson's Bay attorneys cross-examined Jesse concerning his land values. "Do you suppose your judgment to be free from bias?" he was asked. Jesse replied, "I do not feel myself more competent to decide upon the question of my own prejudice than a lunatic upon his own sanity."[335]

After several more months of gathering facts against the British claim, Jesse sent a draft of his information to Judge Cyrus Olney for comments. When the draft was returned to Jesse, he sent his report on to Senator H. Williams of Oregon, instructing him to deliver them to the United States attorney in the matter.[336] Jesse also wrote an article to the *Overland Monthly* concerning the matter. The article was rejected, and Jesse, anxious that none of the evidence be suppressed, urged Judge Deady to use the material for a statement on the matter.

> I willingly concede to you all the honor of authorship or other honors to be derived from it, as I believe it contains the true principles upon which those claims should be adjusted...No matter whether it is worth much or little if they were left in peaceable possession of it—as long as they saw proper to use it, or until the expiration of their license.—I felt it to be my duty to do all in my power to prevent the Gov. from paying an unjust debt... *It is your duty* [to use this information] to prevent a gigantic fraud and swindle from being perpetrated on the Government. You know how much I have it at heart to serve my country in this matter. How happy it would make me if I could only think I had been instrumental in preventing the perpetration of this gigantic swindle upon the government.[337]

Schuyler Colfax paid a second visit to Oregon and Applegate's home. They discussed the three-million-dollar claim against the United States, and Jesse gave him a copy of the rejected *Overland Monthly* article, which Colfax carried back to Washington and presented to the President.

Senator Williams also delivered Applegate's report, presented as expert witness testimony, and his letter to Caleb Cushing, the attorney for the United States. Cushing used both the report and letter in his argument for the government. In September of 1869, the Hudson's Bay Company was granted $450,000 and the Puget Sound Agricultural Company was granted $200,000, much less than the $3,822,036 originally asked for. Of all his public acts, Jesse Applegate was proudest of this service to his country. Joseph Schafer comments, "In this connection, he prepared a voluminous report which is in the nature of a closely reasoned legal brief. It illustrates his justice to opponents, his scrupulous regard for the public welfare, and his extraordinary grasp of the principles of equity which the case involved."[338]

Colfax was not the only one to seek Jesse's advice. Deady often sent him legal briefs for comments, and the Oregon Legislators sent bills to him for his comments on engineering matters as well as legal subjects.

This period of Jesse's life, though not without its frustrations, would prove to be the golden years of his life. He enjoyed the respect of his fellow citizens and was able to pursue his interest in politics, devote himself to public service, and indulge in his philosophical musings without having to neglect his farm or his family.

Winds of Change

In 1858, Jesse took up the task of building his "mansion," the house he had promised Cynthia so long ago in St. Louis. The mansion had never really been her dream; she would have been happy to stay in her little log house on the banks of the Osage River. Nevertheless, her new home was described as the first mansion to be built in Southern Oregon, high-pillared with stately columns across the front porch. The only thing it lacked was a second-story balcony like the one at Charles' house across the valley.

The house was a two-story structure with a forty-foot square foundation. Many tall, narrow windows looked out across the lush valley, some embedded with stained glass birds. The lower floor had eight rooms: parlor, living room, dining room, kitchen, hall, two bedrooms, Jesse's study, and a large, inviting porch. A beautiful wide, curving wooden staircase led from the living room below into the grand music room/library upstairs, which extended the full length of the west side of the house. There were also six bedrooms on the upper floor, the girls' on one side and the boys' on the other, separated by a long hall.[339]

At long last the beautiful 'Gloria de Dijon' rose that Cynthia had carried west in the wagon found its rightful place and soon grew in riotous splendor over the porch. A grand sundial graced the center of the carefully tended rose garden. The Kentucky bluegrass seeds she had so carefully gathered back in Missouri were tenderly sown in the side yard of her grand, new home, and that bluegrass still grows across the valley today.

The house sat back in a little valley that forms a long neck between Mount Yoncalla on the north and a densely wooded hill to the south. In the south of the valley, at the head of this little neck between these hills was a spring, and Jesse's house stood by this spring. He planted an orchard between the house and the road, with a second orchard to the south and a little west of the house, extending up into a little opening in the hills. On the right side of this last orchard, on a hill that faces directly to the east, an acre of ground would be fenced and become the family burial grounds.

Charles and Jesse had purchased one to two thousand books from Harpers in New York, adding to the many Jesse had gathered over the years, so the library shelves were well stocked. Many of the Applegate children in both Charles's and Jesse's families were gifted musicians, so musical instruments had accompanied the book shipment. Alexander McClellan played the flute, William Henry Harrison the violin, Daniel the concertina, Gertrude the melodeon, and Sallie the harpsichord. Edwin Estes, a future brother-in-law, would join them on the piano-dulcimer. Many concerts were performed in the music room with the entire countryside for an audience.

No expense was spared on the furnishings for the house. Splendid, exquisitely patterned Brussels carpets covered the beautiful hardwood floors. A bank of gilded French mirrors lined the walls of the music room. Finely-turned wooden furniture from the far corners of the world graced the rooms. Marble-topped tables were at home in the parlor and the girls' bedrooms, and a large, oak roll-topped desk stood guard in Jesse's office. Jesse was fascinated with clocks, and so there were many interesting clocks in the house, none more fascinating than one on a special shelf in the parlor. This clock had been made in Hamburg, Germany, and had delicate hands encircled with tiny hand-painted roses and pansies of every shade. The large, airy rooms and the beauty and quality of the furniture created an atmosphere of hospitality and refinement reminiscent of the grand homes Jesse had spent so much time in as a youth in St. Louis.

In the entryway of Jesse's grand home was a large, full-length looking glass. In the summertime the front door was often left open to let the fresh air blow through. One sunny day a big, Plymouth Rock rooster strolled through the front door only to discover before him another rooster, just as big as he was. Instantly a battle ensued. Soon the grand looking glass lay shattered on the floor and the offending rooster had disappeared, but before that big Plymouth Rock rooster could crow over his imagined victory, he was chased away with a broom wielded by Mrs. Applegate.

All were welcome at the Applegate home, be it humble travelers in need of a night's lodging, or men of national distinction such as Schuyler Colfax and Samuel Bowles. When a Catholic priest was in the neighborhood, Jesse's home was used for Mass even though Jesse adhered to no religion and Cynthia belonged to the Christian Church. To the children's delight, even the famous Tom Thumb and a circus elephant made their way to the grand house for a night of lodging. For several years, the Applegates prospered and their beautiful home saw many a distinguished visitor. Then the winds of fortune began to turn.

Death Comes Calling

Great heartache came with the death of Rozelle Applegate Putman. Rozelle was Jesse and Cynthia's oldest daughter and by all accounts Jesse's favorite child, since the death of her brother Edward Bates. Rozelle was a very bright child, which delighted her father. After the family came to Oregon, her father discovered in her a real aptitude for mathematics; the two shared a love of solving intricate problems in algebra and geometry. She also displayed a precocious talent for writing poems; many have survived as treasures for her descendents.

Rozelle married Charles Putnam in Polk County, December 28, 1847, when she was not quite sixteen years old. Charles was a printer, and Rozelle assisted him in publishing a journal for Rev. John S. Griffith, the *Evangelical Union*, thus becoming the first female type-setter in western America.[340]

Rozelle and Charles moved to the Umpqua Valley with her parents in 1849. In the spring of 1851, they took up a donation land claim in the Tin Pot Valley west of present-day Drain, where some of her descendents still live. The home was a small, windowless log cabin, and Rozelle helped make the few articles of furniture used in her new home. Roselle's sister Sallie describes her situation: "Rozelle's surroundings were like those of all pioneer women making the work tedious and hard. Yet of evenings she was never too tired to collect her children around her and tell them wonderful tales, to while away the tedium of winter evenings. Some of these were taken from books she had read, and others were invented by herself."[341]

The country around them became settled, and late in the 1850s, the Putnams ran a dairy. Rozelle processed the milk of seventy cows and made butter and cheese to sell to the miners down in the Rogue River Valley. Cheese sold for fifty cents a pound; butter for fifty cents to a dollar a pound. The Putnams now had eight children and their fortunes in life were looking very bright. Then Rozelle contracted tuberculosis. When her health declined, she and her children were taken to the home of her parents in Yoncalla. Cynthia was known for her nursing skills and gave Rozelle all her loving, gentle care, but on May 16, 1861, Rozelle died at the age of just twenty-nine, leaving her husband and eight children behind.[342] Rozelle was buried on the little knoll to the southwest of the house. In time, Cynthia and then Jesse himself found their final resting place in that humble little spot overlooking Jesse's beloved valley. That little plot of ground is still used today as a final resting place by Jesse's descendants.

Rozelle's eight young children stayed with their grandparents for several years, after which Jesse and Cynthia reluctantly sent the children home to Tin Pot Valley and the home of their father so that the oldest girl could keep house for her widowed father.[343]

General Lane's Visit to the Applegates

As Rozelle lay dying upstairs, other dramatic events were taking place in the Applegate household. Downstairs in Jesse's study lay another visitor; perhaps "patient" would be a better word for the white-haired gentleman who lay there.

Just days before, an Irish teamster had arrived at the Applegate house mumbling about General Lane having been shot while crossing the Calapooya Mountain. Jesse must have wondered, as he followed the teamster to General Lane, about what had happened: Lane might have been shot by Indians or even ambushed by political opponents.

It turned out, however, to have been an accidental shooting: in the rugged terrain, Lane's revolver had gone off. The bullet entered through the left breast and exited in the back just below the shoulder blade. The teamster, fearing that the wound was fatal and that he could be accused of murdering General Lane, hurried south looking for help and found the Applegate home. Lane was, in fact, alive, but weakened from severe loss of blood. On seeing Lane's dire circumstances, Jesse comments, "God has thrown him into my care! He is my friend, a sweet and gentle soul who has done brave deeds for his country, I shall protect him."[344] The only hope was to take him to the nearest place of help, Jesse's home.

Lane was carefully carried to Jesse's home and laid on the couch in the study, so as not to disturb those caring for Rozelle upstairs. Once a fragment of the bullet had been removed and the bleeding stopped, Jesse took upon himself the job of nursing his old friend through the days of fever, days that would drag into several weeks. During that time the two old friends, sometimes adversaries, discussed the shocking news that had arrived on the same steamer that had brought Jo Lane home from a failed run for vice-president of the United States: Abraham Lincoln had been elected President, the southern states had seceded, and the Civil War had begun with the firing on Fort Sumter.

Lane was returning home from defeat but had expected to receive a hero's welcome, which he might have received had the captain of the ship not announced the firing on Fort Sumter and the beginning of the Civil War. Suddenly Jo Lane, Oregon's most ardent supporter of the Southern cause, was branded with treason, secession, and disunion, and he found it almost impossible to even hire a wagon or driver to take him home to the Umpqua country.

Some records indicate that Jo Lane was taken first to Charles Drain's home in Drain and that Jesse, upon hearing the news, went to Drain and requested that Lane be moved to his home. Drain was also a Southern sympathizer; therefore, it seems unreasonable to believe that Lane would leave his home to stay with Jesse, the strongest Union man in all the Umpqua area. We may never be able to ascertain the truth of this story, but we do know that Lane lay in Jesse's study for some days with Jesse acting as his nurse, counselor, and friend. Lane did recover from his wounds and returned to his home near Roseburg. Here we see another example of Jesse's fierce loyalty to his friends: at a time when Jesse's heart was breaking at the passing of his beloved Rozelle and great melancholy was seizing him, he took the time to care for his old friend.

Lane's stay with Jesse is documented in a letter written by John Miller, quoted in a footnote in Bancroft's *History of Oregon*: "Jesse Applegate testifies as follows: In crossing the Calapooya Mountain with only his Irish teamster, by some mischance a pistol was discharged, wounding Lane. The Irishman, frightened least it should be thought that he had inflicted the wound with murderous intent, fled to the house of Applegate, at Yoncalla, and related what had occurred. Applegate at once went to Lane's relief, taking him to his house, where he remained for several weeks."

Cynthia Goes Visiting

Jesse's work and involvement with the greater community often took him far from home for extended periods of time. But Jesse shows in a letter from July of 1862 that life was very different for Cynthia:

> By the most accidental I am now at this writing left alone with Uncle Billy sole occupants of this domain. My poor stay-at-home wife has long been preparing herself, her children, and grand-children to visit William Parker. The grand celebration to come off tomorrow at that place-it is the first time in the 14 years we have been here she has consented to go out of sight of Yoncalla—it has made her restless and fidgety for the last month.
>
> Old mother Putnam has been duly notified of the impending event, wardrobes handled and put in order____ and for the last three days the cook stove has been kept at almost a red heat baking, boiling, and stewing the provision needed for the great occasion. This morning being the time for departure came dark and gloomy and it's pouring down rain.
>
> The wagons prepared were without covers, the horses to draw it without shoes … The mud and rain would spoil all the finery with which the children were going to astonish their grand-mother Putnam. To give up the journey on the very day it was to take place was not bearable … the children raised such a clamor to be off that there was no resisting it—*and* off *they went* two wagon loads of them.[345]

Gertrude—the Prodigal Daughter

Jesse and Cynthia would lose a second daughter to illness in 1867, but not before she broke her father's heart by rebelling against all that he held dear. Gertrude and two of her brothers left home in 1856 to attend school at Bethel in Polk County. Her two brothers were to stay at the village inn while at school, but Gertrude was to stay at the home of the Reverend Glen Burnett, an old and highly respected friend of her parents.

Before she left home, both of Gertrude's parents reminded her that as she was only fifteen, she was not to "keep company" with any young man or encourage special, undue attention from the opposite sex. But when the beautiful, very sheltered young Gertrude went off to school, she found a completely new world that was much more exciting than Yoncalla.

The Reverend Burnett's home was about a mile from the school and the walk to and from school in the rain proved very trying, so the kind Mrs. Burnett decided it would be best for Gertrude to stay in town at her son's home. The son was a lawyer whose friends and associates were not the kind of people that Gertrude would have met at the Reverend's home. Young Mr. Burnett's law partner was a bright, reckless young man by the name of James D. Fay. A native of South Carolina, he spoke with an attractive Southern drawl and was a charming conversationalist. Judge Deady describes him as "a little man with a gamy manner—florid, fluent, ready and impudent." Fay was several years older than Gertrude but soon began to "court" her. Even though Gertrude certainly remembered her father's warnings about not "keeping company" with anyone special, she soon gave her heart to the young man whom she knew her father would never approve of: he was a "thorough-going anti-coercion Democrat," a member of the Knights of the Golden Circle, and a secessionist.

Word of this relationship was brought to Jesse, who promptly had Gertrude sent home, telling her she was too young to contemplate marriage and too young to judge for herself who was suitable for a husband. Gertrude was quick to point out to her father that not only had Rozelle been only fifteen when she married, but her Aunt Betsy had also been fifteen when she married Uncle Lindsay.

Jesse replied that in his opinion they had both been too young, but at least they had married honorable men, unlike Mr. Fay.

"But Papa—I don't think I can ever forget him."

Jesse was sure that once she was home and away from the young Fay's attention, she would soon forget him, and that, more important, Fay would soon forget his vow of undying love and move on to a new love.

Against her father's wishes, however, Gertrude continued to secretly communicate with James through cousins. With the help of her friend, Mary Drain, of another secessionist Democrat family, she slipped off to clandestine meetings with Fay. He was elected to the Oregon legislature by the mining camps of Josephine County, and Gertrude might have thought this would change her father's opinion of the young man, but it just gave Jesse another reason to label the young man as a "liar and scoundrel." One October morning in 1864, the stage drew up to Jesse's house, and Gertrude, carrying just one small valise, slipped onto the coach and rode away into the arms of her true love, James D. Fay. They were married October 22, 1864 in Jacksonville.

Jesse was not a man given to anger, but now he fumed. How could his Gert run off with a "damn rebel" at a time when her brothers were marching off to preserve the Union? How could she give her heart to a man who was not even man enough to face her father to ask for her hand? Disloyalty to family, and more important her country, would not be tolerated. Down came the family Bible, and with the fine point of his penknife, Jesse removed Gertrude's name. In a letter to son-in-law Charles Putnam, he explains his action: "Her name is erased from the family record, and her inheritance is taken from her, and even her dead body returned to me, it could not receive burial near the bodies of the honored and upright dead of the family…This may appear to you a hard sentence but it—is a just one—one that is false to country and their God deserves no better fate here, and will receive no other hereafter."[346]

Jesse promptly asked his friend Judge Deady for legal advice concerning Gertrude and the matter of inheritance, explaining that he was not as prosperous as he once had been and was concerned about what he would be able to leave his children, especially because:

> …one of them in defiance of my authority and wishes as a parent has allied herself with a traitor, and thereby forfeited all right to inheritance—I have under a sense of duty and responsibility made a will. In all the purpose of this will my wife agrees with me, and as the most valuable half of our homestead belongs to her in her own right. I wish to know how we had best proceed so as to make her property and mine a common fund to be distributed to our worthy children only, and so strong in law that neither traitor nor the spawn of traitors shall ever enjoy any part of our hard earnings—your advice upon this important matter will be anxiously expected.[347]

Gertrude tried in vain to communicate with her family, especially her dear mother. She sent numerous letters that were never answered. Jesse had decreed that her name was never to be spoken again. Gertrude felt certain that her father would relent when she sent news of the birth of little Jimmy Fay, Jr., but it was not to be.

Sometime in the summer of 1867, Gertrude took sick; her cough grew worse with each passing day. Once she realized she was suffering from the same awful disease that had taken her sister Rozelle, she asked her husband to take her home to Yoncalla so that she could be reunited once more with all that she loved. Fay was pleased with the idea; he was far too busy to care for a sick wife and his business often took him out of town. Word arrived in Yoncalla of Gert's failing health, and with great reluctance, her father relented but declared that the "contemptible and cocky traitor" would not be allowed to come with her.

When they arrived at the grand old family home, her mother raced out to meet her and asked all to come in, even Fay. It is said that as she was carried into the house she told her father, "I have come home to die, Papa."

"No, child, you have come home to be nursed back to health by your good mother." His heart softened some toward his rebellious child upon seeing her frail condition.

Soon after arriving home, she asked that her younger sisters and nieces be gathered around her bed to sing her favorite hymn, something she had not heard since leaving home. When they finished, Fay asked who had taught them to sing so beautifully, and Gertrude replied, "I did."

She then sent for her father, and they were able to spend some time alone, perhaps reconciling before she was taken away. Jesse never spoke of what was shared between the two that afternoon. The following day she died and was carried to the little cemetery on the hill and laid by her sister. Gertrude's date of death, September 5, 1867, was duly recorded in the family records, but the marks of the penknife can still be clearly seen in the family Bible. Gertrude was just twenty-six years old.

Once again, Grandma and Grandpa Applegate would raise little Jimmy Fay, just as they had Rozelle's eight children. His father, James Fay, shot himself on May 30, 1879, at the age of forty-five. His will left money to educate his then fourteen-year-old son, Jimmy.

Hard Times

Ill winds also had begun to blow on the economic front for Jesse, as the southern Oregon mining market began to evaporate. The 1860 census records show Jesse's assets at $15,000 in real property and $10,000 in personal property. Once again, however, he would find himself struggling with the crippling effects of a depression and by 1861, he found himself unable to keep large herds of cattle. He reports to his brother Lisbon, "Finding every other means of making a living about to fail me, I have determined to increase my flock of sheep and have for sometime been scraping together what money I could collect for that purpose." About this same time, he tells Deady, "Stock was a mere drag on the market."

It must have seemed to Jesse that God Himself was against him during the winter of 1861–62, which was unusually severe; he lost most of his recently purchased sheep and many of his remaining cattle. Once again he writes to Deady, telling him of the "great calamities we have all suffered from the floods and are now suffering from the severe frost.... It would make your heart sick to visit your neighbors at this time." In April of 1863, he reports to Deady that the economic situation has not improved:

> My income from all sources has failed, just when my expenses are necessarily increased by having to provide for Rozelle's eight orphan children. And as I conceive to be a man so circumstanced that doubtful speculation are forbidden, there is nothing left to me but earnest, constant, and persevering labor with my hands. In this I am nobly supported by the children at home ... So that if we are numerous as bees, there are no drones in the hive, and when you come to see us this summer (as we hope you will) you will find us as happy and prosperous as heart could wish.[348]

All through the Civil War, Jesse kept hoping the economic situation would turn around in his beloved Yoncalla Valley, but by 1867, he had left for the Clear Lake area of Northern California to go into the sheep business with his friend Jesse D. Carr. By this time, he had deeded much of his donation land claim to his children. He did continue to use his Yoncalla home as "home base," but the financial returns from it did not improve. In fact, in the summer of 1868, he harvested three thousand bushels of wheat that he could not sell at any price. This must have brought back memories of the time in Missouri when he could not sell his butchered hogs; but this time there was no "promised land" waiting on the horizon.

However, by 1873, Jesse had increased his sheep herd to 1,700 head. The Dorris Brothers of California, who owed him $20,000 for a herd of cattle they had bought on note in 1858, finally paid him $2,000 and assured him he would soon get the rest. Jesse had sold almost all of his cattle to the Dorris brothers in 1858 with the agreement that he would be paid as soon as they were able to sell the meat to the mining camps. However, they were unable to sell the meat, and ten years passed before they paid him the $2,000 and he never received the $18,000 balance. At this time, he also was receiving a salary of $200 a month from the Oregon and California Railroad for surveying its route through Northern California and Southern Oregon.

An article that appeared in the *Daily Oregonian* on Saturday, June 11, 1870, gives us some details about Jesse's work for the railroad:

> The preliminary survey for the Oregon and California railroad has been pushed through to Rogue river. From the head of the Wallamet [*sic*] valley it takes the Pass creek route to Umpqua valley; thence through the Umpqua Canyon to the valley of Cow creek, where it deflects from the route formerly traced, and instead of following down Cow creek and passing over the divide to Grave creek, which has always been deemed a very difficult route, it takes an easterly direction, ascends Cow creek valley and finds a comparatively easy way by passes through the mountains to the valley of Rogue river, which it enters near Table Rock.[349]
>
> Mr. Jesse Applegate, who has made this preliminary survey, says the route is even more favorable then he had ever supposed it. It is also much shorter.

If this gave the complete picture of Jesse's life at the time, it would seem as if his situation were improving; however, Jesse's life was as complicated as the man himself and in reality the consequences of past decisions would soon erase all gains and consume his life.

Drums of War

With so much hardship and drama in Jesse's life during the 1860s, he might have wanted to ignore the war raging in battlefields hundreds of miles away; however, the Civil War affected the Applegate family as it did every American family of the time. The Applegates learned the momentous news of Lincoln's election and the start of the Civil War when Lane came to stay with them after his accident. This news brought both joy and great sorrow to those in the Applegate households. Lincoln president! The Applegates rejoiced at this news. Lindsay in particular walked a little taller; after all, he had played with Lincoln as a boy and fought with him in the Black Hawk War. Yet the news of the war was sobering. Jesse had fought hard to help preserve the Union, but now his worst fears were realized: brother would fight brother. There were many young men in the Applegate households of "soldiering" age; it was only reasonable to believe that some of them would march off to defend Old Glory.

Jesse and Lincoln

Family history holds that Jesse played a part in electing Lincoln as president. Some historians cast doubt on the following story, but my research finds nothing that would discredit it and much to prove that the basic facts are correct.

In the year 1860, Edward Bates was a prominent Republican running for his party's nomination for president of the United States. Jesse was excited that his old friend from his St. Louis days was running for president and certainly planed to vote for him if given the opportunity. Jesse explains this bluntly to Joseph Lane in 1860: "Douglas' popularity in the north is unavailable as he will be rejected by the south, and next to him you are the most popular man in the free states, and as acceptable to the south as a native. For these reasons I feel almost certain that I shall cast my vote against you next November, and in my opinion there is but one man in the Union that can beat you for President—Edward Bates of Missouri."[350]

Leander Holmes, who had been the Republican nominee for secretary of state in 1858, Dr. Warren, and A. G. Hovey were elected delegates from Oregon to the Republican National Convention in 1860. Holmes, however, was unable to attend the convention, and his friend, Jesse Applegate, convinced him to send his proxy to Horace Greeley of the *New York Tribune*.[351] Greeley carried a good deal of influence throughout the country north of the Mason-Dixon Line, and Jesse had great respect for him. Greeley was not backing William H. Seward for president, and thus had fallen out of favor with the Seward and Weed political crowd. He had been barred from being a delegate to the convention from New York. The instruction that went with the proxy from Oregon was "use it in the interest of Edward Bates."[352]

The New York delegation had no idea that Greeley was to have a voice in the vote and were shocked when he stood up and responded as a delegate from Oregon. On the first and second ballots, the Oregon vote went to Edward Bates. Lincoln and Seward proved to be the leading vote getters: first ballot, Seward 173, Lincoln 102; second ballot, Seward 184, Lincoln 181. There were 465 votes in the convention, with 233 needed for confirmation. It is reported that "During the third ballot there was tolerable order until Oregon declared its five votes for Lincoln, rendering his nomination almost certain. At this point the enthusiasm became irrepressible; the Wigwam was shaken with cheers from twenty-three thousand Republicans as state after state declared its unanimous vote for 'the man who could split rails and maul Democrats.'"[353] The vote was now 231 for Lincoln, within two votes of nomination, and before the vote was announced, other states changed to Lincoln; thus the Applegates' claim in having helped to elect their old friend, Lincoln, President of the United States.

In his autobiography, Seward himself lays his defeat at the 1860 convention to the influence of Horace Greeley, who had a voice at the convention only because of the influence of Jesse Applegate on his friend Leander Holmes.[354]

Jesse and West Point

As his beloved country moved deeper into the Civil War, Jesse's son Dan decided he wanted to go to West Point, and so Jesse sent off at least three letters to friends who might be able to help with this endeavor.

> July 22 1863
> Dear Sir,
>   Dan wants to go to West Point. He is the proper age an Oregonian by birth, a good head and strong body—in a word I believe he will be able to make his way at West Point, become a useful man to the country and perhaps an honor to the State and friends that sent him there.
>   Wishing you to share in all the honors going I give you this chance to share in honor of Dan's elevation to perhaps Major Generalship.
>   At the same time be assured you will confer a great favor upon his father by your assistance.

Hon.   Yours truly
Sam E. May   Jesse Applegate

Four days later Jesse wrote to his friend Deady asking for his help in getting this appointment for Dan:

> 35 years ago, I was an applicant for a cadetship, it was the only position I ever sought.
>
> The law of rules have not been changed since except to require 5 years of service from the graduate.
>
> Dan bears the name of his grandfather Daniel Applegate who was a soldier of the Revolution—first under fire at the battle of Brandywine—was at Trenton, Princeton and received a bayonet wound at Monmouth Court House … Dan's Great-Grandfather was a Captain of volunteers in the same war … *His father* "would have fought, bled and died for his country" if it had been ordained.[355]

In Abraham Lincoln's collected notes, on a letter dated July 22, 1863 from Jesse Applegate to Edward Bates, there is a notation from Lincoln on the side of the letter asking Bates to help in obtaining the appointment of Jesse's son Daniel to West Point.[356] However, there is no record that Daniel went to West Point. This next letter, from Jesse to Deady dated November 19, 1863, explains why:

> When informed Oregon has no vacancy at West Point and a billet there if one was obtained would be a *favor* from the administration he or more truly I for him at once gave up the notion.
>
> I informed McBride "I could receive nothing for myself or family which in the remotest degree could be construed a *favor* from powers that be." This you may look upon as foolish or false pride but you must allow your humble friend to be foolish in this direction, it is essential to his manhood and has been so long cherished and practiced that it has become a part of himself.

This incident again illustrates Jesse's strong but conflicted sense of honor: he was willing to ask for help from friends, but not to receive special treatment. Certainly his life and the life of his son would have been so much simpler if he had walked the path of most men and accepted this favor from an old friend.

Jesse seldom gave public speeches but broke that self-imposed rule on March 4, 1865, in Oakland, Oregon. The speech was prompted by a patriotic call to young men to enlist in the army. He stressed the duties of patriotism and maintained that since, "death must be met somewhere, sometime, where could it be met with less pain and more glory, [than] battling the cause of the right?" Jesse went on to explain that war was not all evil:

> Like strong medicine it renovates and improves, and as the thunder storm purifies the air…so does war arouse men from the lethargy of an enervating peace; it stirs their energies, it purifies their hearts and draws them away from the corrupting pursuits of pleasure or of lucre. It stimulates noble deeds, and heroism. A war like ours of principle, infuses principle, and like the atmosphere purified by the storm, men for generations after such a struggle act in all things from higher and better motives.[357]

Daniel and his brother Alex did volunteer along with twenty-five other young men from the Yoncalla area, serving under their cousin, Captain Ivan Applegate, Lindsay's son. The war ended only six months later, but the young men from Yoncalla were not mustered out until sometime the next spring. When her sons finally returned home from the war, Cynthia convinced Jesse to divide a portion of his donation land claim and give it to Daniel and Alex with the hope that it would keep them close to home, as her heart had ached every day they were away from home and possibly in the line of fire. Jesse had told the boys from a very young age that someday they would receive a portion of the land, and Cynthia urged him to simply do it sooner rather than later. Unfortunately, this kind gesture turned out to be a mistake, as we shall see in later chapters.

Jesse captures the spirit of that time in the following letter to Governor A. C. Gibbs on July 5, 1864.

Yoncalla celebrated the National anniversary yesterday in the old and homely style of our ancestors. I did not participate in the preparations, being too melancholy and despondent to hold a festival in commemoration of our Nation's birth when so many of our fellow citizens are lying in glory beds of the battlefield to maintain the Nation's life.

In the evening, however, after the mail passed, I went upon the ground chosen for the picnic and was both surprised and delighted to find almost the entire population of the district, men, women and children assembled listening with earnest attention to an impromptu oration by the Rev. P. C. Parker, one of the representatives-elect, and I must say, though the discourse was not in well chosen language, nor delivered in accordance with the rules of elocution, it was one of the most stirring and inspiring I ever listened to.

The People were powerfully moved, not by that lighter emotion which expresses itself in noisy demonstration but by the strong and deep feeling which animated Cromwell's soldiers when they felt themselves the champions of religious as well as civil liberty. In a word, tears flowed freely from eyes not accustomed to weep.

As you would expect, no intoxicating liquor was on the grounds; a barrel of lemonade and pure water constituted the drink. The dinner, which was excellent and abundant, was all brought from the homes, and nothing but some roast meats and some coffee was cooked on the ground.

Near the speaker's stand there was erected a tall flagstaff from which floated the ensign, very handsomely gotten up. In the center of its blue field was a large star intended to represent the Union. Clustering around it in close proximity circling the whole were 21 stars for the States admitted into the Union.

I describe this particularly because, in the procession each of these stars represented by a lady bearing a banner upon which was the name of the state represented by the bearer—with the date 1776 on those representing the old states, and the date of its admission into the Union on those representing the new states.

None of these banners had mottoes except that one representing the central star, "The Union," "The Union: it must and shall be preserved!" Old ladies, really the mothers, 14 in number, represented "The Union" and the 13 original states; 21 of their daughters represented the states since admitted, and a bevy of little girls carrying appropriate banners, represented the Territories.

Behind these followed, first the females, then the males, making a procession of about 300. The spectacle was very pretty, particularly so because the clouds, which had hung threateningly in the heavens all morning, gave way, and a glorious burst of sunshine saluted the procession as it circled the flagstaff, amid the singing of the national airs.

There was one circumstance that was very remarkable. The committee, in order to remove all doubts of partiality in the distribution of the banners representing the States and Territories, assigned them by lot. The banners were numbered and corresponding numbers put into a hat, the lady consenting to march drawing her number without seeing what she drew. Of the 14 older ladies representing the Union and the old states the most politically intelligent and patriotic lady, Mrs. John Hedrick, drew the Union banner. My wife, the fattest and Dutchiest looking, drew New York State. Many others drew their native states. Mrs. Estes, the least of the mothers, drew little Delaware; and Mrs. Charles Drain, the only lady of Southern proclivities, drew South Carolina. Alike appropriateness was observable in the distribution of the younger States and Territories.

And lastly, when it was made known that Your Excellency desired a volunteer company which could hold itself in readiness for immediate service, almost every man and boy capable of bearing arms formed in line under the flag.

I think if you had been present you would have felt as I did, that "Surely the hand of God is in it, and the victory will be ours, for He has put it into the hearts of the people.[358]

Jesse's seven-year-old granddaughter, Susan Putman, would never forget one day in April of 1865 when she carried the mail into the house and handed it to her grandmother, Cynthia. Her grandmother took one look at the paper and handed it to Susan, telling her, "Take this out to your Grandpa."

Little Susan ran out to the garden and handed the paper to her grandfather. Susan said she would forever remember how her grandfather looked at the paper, leaned his head on the handle of his hoe and wept, great sobs shaking his body. The newspaper told of the assassination of Abraham Lincoln. Jesse wept for the man he admired, but most of all he wept for his country.

Jesse's attitude toward the Civil War once again shows his complex thought process: "As much as I deplore the terrible sacrifice of human life and treasure, it seems to me that in the history of the world there is no record of any great reform except that comes through the baptism of blood."[359]

Betrayal by a Friend

No history of Jesse Applegate would be complete without some mention of the complicated, controversial events known as the "May affair." There are many legal details involved in this story; the following account is an attempt to give a full and honest picture of this chapter of Jesse Applegate's life, a chapter that would affect the rest of his life.

In 1862 and again in 1866, Samuel E. May, a southern Oregon Republican, was elected secretary of state for Oregon under the governorship of Addison Gibbs and George L Woods, respectively. Jesse had nominated May at the Republican State Convention in 1862 and again four years later placed May's name on the ballot.[360] Some contemporaries claimed that "Samuel E. May was dark, dapper, and a rather Dickensian rogue,"[361] but Jesse Applegate considered him a close friend. Jesse and May were both Republicans and involved in the political life of southern Oregon. May lived in Jacksonville and Jesse met him through his brother Lindsay. Thus, when a bondsman was required by the state, Jesse agreed to sign the bond for May's first and then second term in office. A bond was required by the state because Oregon was a new state and had no treasury of its own to back the expenses of the state and could borrow money only on the guarantee of a bondsman.

On the first bond, Jesse signed along with Orange Jacobs and James Kilgore. The signatories on the second bond were Jesse Applegate and B. F. Dowell, a Jacksonville lawyer. The following is a quote from the first bond: "KNOW ALL MEN BY THESE PRESENT: THAT WE SAMUEL E. MAY, JESSE APPLEGATE, O. JACOBS AND JAMES KILGORE, ARE HELD AND FIRMLY BOUND UNTO THE STATE OF OREGON IN THE SUM OF TEN THOUSAND DOLLARS FOR THE PAYMENT OF WHICH, WELL AND TRULY TO BE MADE, WE JOINTLY AND SEV-ERALLY BIND OURSELVES, OUR HEIRS, EXECUTORS, AND ADMINISTRATATORS, FIRMLY BY THESE PRESENT. DEALED WITH OUR SEALS, DATED THE 6TH DAY OF SEP-TEMBER 1862."[362] All four men signed the bond. As this story progresses, it is important to keep in mind that four men signed this pledge, yet only one had to forfeit all he owned to pay the bond.

As early as 1869 there was speculation that May had used state funds to finance an extravagant and luxurious lifestyle. However, the extent of his embezzlement was not known until a new legislative committee had been appointed in 1871 and an official investigation was conducted. After a year's investigation it was determined that May had embezzled $3,600 during his first term and a total of $8,524.25 during the second term. May, who was now living in Utah, reluctantly returned to Oregon for a trial in Marion County.

Jesse and his daughter Sallie traveled to Portland in March of 1871 and called on Judge Deady, who the next day made the following entry in his diary: "Jesse A. called to see me yesterday. I advised him that he was not responsible for the money that Sam May received from the US as S. S. of Oregon and embezzled."[363] Unfortunately, Deady seems to have forgotten this advice over the ensuing years.

The new Secretary of State, S. F. Chadwick, reported on the trial in 1872: "Counsel have been employed on behalf of the State in the prosecution of S.E. May, formerly Secretary, and in conducting civil actions brought by the State against him and his sureties for the recovery of moneys of the state not accounted for by him. The prosecution in the criminal cases, after three trials and no conviction, abandoned further proceedings on the remaining Indictments against Mr. May, but the civil actions above mentioned are still pending."[364] The criminal trials against May were held in Marion County and the first one started on December 6, 1871, and the last one was in July of 1872. On every indictment for which he was tried, a full jury failed to find him guilty.[365]

Civil action was brought against May for the debt; however, he had left the state and been declared insolvent. Jacobs no longer lived in Oregon, and Kilgore had neither appeared nor been represented by council, so the state sought satisfaction in the amount of $1328 for the first term's embezzlement from Jesse Applegate alone.

On November 11, 1873, two actions were commenced in the Circuit Court of the State of Oregon for the County of Marion in favor of the state of Oregon and against May's sureties—Jesse Applegate and B. F. Dowell.

At first Dowell fought the action with all he had and urged Applegate to join him to "fight to the finish." He filed a lengthy brief arguing that he was not responsible for the second bond and claiming he had signed the agreement with the understanding that Applegate, Jacobs, and Kilgore would all sign it. In the end, only Applegate and he, Dowell, had signed; therefore, he argued, it was not a valid bond.[366] Jesse, on the other hand, never attempted to evade his portion of the bond, waived trial by jury, and agreed that he would abide by the decision of the referee for the Oregon Supreme Court, Matthew P. Deady.[367] If Deady found the state was entitled to recover under the judgment, he was to determine the exact amount of liability for the sureties. Jesse, with his usual lack of self-interest, said that he felt not only legally but also morally responsible for May during the first term, and if held legally liable, all he possessed was at the disposal of the state. In fact, while the case was pending, Jesse left almost everything he owned at the state's disposal, keeping only his surveying instruments and scientific equipment, which he would need to make a living.

The case was submitted to Deady, and months went by. The new secretary of state, S. F. Chadwick, felt secure enough in his conviction that nothing would come of the suit that in May of 1873, he returned money to Jesse that had been on deposit for the state, telling Jesse to invest it in something that could make him money. Jesse used the money to buy more sheep and took them to the Clear Lake ranch of his friend Jesse D. Carr. More months went by in which Jesse heard nothing about the May case. In the meantime, the Modoc Indian War had broken out in the Clear Lake region, and he was very involved with this crisis, serving as a member of the peace commission. This left him little time to worry about the May situation. Jesse hired David Logan, a lawyer, to deal with the May situation in his absence. However, Logan died in March of 1874, almost three months before Deady rendered a judgment, leaving Jesse without legal representation.

It was nearly eight months before Deady submitted his decision in favor of the state on June 12, 1874. On the first bond, Jesse Applegate was held solely responsible for $1,328.29. On page four of Deady's decision, item number eleven, he states "that by reason of the premises, the plaintiff is entitled to have and receive from the defendant Applegate the sum of $1,328.29 of said damages, but not the remainder thereof, for the reason that it is not alleged in the complaint that the defendant May received and failed to account for any other or greater sum of money belonging to the plaintiff than said $1,328.29." On the second bond, Deady ruled that Applegate and Dowell together owed $8524.25, plus $405.60 costs and disbursements.

Jesse owed the state a total of $5793.21 for having served as one of May's bondsmen. Four years after May was first suspected of embezzling funds, he had been found not guilty and left the state, and yet Jesse Applegate was being asked to produce $5793 for his "friend's" wrongdoing. The entire country was suffering from the weight of a depression after the Civil War and ready cash was hard to come by. Ironically, the state of Oregon owed Jesse $1871 for survey work,[368] and the Dorris Brothers of northern California owed him $18,000 dollars; however, these obligations could not be turned into ready cash to pay the $1,328 for the first judgment. Therefore, in the fall of 1874, the state confiscated Jesse's 1,080 acres and sold the land at public auction to cover the bond for the first term. Two of Jesse's sons were able to scrape together enough money to buy back the house from the state for $500.

It was unfortunate that Jesse had been misled about the possible consequences of the bond; in 1871 he could have scraped the funds together to pay the debt and save his property. Sadly, this was not to be: "Gone were the beautiful Donation Land Grant, the fertile fields, the rolling hills of pasture land, the carefully tended orchards ... the first mansion built in Southern Oregon, high pillared with stately columns shining afar like Arlington or Monticello against the Calapooya foot hills ... the loads of furniture brought by ship to Scottsburg and hauled by mule teams to Mt. Yoncalla."[369]

It had been Deady's habit for years to send Jesse copies of his briefs for Jesse to critique, but this one was slow in coming. When Jesse finally did get it, he responded that it seemed a "monstrous perversion of justice" that bondsmen should be held liable when May had been declared innocent. "This may be the law, but to those not looking at the case through legal spectacles it appears a monstrous perversion of justice." At the same time, he acknowledged the report: "I have to thank you for a copy of your decision as Referee in the Sam E. May case. I am glad to receive it, as it contains a full statement of the facts, which differ materially from those reported to me by interested parties. I have nothing to object to the justice of the decision, except that I have not the means to respond in the only way that will be satisfactory."[370] May had not been found guilty on criminal charges but Jesse was being held responsible on civil charges because of May's default.

George Riddle, in an address to the Oregon Pioneer Association, comments on the "May affair" and how it illustrates Jesse's code of honor:

> To show the stubborn honesty of Uncle Jesse in this matter, when the collection of these bonds was pending I was a member of the legislature. Our delegation from Douglas County submitted a bill for relief of Uncle Jesse from liability to the state under the May bonds. We thought his many sacrifices and services to the state in its formative period entitled him to this. We had not consulted him and, to our surprise, we received a letter from Uncle Jesse asking us to withdraw the bill at once. He felt insulted to think that we would think he would accept relief of that kind.

The legislature did have the authority to dismiss the charges against Jesse, but once again, we see Jesse's sense of honor get in the way of his and his families' best interest. Accepting this loving gesture from his fellow Oregonians could have saved him and his children a lifetime of grief, yet in his mind it would have been a betrayal of all he held dear.

Repercussions

After some delay, B.F. Dowell, the Jacksonville lawyer, paid the entire second bond. In 1874, he brought suit in Douglas County against Jesse Applegate, Cynthia Ann Applegate, their children, and Charles Putnam, a grandson, alleging that the deeds Jesse had made to his sons, to daughter Sallie Applegate Long, and to his grandson some ten and twelve years before were executed with intent to escape liability as a surety of Sam May's bond.[371] The deeds were dated in April of 1867 and May of 1869. Because Applegate had transferred his property to his children, Dowell claimed, he was rendered insolvent; therefore the plaintiff, Dowell, demanded that the instruments be declared fraudulent and void.

Jesse was sure that no one would ever believe there was any truth to Dowell's charges that the deeds to his children were made to defraud the state. In the first place, when they were made, no one had any idea that May had embezzled funds; May was one of the most respected public figures in the state. Secondly, at the time that the deeds were drawn up, Jesse had more than enough resources to pay his part of any bond. Deady was aware of this because in June of 1869, Jesse had sent Deady a letter including two thousand-dollar checks from Wells Fargo Bank and asking him to have the money paid out in gold coin. Thirdly, and most important to Jesse, anyone who knew him understood him to be the model of an honest man.

Jesse explains the deeds in his testimony in the ensuing trial in the Circuit Court of Oregon for the County of Douglas:

> The contract with all the parties mentioned Wm. Henry, Daniel and Peter Applegate and Charles Putnam was the same, that if they remained with me and worked on the farm until they were married or 21 years of age, I would give to each of them the same that I had given to the elder brothers, Robert and Alexander. Charles Putnam is my grandson and the contract with him was made with his father Charles F. Putnam as well as himself. I had given to Robert and Alexander on the same kind of contract, a tract of land each with stock and so forth.[372]

When asked when this contract had been entered into, Jesse replies, "It was understood between my own sons and myself as soon as they were old enough to clearly understand the conditions, the younger understood them more clearly from what I had done for their elder brothers Robert and Alexander."

It is evident from these answers that Jesse had intended from the time each son was born to give them a portion of his land holdings when they reached the age of twenty-one. Jesse had accepted that he was liable for May's defrauding of the state and had allowed his assets, 1080 acres and the contents of his beautiful home to be sold at auction to pay that debt, but he could not bear that Dowell was now going after the rightful inheritance of his children.

To the next question, "Mr. Applegate, state what was your condition after the execution of these conveyances and the transfer from you of the property therein conveyed, as to solvency or insolvency, state fully," Jesse gives this answer:

> I owed no debt of my own contracting, I did not believe Mr. May would be a defaulter, he had undergone the most rigid investigation by three legislatures, and nothing found against him, if I had known Mr. May to be a defaulter I would have fulfilled my obligations to these young men just the same, I had however some money in the bank, a tract of land on Mount Yoncalla containing 1080 acres and debts owing to me to the amount of at least $40,000. One party, drovers in California, owed me about $20,000 exclusive of credits amounted to about $3000, the men I believe today to be honest and probably will pay the debt at some time, one of the parties, P.A. Dorris, came to see me at Clear Lake in 1872 after the state had commenced against Mr. May for defalcation. I told him of the suit commenced against May and his sureties and if he would stand between me and any responsibilities growing out of it, I would give him his note. About 18 months ago when his note and interest was worth $25,000, I cancelled his note and sent it to him, with the amount of May's debt. The debt of Mr. Dorris to me was 4 times the amount of my part of Mr. May's.[373]

There is at least one published work claiming that Jesse Applegate owed the Dorris Brothers $25,000; however, the record clearly shows that they owed Jesse the money. The court testimony above shows his hope of using this debt to him as a way of paying the May debt. Further verification of this debt can be found in a letter to Judge Deady. In June of 1869, Jesse writes, "Mr. Dorris proposes to send me drafts payable in San Francisco as fast as he receives money from his butchers until my debt is paid it will amount to about $15,000. I will send the drafts to you as fast as I receive them to be invested in Coupon Bonds of the denominations of $500 and over ... the interest upon it ought in a plain way support my wife and unmarried children."[374]

The court record then indicates that Jesse was asked to state what other property, if any, he had at the time of making these conveyances. His answer:

> A small band of cattle, I do not remember the number of any particular year. I was employed by the Oregon and California Railroad Company at $200 per month. I invested some of this money in swamp lands, after this suit against May and sureties commenced, I abandoned my swamp land and placed the money paid upon it in the hands of Secretary Chadwick to be applied upon any judgment that might be recovered against me as surety for S. E. May. The amount was about $1,800. After my deposit with Secretary Chadwick a year or more, Mr. Chadwick wrote to me that the suit against May did not progress but slowly and might never reach a judgment against him; he advised me to draw my money and invest it in something that would make it profitable which I did; and made a great loss, not only taking the last money I had, but the last of my personal property also.

Jesse had invested that money in sheep, all of which were lost in the winter of 1874, in a series of severe winter storms in Clear Lake. In cross-examination Jesse gave the following answer, "As a last effort to meet this obligation I invested all my remaining means except the tract of land sold to satisfy the first judgment, in a sheep speculation and they were swallowed up by an act of providence."

Dowell lost his attempt to have Jesse's sons' deeds overturned in Douglas County. He then appealed the case to the state supreme court, where the case was remanded back to Douglas County. When he lost again, he appealed to the U.S. Supreme Court on the technicality that the deeds were improperly stamped and therefore violated the federal excise tax law. This time, the ruling was in his favor and the deeds for the land Jesse and Cynthia had given to their sons and Sallie Long so many years before were overturned. Only his grandson, Charles Putnam, was allowed to keep his land. The judge ruled that it was in payment of services rendered and therefore valid.

Dowell, now in possession of the land deeded to Jesse's sons, went back to court demanding that they pay Dowell rent for the past six years and turn over any profits made from the land. The Applegates appealed this decision, fearing that Cynthia would lose the forty-acre tract of land near the top of Mt. Yoncalla that the boys had deeded to her so that she would always have a place to call home. They balked at letting the humble little three-room house on the hill be given to Dowell.

In 1878, Governor Thayer intervened on the behalf of the Applegates concerning the little house on the hill. Thayer, feeling that the Applegates had suffered great injustice at the hands of the state, gave Cynthia, in lieu of her dower in the donation land claim, forty acres and some of the notes the Applegates had turned over to the state to settle May's debts. Jesse explains the situation in a letter to his son Henry:

> The Governor wrote in reply to my letter that if I would send him a description of the 40 acres including the vineyard that the state would make your mother a deed to it on the same terms Bob and Dan agreed to do it. I have sent the description and the deed has been made by the state so that your mother once more has a home of her own and she keeps me as her servant.

This kind act of the Gov. has lifted a load of uneasiness off our minds. As long as I am able to work I feel sure of making our support and when I cannot work any longer the sale of the vineyard will bring something to keep your mother in her old age. [375]

Justice Sawyer of the United States District Court explains his opinion on Jesse's deeds to his children, "I think those conveyances were made in good faith, and without any attempt to defraud the state." Still the court held that Jesse's transfers of land to his children were invalid because the land was encumbered by debts before the deeds were made. Sawyer ruled that although Samuel May's defalcations were not known until 1869, after most of Jesse's land had been transferred to his children, each and every time May made a theft between 1863 and 1869 there was a breach of the bonds, dating from the time of the theft. Jesse had twenty days to pay Dowell $7,488 or the land would be sold at auction. Jesse's children exhausted all means to raise the money and were able to save a portion of the land, including the acreage where the little family cemetery was located.[376] Dowell bought the remaining portion from the state for $7,400.

Jesse reports to his brother Lindsay on June 17, 1883: "I am happy to inform you that my children, tho at great pecuniary sacrifice, have paid off Dowell and are now out of the clutches of that deamon [sic] incarnate and tho they have lost money by the lawsuit—they have gained an ample equivalent in character as upright honorable men, which is of far more value than gold."[377] Unfortunately, Jesse was incorrect in this letter because Dowell would continue to press suits against the Applegate children that would drag on for another nine years.

Justice Thayer addressed the issue of insufficient revenue stamps in an address before the Oregon Supreme Court in March of 1879:

The only grounds, as before observed, upon which it can be claimed that the Circuit Court of the United States for the district of Oregon has jurisdiction of the suit of *Dowell v. Applegate*, in which the said decree was given, were the allegations in reference to the insufficiency of the revenue stamps upon the deeds, executed by Jesse Applegate and wife to their children ... The jurisdiction of the said United States court was invoked as auxiliary to the process of the State courts, and the federal question involved in the case, if it deserves to be considered as such, was not regarded of sufficient importance to receive from the court the opinions delivered more than a passing remark, and was evidently thrown into it as a mere subterfuge upon which to claim the benefit of federal jurisdiction ... How Dowell's right to have the deeds referred to set aside, and the land conveyed thereby sold, and the proceeds applied in payment of the two judgments, was affected by any construction of any act of Congress, might be explained by metaphysical subtleties, but no ordinary logic can demonstrate it.[378]

An editorial written in the *Rogue River Courier* of August 6, 1886 expresses outrage on the affair: "The whole system of requiring an innocent person to suffer for a guilty one is wrong. The State has the power to do it, but the exercise of that power is not only wrong, but also cruel and wicked in the extreme. There is no justice in it. There is no morality in it. It is legalized robbery, a relic of heathenism."[379]

Jesse had always taken great pride in paying his debts and had taught his sons that this was one of the greatest virtues, a mark of a true man. But now Jesse was brought to abject poverty in his old age for another man's dishonesty: "Now, for another man's sins I have been deprived of all my earthly possessions. I have besides the tools of my craft nothing, nor even a spot to hide away my body. It is not imaginary privations about which I am so anxious—but the actual wants of the animal, food, and clothing and where I shall lay my head."[380]

One of the ways that Jesse tried to earn money to pay his debt to Dowell was by applying for surveying work in Oregon and California.

When I saw Dowell at Jacksonville last June He said he had political influence enough to obtain profitable contracts of surveying and proposed if I would do the work to obtain enough to pay our joint debt his "influence" to balance my labor—tho a hard bargain on my side I agreed to it because I had just as well spend the remainder of my life in the woods as any where else, and if in the prosecution of its only object I think I will be better contented than in any other way. As I have heard nothing further from Dowell I presume he over rated his influence.[381]

Dowell's influence never brought any surveying jobs, and Jesse was unable to obtain jobs in Oregon because the staunchly Democratic surveyor general, Ben Simpson, refused to give him work. He was able to secure limited work in California for the state surveyor general's office and often spent extended times in California completing the work. One of his surveying jobs involved the Jesse D. Carr ranch in Modoc County:

Since this May matter has made it my duty to find money to pay it if I can, I have each year formally applied for surveying both in Oregon and California. Presenting references to the satisfaction of the Sur's Gen. of both states of my performance as a Deputy—but notifying then that I will neither bribe them with money or political service in consideration of employment…the Sur. Gen. has twice in this spring selected work for me to do—and each time been forced to give it to others, one of whom he knows to be both dishonest and incompetent, for he told me this himself.[382]

Dowell continued to harass Jesse's sons, Daniel and Alex, over clear title to a forty-acre plot they had bought from their brother William, finely managing to get the case before the US Supreme Court. Alex gave up in frustration and deeded his interest to Daniel. Daniel, under the weight of debt, was forced in June 1888 to sell the south half of the donation claim so as not to lose all the land. The grand old house on the land he sold had lost its grandeur: it sat neglected for lack of funds and empty because the furniture had been auctioned off years before. The need for money to continue the never-ending legal battle forced Daniel to work for wages, and the strain became too much: on March 14, 1896, while returning home from work, he collapsed and died at the age of fifty-one. Shortly thereafter, Dowell, now seventy-five, also died. There had been no judgment concerning the contested forty acres; the case was dismissed, and Daniel's widow retained the contested forty acres, including the family cemetery.

Family tradition holds that when the first auction was held by the state for the first term bond, most of the furnishings from the house were sold for mere pennies on the dollar. Sallie Applegate was able to save a few pieces for the family by slipping into the house on the morning of the sale and writing the names of family members on the underside of some pieces of furniture. Some of this furniture, like the table in this picture, indeed remains in the family, and the names are still clearly etched into them.

One of the tables saved by Sallie Applegate Long during the auction.

The Applegate descendants have long debated the fate of the Jesse's house. Some historians have said that it burned down. A letter from Sallie Applegate Long to a Mr. Ackerman dated March 5, 1892 says, "The house was torn down by the present owner Mr. Coffey." Since the house was too big for an ordinary family, more value could be gained by tearing it down and selling the wood from the grand staircase, the moldings, and the stained glass windows. At one time the home site could be identified by a large, flat stone, part of the base of one of the fireplaces, but even that is gone now, and thus an important site in Oregon history has vanished forever.

This entire episode is an example of Jesse's sense of honor and how that sense of honor was not shared by those around him. He acted in good faith, trusting May, his co-signatories, and indeed the state of Oregon to demonstrate the same honor. He trusted his friends Deady and Chadwick to give him good advice in the matter, and they did not. Jesse's utter lack of self-interest and trust in the honor of others left him a broken man.

The "May affair" weighed heavily on Jesse and drove him deeper and deeper into depression. One more blow would take him over the edge for a short period.

Clear Lake — Modoc War Years

During the drawn-out course of the May episode and its aftershocks, Jesse had moved to new ventures in California. As we have seen in earlier chapters, Jesse's economic fortunes had dwindled after the Civil War. Two of Jesse's sons, a grandson, his brother Lindsay, and several of his nephews were now living on the northern California-Oregon border in the Clear Lake area, and Jesse set his sights on this area, hoping it would be a more profitable area to raise sheep. It would place him closer to the northern California mining district and a market for his sheep. Having deeded his Oregon property to his children, Jesse then transferred his flock of sheep to a piece of swampland located on the old emigrant road on the north shore of Clear Lake, not far from the Lost River Modoc country. Jesse used a technique he had perfected on his Yoncalla farm to reclaim a low, swampy area: he cut the tule reeds, packed the swamp land with them, then covered them with soil, turning useless swamp land into useable grazing land. Jesse continued to maintain his Yoncalla farm as a base of operation, living there most of the year.

History of the Modoc Conflict

George Nurse and a number of other stockmen had begun to settle in the Clear Lake area as early as 1863, and in 1864, the Modoc, Klamath, and a Snake band known as the Yohooskin band signed a peace treaty ceding their land at Lost River, Tule Lake, and Lower Klamath Lake. However, during 1871, Jesse and many of his neighbors in the Clear Lake area began to have problems with the Modoc Indians, who had left their Oregon reservation in April 1869. The Indians were constantly sniping away at the white settlers' flocks and Kientpoos, a young Modoc warrior known to the whites as Captain Jack, came on to Jesse's land at one point demanding that Jesse pay him a stated allowance of subsistence in consideration of having permission to settle in the country. Jesse refused to encourage this behavior,[383] as the Indians had deeded their land to the United States government in 1864, when they signed the treaty giving up the land in exchange for reservation life. The conflict growing between the settlers and the Indians in the Clear Lake area was common to all Indian and settler conflicts; the encroachment of whites upon traditional Indian land until the Indian way of life was threatened with total extinction.

The bitter roots of this conflict went back to the opening of the Applegate Trail and the introduction of whites into the area. The Modoc were fierce warriors who jealously guarded their territory and despised outsiders even passing through their region. Over the next few years, the Indians killed a number of whites traveling in the wagon trains over the area. Many were killed at a spot that became known as Bloody Point. Bloody Point was a popular campsite because of its location at the edge of Tule Lake, providing settlers and livestock with water after a long, hard, dry day of travel. Unfortunately, the area was surrounded by huge lava outcroppings with a number of large boulders within a hundred yards of the lake, where the Indians could easily lie in wait for their attacks.[384]

There had been a particularly terrible massacre in the late summer of 1852; some sources say thirty-three were killed, and others say thirty-six.[385] After this event, a young volunteer from Yreka by the name of Ben Wright was enlisted to lead raids on the Indians. In early November, Wright and a small party of men went out to Bloody Point and camped for several days before Wright told his men he was going to march into the Indians' camp and demand that two white female captives be returned along with the supplies taken from the emigrants. Wright carried a pistol under his coat and gave the instructions that if his demand was not met, he would shoot the headman and drop to the ground while his men opened fire on the camp. Wright's demand was refused, so he promptly shot the leader and dropped to the ground, and his men, hidden on the banks around the camp, opened fire. Later the Indians said that forty-two Modoc died that day.[386] The Modoc never forgave or forgot this treachery.

The hostility continued until October of 1864, when a peace treaty was signed with the Indians of the area, moving them to a reservation on a portion of the former Klamath Indian range on Upper and Middle Klamath Lakes. The treaty was a standard Indian agreement of the time.[387] The Klamath, Modoc, and Snake of the area gave cession of all tribal land to the United States Government and agreed to move onto the land set aside for them. Murray, author of *The Modoc and their War*, explains, "A major reason the Indians were willing to sign, even though many were dubious about doing so, was that another group of Paiutes, called the 'Walpape Snakes' under the leadership of their headman, Paulina, was raiding both Klamath and Modocs as well as attacking any white man who came through the Silver Lake-Summer Lake country about fifty miles north of Goose Lake."[388]

What the government had not taken into consideration in the treaty was that the Klamath and Modoc had been traditional rivals for centuries. Almost from the beginning of their time on the reservation, there were problems between the Klamath and Modoc. It was not long before Captain Jack led a small group of braves and their families back to Lost River, their traditional homeland. When Captain Jack and his band returned to Lost River, he found a number of Americans had moved onto their traditional tribal grounds at the urging of the Oregon government. The Oregon settlers were uneasy having Jack living among them. Murray explains: "Jack's whole way of life conflicted with that of the Oregon settlers, who wanted title to the land for farming and stock raising. As long as the Indians roamed their traditional hunting grounds, there was always the possibility of conflict."[389]

Trouble with Captain Jack

The former Indian agent and Yreka lawyer Elisha Steele had promised Jack a small reservation on Lost River, but did so when he no longer had this authority, having lost his position as Indian agent due to political wrangling. Over the next several years, Jack often went to Yreka to seek the advice of Steele and continued to believe that his friend would be able to secure his little band a permanent home on Lost River.

On March 4, 1869, Ulysses S. Grant became President, and with the new administration came new appointments. On May 1, J.W.P. Huntington was replaced with a new Indian superintendent for Oregon, Alfred B. Meacham. Lindsay Applegate was replaced as Indian Agent for the Klamath reservation because it was put under the control of the army with Captain O. C. Knapp, a veteran of the Union Army, in charge. Meacham did not think highly of the military at Klamath: the desertion rate was very high, and Meacham said that half the troops were needed to guard the other half, and when one group was sent to search for deserters, that group soon joined the deserters themselves. Meacham had no faith that this kind of soldier would ever be of any help in forcing Jack to come back to the Klamath reservation.[390] However, in mid-December of 1869, Meacham, Knapp, and a small band of soldiers, along with an Indian woman to translate, went out to Jack's camp to convince him to come back to the reservation. At first, Jack denied that he had ever signed the treaty of 1864 and claimed he could therefore not be forced to leave his land. After some negotiation, however, he did admit that he had signed the treaty and Jack and his band returned to the reservation.

Peace on the reservation was short-lived, and before long the Klamath were once again ridiculing and harassing Jack's little band of Modoc. The Klamath claimed that the Modoc could survive only with the charity of the Klamath. To Jack's credit, he appealed to Agent Knapp for relief from the harassment, but nothing was done, and Jack was told that if he could not get along with the Klamath, he could move to a remote part of the reservation where there were no Klamath Indians. Jack moved his little band, but the harassment continued. Thus, Jack and the band of Modocs felt they had no other option but to go back to Lost River and hold out for a reservation of their own.

The return of Jack to Lost River was not well received by the white homesteaders, as Jack began to demand that the whites either leave or acknowledge his suzerainty over their holdings by paying him "rent" in the form of produce for their use of the Modoc's land.[391] Once again, one of his stops was at Jesse Applegate's ranch, and once again, Jesse refused Jack's request. Jesse understood that giving in to their request at this point would only encourage them to become more arrogant and insolent.

Jesse's surveying for the railroad was taking him across much of Oregon and Northern California; early on the morning of July 4, 1871, he paid a visit to Alfred B. Meacham, the superintendent of Indian affairs for Oregon. They discussed the state of affairs in the Clear Lake/Lost River region and how Captain Jack and his loyal band of Indians refused to return to the reservation. They discussed the merits of giving Jack and his band a reservation on Lost River, which Jesse seemed to favor at the time. Meacham submitted a report to the commissioner of Indian affairs in Washington D. C. proposing this idea.[392]

The next evening Jesse was already in Yreka, California, to confer with some of the local citizens concerning Captain Jack and a recent incident that was sure to cause Jack problems. Jack had killed an Indian doctor (shaman) on the reservation; the Klamath shaman had been called to treat Jack's children who were ill. The children died and Modoc tradition believed in the concept of an eye for and eye. Therefore, Jack felt he had the moral right to kill the shaman because he had allowed his children to die. The army, by law, was required to arrest Jack for the offense. Most of the locals feared that such a move by the army would start an all-out war, which they wished to avoid. The following statement was issued after a conference with Captain Jack:

> We, the undersigned have had an interview with the Modoc Chief known as Capt. Jack. He wishes us to make known to who it may concern that he will not resist the soldiers, nor in anyway disturb the settlers in the Modoc country.
> July 5th, 1871 (Signed.)
> A. M. Rosborough
> Judge 9th District, State of California
> Jesse Applegate
> Henry F. Miller, (of) Tule Lake.
> John S. Miller of Jacksonville.[393]

At this conference Jack indicated that he would not resist arrest for the killing of the shaman, but his actions did not follow his words. The following letter from Jesse shows some of Jack's reasoning and the results of the resistance.

On July 27, Jesse sent a letter to Meacham from Ashland, Oregon, reporting that he had just completed a tour of the Lost River area and that its inhabitants, both Indian and settler, were in a high state of excitement. Jesse felt duty bound to tell Meacham what he had observed:

Beside the defiant attitude assumed by the rebellious band of Modocs in regard to returning to the reserve, it seems Capt Jack their chief has added another offence by killing an Indian of the reservation. For this it seems some abortive attempts have been made to arrest him by the military.

As Jack seems to have the unanimous support of his people, they have made his cause theirs to the extent of standing unitedly in his defense. They have concealed their non-combatants in some unknown retreat, and the men of the band fully armed, in parties of 10 or 15, rove over the settlements declaring their intention to fight the soldiers should they come to arrest Capt. Jack, and living well upon the charities of the settlers which is much improved by the fear the Indians inspire. As the Indians are very saucy and in some instances menacing, and the widely scattered settlers both themselves and their property at the mercy of marauders a state of terrorism exists among them hard to realize except by those who have been exposed to a like danger. Hence the settlers are greatly exasperated not only against the Indians, but those in authority whose duty they conceive it to be to protect them from such dangers and exactions.

That the settlers had been for two seasons annoyed and their women and children kept in terror by these Indians. That their petition for protection had been wholly disregarded both by the agents and the military, until the Indians have grown confident by impunity had become so impudent and menacing that the state of terrorism in which the settlers lived was no longer endurable and they were going to take their defense into their own hands.

Jesse continues the letter, explaining that he was at the head of Langell's Valley with a wagon and cattle when a band of Indians rode into the camp fully armed and led by Captain Jack's second-in-command, Black Jim. They mistook him for an emigrant and demanded food and ammunition. When they realized who Jesse was, Black Jim demanded to know why the soldiers were in pursuit of Captain Jack since Jack had done them no harm; after all, he had killed an Indian. Jim also demanded to know why they could not live in peace on the home of their fathers.

Jesse tried to explain that the soldiers were after Jack because it was the custom of white men to arrest the person who had killed someone and have a trial to determine if he was guilty. "I also explained to him that you were the high chief over Indian Affairs in this state, and that you were not disposed to punish Capt Jack, or any other Indian unless they were guilty. That I knew you had no enmity towards the Modocs... and knew you to be their friend and disposed to treat them kindly if they were good Indians and behaved themselves peaceably towards the whites."

Jesse then listed Jim's concerns and rationale for why the Indians were off the reservation. First, Jim explained that Captain Jack had killed the Indian doctor in the belief that he had given strychnine to Jack's children, causing their death. Second, the Modocs refused to live on the reservation because, as they saw it, they had been tricked and all the advantages were given to the Klamath, leaving the Modocs nothing to live on. Third, they preferred to live on their old land at Lost River and wanted nothing from the government but peace. Fourth, Jim shared that at present they had no home and no country, and now the whites were pushing aside their wigwams to build houses for themselves. Fifth, the soldiers had chased them to the mountains where there were no roots or fish for their hungry families. Finally, life had no more pleasure for them and they were ready to die: "Here is the dust of my fathers. Better for me to die here than be removed to any other country. If I die here I go down to dust with my father and my people. If I die in some other land I shall be lost forever." Jesse explains his reaction, "Remembering the suggestion you made to me at Salem of giving these people a small reserve on Modoc Lake I mentioned it to him, it seemed to fill him with joy. He said it was all they asked for—a place at the mouth of Lost River for a home—the whites might have the balance of the country in welcome. Their young men and boys by working for the settlers and herding their cattle could earn shirts and blankets."

After giving a detailed report of the Indians' point of view, Jesse explained that most of the whites would not be happy with the Lost River reserve; they wanted the Indians absolutely removed from the country, or at least strictly confined, which could not be done on a small reservation at Lost River. The settlers felt that such a reservation would become the refuge of every vicious and vagabond Indian in the country and soon become a greater nuisance to the settlements than even the present marauding of the Modoc. Jesse ended the letter by saying it was not his desire to make suggestions, but to state the facts. "I shall close by saying that the situation is extremely critical and needs your prompt attention."[394]

Meacham replaced Captain Knapp with his brother, John Meacham, at about the time he received this letter from Jesse. In *Wigwam and Warpath*, Meacham recalls:

> About this time I received a letter from Hon. Jesse Applegate in regard to Modoc matters. His long experience as a frontier man gave his opinion weight. He represented the Modocs with whom he had met, as willing to meet me in council for the purpose of settling the difficulties then existing. He further suggested, that the only sure way for permanent peace was to give them a small Reservation at the mouth of Lost river, the old home of Captain Jack. He, being a practical surveyor, furnished my office with a small map of proposed Reservation.[395]

Because of his confidence in Jesse Applegate's judgment, Meacham forwarded Jesse's letter to General Canby, commander of the Department of the Columbia, asking that military action be delayed until another effort could be made to settle the problems with Captain Jack and his band of Indians.[396] A.B. Meacham then sent a letter to his brother John at the Klamath agency, telling him to proceed at once to the Modoc country and make one more effort for peace:

I am induced to make this request on reading a long and intelligent letter from Hon. Jesse Applegate, who has had a talk with Captain Jack and Black Jim ... You can say to him that, in the event I succeed in getting a home for them on Lost river, they will be allowed their portion of the Klamath and Modoc treaty funds ... I will request General Canby to delay any order now out for the arrest of Jack until you have made this effort to prevent war ... Jesse Applegate is somewhere out in that country. He is a safe adviser. I have no doubt he will assist you in this hazardous undertaking.[397]

Meacham's final statement in this letter shows his compassion for the Indians and desire for a peaceable solution to this problem: "Go on this mission realizing that you carry in your hand the lives and happiness of many persons and the salvation of a tribe of people who have been much wronged, and seldom, if ever, understood." Meacham had hopes of a peaceful solution that would serve the best interest of both the Indians and the white settlers.

Jack let it be known through Jesse Applegate that he would meet with the men from the Klamath Agency if they would come to Clear Lake attended by no more than four men; he would have the same number of braves with him. Ivan Applegate, Lindsay's son, and John Meacham, along with two Indians from the reservation, went out to the rendezvous. "No agreement was made in reference to arms, each party following the dictates of common sense,—by being ready for *peace*, but prepared for *war*."[398] When they arrived, they found Jack surrounded by twenty-nine warriors painted for war. Jack set forth his grievances, mainly the treatment by the Klamath on the reservation, and his view that killing the Indian doctor was not a crime under Indian laws and that therefore he should not be held accountable to laws that were not his. Jack had witnessed whites killing Indians and they had not been arrested, so why should he be arrested for killing an Indian. He said he had tried twice to live with the Klamaths and would not try again. Jack then declared that he had no objection to the white men settling in his country and that he would keep his people away from the settlements and prevent any trouble between the whites and Indians.[399]

Ivan Applegate and John Meacham once again offered Jack and his followers a home on the Klamath Reservation, and Jack once again declined, even when assured of protection. In the end Jack was given permission to remain at Lost River until the superintendent, A.B. Meacham, could be brought down to discuss a small reservation at Lost River. John Meacham agreed to write his brother and tell him that the situation with Jack and the Modoc was under control.[400]

Meacham would later state that hostilities were averted then and could have been for all time if the authorities in Washington had simply granted the request before them for the Lost River reservation, a tract of land a mere six miles square.

Jesse would send one more letter to Meacham arguing in behalf of the Modoc, "I am as you know much in favor of treating the Indians with forbearance and humanity, and as there were some just grounds for the discontent of the band of Modocs, I fully approve of your proposal last summer to place these Indians on a reservation to themselves." [401]

In November of 1871 a new road was built from Yreka into the Modoc country. With the new road, the area was now more attractive to settlers, but before many would come, the Modoc question needed to be resolved. A group of forty-four citizens from the Lost River, Klamath, and Tule Lake Country sent a petition to A.B. Meacham requesting that the army remove Jack and his band from the area. Jesse was not among the petitioners. The statement reads in part:

> We have been repeatedly on the verge of a desolating Indian war with this band of outlaws, who by your delay to enforce the treaty, have been led to despise rather than respect the authority of the Government, their long continued success in defying its authorities has emboldened them in their defiant and hostile bearing until further forbearance on our part would cease to be a virtue; that in many instances our families

have become alarmed at their threats to kill and burn until we were compelled to remove them for safety across the Cascade Mountains, thereby suffering great loss of time and property.[402]

The settlers went on to complain that the Modocs were "demanding rents for the lands occupied by white men; claiming pay for the use of the stock ranches; demanding horses and cattle; visiting the houses of settlers, and, in the absence of the husbands, ordering the wives to prepare meals for them, meanwhile throwing themselves on the beds and carpets, and refusing to pay for the meals when eaten; feeding their horses with the grain of the settlers, and, in some instances *borrowing horses without asking the owners.*"

After receiving this petition, Meacham felt he had no choice but to ask General Canby, commanding general of the Columbia, to remove Captain Jack's band of Modoc to the Klamath reservation. The request was forwarded to General Schofield with the suggestion that before using force with Jack, one more attempt should be made to convince him to return voluntarily to the reservation.

Early in the fall of 1872, T. B. Odeneal replaced Meacham as Superintendent of Indian Affairs for Oregon. He felt that Captain Jack's band must be moved back to the reservation or there would be serious consequences and he stressed that military force would be necessary. Canby reinforced this idea by stating "if the intervention of troops becomes necessary, the force employed should be large, as to secure the result at once and beyond peradventure."[403]

On November 29, Captain James Jackson and thirty-six troopers left Fort Klamath for Jack's camp on Lost River. Ivan Applegate joined the group as guide and interpreter.

Jack's winter camp, consisting of about fifteen families, was located on the south side of a sharp bend in Lost River. There was a second Modoc village of about the same size across the deep river and down stream about one-half mile. Captain Jackson and his soldiers surrounded Captain Jack's camp while a citizen's party arrived on the opposite bank near the camp of Curly-Haired Doc. Captain Jackson, through Ivan Applegate, called to the Indians to surrender and for the leaders to step forward. The Indians, wishing to avoid conflict with the army, agreed to go to the reservation. However, the situation became tense when Captain Jackson demanded that the Indians disarm. Jack was indignant, but lay down his weapon. The other warriors were doing the same when a shouting match started between one of Jack's men and one of the cavalry men; both pulled their revolvers and shot at each other, but missed. The Modoc warriors scrambled to regain their castoff weapons and a short battle ensued. As the Indians fled the camp, Captain Jackson ordered his troops to retreat and wait for reinforcements.

When the first shots rang out at Jack's camp, the Modocs on the opposite side of the river caught up their guns and rushed toward the battle down river, intending to help Captain Jack. The citizen group that had came out from Linkville (Klamath Falls) to watch the removal of the Modocs quickly swung into action and tried to prevent the Indians from going across the river to Jack's aide. The ragtag group of citizens quickly realized that they were at a disadvantage and began to withdraw as quickly as possible, firing into the lodges as they fled. The Modoc returned fire and pursued the whites to a nearby cabin. Meanwhile, the women and children of the village escaped down river. Years later Jeff Riddle claimed that an Indian woman and her baby were killed in the skirmish as the whites fled the village.[404]

Ivan Applegate, along with several others, afraid of what the highly agitated Modocs might do as they rode away from this confrontation, rode across the country like contemporary Paul Reveres warning the settlers to get out or take steps to protect themselves. They were able to warn many, but not all. They arrived at Jesse's place on Clear Lake at about sundown on November thirtieth, exhausted after thirty hours in the saddle. Jesse had known that something was wrong because he had seen many Modoc signal fires burning in the direction of Tule Lake the night before.[405]

A small band of Modoc, under the leadership of Hooker Jim, fanned out across the north and eastern shore of the lake and proceeded to murder fourteen (some records say eighteen) male settlers living in the isolated country over the course of the afternoon of November twenty-ninth and the morning of November thirtieth. The Indians then fled to "The Stronghold" in the lava beds on the south shore of Tule Lake, a vast lava bed honeycombed with caves, making it a mighty natural fortress. Captain Jack had boasted for some months that in the event of war, his band would retreat to the lava beds and be able to hold off any army sent against them. The fate of Captain Jack's little band was sealed now; there was no turning back.

It took some time to marshal an army, but finally the army moved on the stronghold on the foggy morning of January 17, 1873. The troops never saw a single Modoc Indian, but at the end of the day, the U.S. Army had lost thirty-five men and five officers; twenty were wounded. The fifty-three Modoc warriors at the stronghold suffered no casualties in the fight: Captain Jack had chosen well for his little band of Indians.

The Peace Commission

Lindsay Applegate and ex-Superintendent of Indian Affairs, A. B. Meacham, were in Washington D.C. as members of the Electoral College for confirmation of Ulysses S. Grant's second term when the word of the defeat reached Columbus Delano, Secretary of the Interior. Lindsay was the first to suggest the formation of a commission to talk with the Modoc, commenting that "jawboning is cheaper than ammunition."[406] Delano agreed that it was a good idea. Delano named A. B. Meacham head of the commission. Meacham accepted, stating, "I did not believe that doubling the number of widows and orphans would make the griefs of the mourners less or lighter to be borne."[407]

Meacham requested that Jesse Applegate, "a man of long experience on the frontier, well qualified and personally knowledgeable of the current conflict" be named one of the commissioners, along with Samuel Case, an Indian agent at the Alsea reservation situated on the Oregon coast, who had long experience in the management of Indians. General Canby was to act as counselor to the commission.

Jesse was on his way home to Yoncalla when he received a telegram informing him of his appointment to the commission. He returned at once to Linkville, and as always, he took his duties seriously and worked diligently for a peaceful settlement.

On February 15, General Canby met with Jesse Applegate and Case at the Linkville Hotel. A young reporter from the *New York Herald* was present and commented in a report to his paper that Jesse Applegate was one of the oldest settlers and explorers of Oregon and, in pursuit of his profession as surveyor, had traveled over the greatest part of the state and was personally acquainted with the Modoc Indians. The article about Jesse continues:

> He is said to be on good terms with Captain Jack and some of the party, but there are some of the men who do not entertain the most kindly feelings toward him and are reported to have expressed an extreme interest as to the length of his hair, with a view to adorning their wigwam with those revered gray hairs. I have talked with Mr. Applegate on the likelihood of peace, and he evidently appreciates the difficulties that are before him in the attempt to make a treaty with the Modocs that will prove satisfactory to the government and the settlers.[408]

Soon after Applegate and Case arrived at the hotel, the private secretary of Oregon's Governor, LaFayette Grover, presented an official letter outlining several directives to the commission. The commissioners appeared rather "flabbergasted" at the letter, and some remarks were made respecting the governor's sanity.[409] The reporter at the scene explains, "Finally 'Uncle Jesse,' as he is best known in this section of the country, took the bull by the horns, and the objectionable document was laid on the table."[410] Jesse replied to Governor

Grover in an open letter as a private citizen, pointing out that the commission was a federal body and could not receive instruction from any state executive.

Meacham had not yet arrived from Washington, D.C. After one day of meeting in the hotel, the Commission agreed it offered them no privacy from the reporters swarming all over the town, so they moved to Fairchild's ranch across the border in California and set up their headquarters in army tents. This move angered both the reporters and the government of Oregon. Edward Fox, the *Herald* reporter, wrote, "It is the general opinion in the neighborhood that the peace commission will fizzle out, as the right men are not on it." Many of the locals complained because California had no representation on the council: all three members were Oregonians.

The grand jury in Jacksonville, Oregon, had issued an indictment for eight of the Modoc Indians involved in the murders of the white citizens on November 29 and 30. They feared that the commission moving to California was an attempt to negate that indictment. One of the Oregon governor's demands in his letter to the commission was that the eight Indians be placed under the jurisdiction of the state and not be removed to a reservation. The letter also stated that a reservation at Lost River was out of the question; the commission could "no more give away the settled and surveyed land at Lost River than any other settled lands in other portions of the state."[411] By this time, Jesse had changed his mind about the Lost River Reservation and felt that all concerned would be best served if Jack and his band returned to the Klamath reservation, or were removed from the general area.

The full peace commission held its first meeting at Fairchild's ranch on February 19. A messenger went to Captain Jack's camp to arrange a meeting, which he agreed to attend if his California friends Rosborough and Judge Elijah Steele were part of the commission. President Grant appointed Rosborough to the commission and agreed that Steele could be present as a consultant to help negotiate peace.

On February 23, a messenger went back to Jack's camp and returned to the Fairchild's ranch late at night with an Indian who was immediately rushed to the commissioner's tent. The reporters present became curious and attempted to enter the tent, but Meacham closed the meeting to reporters. This action angered the reporters and added fuel to an already growing feud between Oregon and California newspapers. The feud would become personal at the end of February. The Applegate family had played a large role in the settlement of the Klamath Basin, from bringing white settlers to the area via the Applegate Trail, to being themselves among the first settlers in the area. Two of Lindsay's sons, Oliver and Ivan, were Indian agents for the area. The *San Francisco Chronicle* had opposed the Oregon point of view on the war from the beginning, and now their reporter, Robert Bogart, accused the Applegates of cheating the Indians at the agency and having a financial interest in removing the Indians from the country. This story, reported in the San Francisco paper and repeated in other newspapers along the coast, caused a great sensation.[412] Meacham and Case determined that the commission had to resolve this issue before it could go on to other matters. When Jesse learned of this decision, he promptly resigned from the commission, stating that it would be impossible for him to be impartial in the matter.[413] Samuel Case also resigned from the commission, and Rev. Eleazer Thomas and L. S. Dyer replaced the two men. No evidence was ever presented to support the claim that Ivan and Oliver Applegate were in any way involved with cheating the Indians at the agency. Bogart, the *San Francisco Chronicle* reporter, was recalled by the paper and later court marshaled by the U.S. Navy on an embezzling charge.

Jesse submitted a report of his own on March ninth that makes it seem likely that he would have resigned from the commission even if his nephews had not been accused of wrongdoing:

The commission appointed to examine into the causes and bring to a conclusion the Modoc war, having concluded its labors, it was agreed that each member should submit his own views and opinions of the subject as a final report. In pursuance of which agreement I submit the following opinions: 1st. The causes leading to the war were the dissatisfaction of Captain Jack's band of Modocs with the provisions and execution of the treaty of October 14, 1864, and refusal to abide thereby. To what extent wrongs justified resistance, the commission, having no power judicially to investigate, cannot say. 2d. The immediate cause of hostilities was resistance by the Indians to military coercion. 3rd. Unconditional surrender of the Indians, and the trial and punishment of the guilty by the civil authorities, would have been more satisfactory to the whites, and a better example to the Indians, than more lenient conditions. The terms agreed to by the commission were suggested and must be carried into effect by the military. A commission to negotiate a peace was therefore unnecessary. I therefore consider the commission an expensive blunder.[414]

The commission members were to be paid ten dollars per day, plus expenses. Jesse was hard pressed for ready cash at this time; nonetheless, the ever-independent Applegate accepted the responsibilities of the job, but refused the pay. Jesse believed that service to one's fellow man was a duty not to be corrupted by monetary gain. Jesse seems to disappear from the Modoc War story at this point. Family history indicates that he was on his way home to Yoncalla when he received the telegram appointing him to the commission and, now that his role as a commission was over, he did return to Yoncalla.

On the morning of April 11, General Canby, Meacham, Rev. Thomas, and L.S. Dyer, along with Frank and Toby Riddle as interpreters, met with Captain Jack, Black Jim, Hooker Jim, and several other prominent men from the camp. General Canby opened the meeting by passing out cigars. He soon realized the Indians were armed and informed them they could not meet Jack's demands until they received orders from the great white chief in Washington. The mood turned angry and Captain Jack got up, walked away a few steps, and then turned and gave a signal to fire. The first shot killed General Canby, and then Reverend Thomas, Jesse's replacement, fell mortally wounded. Meacham leaped to his feet and frantically searched for his derringer. Running backward as he tried to fire his gun, he tripped over a rock and fell wounded. The Indians were upon him, stripping him of his clothes and attempting to scalp him when Toby Riddle cried out, "The soldiers are coming." This was not true, but the Indians turned and ran; Meacham's life was saved.

While Jesse tended his Yoncalla farm, the Modoc War raged on, ending with Captain Jack's capture at Willow Creek on June 1, 1873. He was taken under guard to the army camp at Applegate's ranch, where the rest of the prisoners were housed. Jack and his band of sixty or less warriors had held a far numerically superior army at bay for seven long months.

Captain Jack and his little band of prisoners were sent to Fort Klamath for trial and found guilty on July 8. On October 3, 1873, Captain Jack, John Schonchin, Black Jim, and Boston Charley were hanged at Fort Klamath. The remainder of the Modoc tribe was sent to a reservation in Indian Territory (Oklahoma.) The Modoc War was the last major Indian war in America and the only one in which a general of the United States Army was killed.

Declining Years of an Old Patriot

In 1871, when Jesse realized that he might be held accountable for May's debt, he sold his swampland to Jesse D. Carr. He then deposited $1,800 with the secretary of state, Chadwick, as an assurance that he was willing to pay his portion of the bond. Long after Jesse had sold his land to Carr it appeared on maps as the "Applegate ranch." This may have been by design on Carr's part as he amassed a very large tract of land for his grand "rancho" over the following years; the original "Applegate ranch" would be a key part of his eventual empire.

No known documentation shows how and when Jesse Applegate and Jesse Carr met, but their lives would become very much intertwined in the Clear Lake area. It is most likely that they met when Jesse Carr ran a stage between California and Portland. The stage line often stopped at Jesse's Yoncalla home for a meal or to spend the night, and it seems reasonable that the two Jesses would become acquainted. They shared many of the same interests: both were interested and involved in politics, both were interested in cattle ranching, and they had mutual friends in California, including Peter Burnett.

Years later, the *San Francisco Chronicle* would run an article stating that Jesse Applegate surveyed the land at Clear Lake for Jesse D. Carr.[415] Public record indicates that Jesse Applegate was hired to survey some land for Jesse Carr sometime in the early summer of 1872. The contract reads:

> For the exterior boundary lines of Township 46,47 and 48 North of Ranges 3, 4, 5, 6, 7, and 8 east of Mount Diablo Meridian subdivision and bounds on Rhett or Tule Lake and Wright or Clear Lake.
> [Signed] Jesse Applegate
> Contract not to exceed $2,500 to $3,000. [Signed] J.D. Carr Monterey Co.[416]

It seemed that no matter what Jesse did to recoup his loses in his old age, failure seemed his lot in life. Jesse had hoped that his investment in sheep would repay him enough to get him back on his feet, but this was a sore disappointment. A newspaper article in the Sacramento Daily Union on March 18, 1874 starts with the headline: "Destruction of Stock in Siskiyou County—Jesse Applegate Freezes His Feet and Loses 1,800 Head of Stock."

> The loss of cattle and sheep has been fearful, and probably One-half of the stock in the county is dead. A letter from Linkville dated on the 8th, says the snow is 2½ to 3½ feet deep all over the County, and still storming. Cattle were dying fast, and the sheep were nearly all dead and some horses. Jesse Applegate lost 150 head of cattle in one day. After freezing his feet badly, he was obliged to abandon his herd to their fate, having lost 1,800 head [sheep].

This storm was the final blow to Jesse's attempt to regain his fortune; from this time on he struggled merely to keep food on the table and a roof over his head. He depended on a few surveying contracts and work as a hired hand for Jesse D. Carr. He writes to his friend Deady, "But while I live I cannot escape the duties imposed by life. I have frequently prayed to die in harness and it seems my prayer is likely to be granted when no longer desired—if this Contract has the promise of money in *it I must undertake it*. If no one will take my place in the management of Mr. Carr's Modoc property *I must continue to do that*. Out of this contract money may come to pay my debt."[417]

Sometime in 1872 Jesse made a trip to San Francisco on business. While there he went to the Pacific Bank to see his old friend Peter Burnett. Mr. Burnett describes that meeting:

> I left him (Applegate) in Oregon in 1848. He was a rich man, for that time and that country. I did not see him again until 1872, a period of nearly twenty-four years. In the mean time he had become a gray-headed old man. He and myself are near the same age, he being about two years younger. One day, without my knowing that he was in California, he walked into the Pacific Bank in San Francisco. I knew, from the serious expression of his face, that he was an old friend; but, for the moment, I could not place him or call his name. He was so much affected that his eyes filled with tears, and he could not speak. I shook his hand cordially, invited him to sit down, and sat down by him, looking him full in the face one moment, when it came into my mind that he was my old friend, and I exclaimed, "Applegate!" And we embraced like brothers.[418]

In the summer of 1875, having lost their homestead to the state, Jesse and Cynthia moved to a little cabin about one thousand feet up the eastern side of Mt. Yoncalla. This was the property first given to Cynthia by her sons Robert and Daniel and later deeded to Cynthia by Governor Thayer. Jesse had resisted the offer from his sons at first, but in the end accepted in part because the property was remote from the world of which he had grown weary. He describes his life in the little mountain abode to Deady: "I think we can make a living, and if we fail the children say we shall not suffer for food and clothing. So you see the great struggle for a living which has occupied us for well nigh fifty years of wedded life is at length ended happily. Most happily... for now after a day's work I am free! Both in mind and body until the dawning of another day. Thank God for even this much release from the cares of the world."[419]

In his diary, Judge Deady records a visit to "the Sage" in Yoncalla:

> It had rained and the mountain was slippery. After a good mile of walk up the mountain to the west and south I found him camped under a shed with his wife and engaged in building a new house and I suppose his final home on earth and above ground. The spot is lovely and picturesque one, at the head of a cove filled with a beautiful and untouched grove of black oak. We spent the night until 12 in pleasant converse, and then retired but as our beds were within an arms length of each other the conversation was continued long after until I fell asleep.
>
> Was up at 6 in the morning, ate breakfast and down the mountain to Snowdens by 7. Jesse accompanied me and we parted warmly—it may be, but I hope not forever.[420]

Jesse and Cynthia built their little three-room cabin there on the mountain. Their nephew, George Applegate, who was living in the mountains east of Sacramento, California, brought them 1200 grape vines and helped them plant the first vineyard in Douglas County. They also planted a small garden and fenced the little plot of ground. Life was simpler now; gone was the grand house by the roadside that had attracted so many visitors. Cynthia had never really wanted all the hubbub of the grand lifestyle; she was perfectly happy with her little home on the mountainside where only her children, grandchildren, and a few dear friends bothered to make the trek up the mountainside to her door. Jesse once again had time of an evening to read to her and discuss the day's events as he had in the early days of their married life. She now had time to sit on the porch in the evening, look out over the valley, and listen to the night birds calling. She could look down on the peaceful, little graveyard where her dear girls slept and watch the tall firs sway in the breeze as they stood guard over that sacred ground.

Jesse and Cynthia's mountain cabin

Jesse describes the cozy scene to Deady in a letter written on Christmas Eve 1877: "We have got into a comfortable little cabin. My wife keeps it clean and tidy. I have some of my favorite authors (mostly science and history.) Get the Oregonian, S.F. Bulletin weekly, and the children send us Harpers Monthly and Weekly. I am bent on making my vineyard a success, and work all the time in it, except what is taken up by getting firewood and doing chores."

Some of Jesse's old friends worried that the isolation on the mountain was not good for him and might drive him deeper into the melancholy that they saw increasing in him. For example, in December of 1874, the Oregon Pioneer Association had invited Jesse to give the annual address to the group in June. Jesse declined, stating:

> I will not be present. Did my circumstances permit, it would afford me great pleasure to meet old friends and neighbors on that happy occasion...It would be a great enjoyment to meet them and present them with an address. There are many pleasant and flattering things I could truthfully say to them, and some scraps of history in which some of the early settlers of Oregon deserve honorable mention yet untold, which I should like to see go on the record...[the settlers were] precisely adapted mentally and physically to perform the part assigned us in the march of civilization...But like the scythe, the sickle, and shovel plow, the best of tools among the roots and stumps of a new land, we will be thrown aside and forgotten now our work is done.[421]

The next year the offer was made again, and again Jesse declined. S. F. Chadwick wrote to Deady urging him to convince Jesse to accept the invitation. "It will do him good to come out of his house and circulate among his old associates...We must get him out and cheer him up."[422]

Jesse was not in the mood for these gatherings, not only because he regarded the Pioneer Association "as a kind of mutual admiration society which assembled annually to praise and be praised by each other," but also because money had become a problem again. Insects destroyed the first crop of grapes that he had so counted on to help him recover some of his losses. Now he was nearly desperate, yet he refused to ask his children for help, even though they would have willingly given what they could. The state of Oregon had owed him $342 since 1873 for a surveying job, and Jesse wrote a terse letter to his old friend Deady asking him for help in collecting the debt. He wondered if the money owed him had been forgotten in the interest of economy: "I am much in favor of economy and for the sake of so good a thing my old woman and myself may well afford to live a little harder, and dispense with the luxury of warm clothing next winter."

The money was not forthcoming, and thus Jesse and Cynthia were forced to abandon their little house on the mountain and return to Clear Lake and the employment of Jesse D. Carr during the winter and spring of 1876–77. Jesse and Cynthia both worked for Carr: Jesse surveying, building fences, keeping books, and herding sheep; Cynthia was cooking for a crew of fourteen ranch hands. In the spring of 1877, the work became too much for Cynthia and her health began to fail. Just as it seemed they would have to terminate their work for Carr and return home empty-handed, the state finally paid Jesse $471 for a surveying contract of 1874. Jesse reports to Deady: "So I can now return to Yoncalla with a few hundred dollars needed to supply the simple wants of my good and ever faithful wife and myself and be in the midst of our numerous and loving family without feeling ourselves a burden upon them."[423]

Jesse did finally attend the Oregon Pioneer Association meeting in 1876 and he delivered his famous "A Day with the Cow Column in 1843" paper. Jesse met Mr. Bancroft at this time and was interviewed by Bancroft. Bancroft states in the interview that Jesse agreed to the interview in part to clear the record concerning Dr. Whitman's part in securing Oregon to the United States. It was also at this time that Jesse agreed to write out his comments on F.F Victor's *River of the West* and other related topics concerning Oregon's early history.[424]

At the1878 meeting of the Oregon Pioneer Association, Jesse Q. Thornton offered an "apology" for his tirade against Jesse Applegate and the Southern Route thirty-two years before:

We cannot explore the recesses of Jesse Applegate's mind for the purpose of discovering the hidden forces which in the end wrought such disastrous results, yet, even the thirty-two [years] of subsequent opportunity for bringing clearly into view a motive, if such had an existence, that could have influenced him to make a willfully false statement respecting the road, has failed to discover anything that would have been likely to induce him thus rashly to forfeit character, formed upon the model of a man of high sense of honor, but smarting under a present sense of loss, the emigrants, in the fever and delirium of excitement, denounced him in terms which indicated the gangrene of a resentment that was in a high degree unfavorable to a cool judgment upon acts which they saw indeed, but respecting the motive, for which they could only form an opinion. Nor was your speaker less affected [in] this infirmity than his fellows. But having since traveled very far toward the sunset of life, and standing now in the rapidly lengthening shadows of old age to which brings with it an ever increasing sense of life's responsibilities and of the great duty to charity to all, I look backward through the vista of thirty-two years, and see how possible it was for Jesse Applegate to have been led into erroneous estimates of distance of the general character of the road by the overwhelming influence of strong desires that clouded his judgment, and thus disqualified him for correctly describing the route he persuaded us to follow.[425]

According to family tradition, Jesse Applegate's response to Thornton's questionable apology was, "When he makes his apology as public as his condemnation was, I will accept his request for absolution."

Jesse the Historian

Sadly, Jesse was mistaken in believing he could now settle into a quiet, uneventful life on the mountain. Dowell filed his suit against Jesse and his children in 1878, and that long, wearing battle would consume the rest of Jesse's life. However, Jesse also began his pleasant distraction of writing some notes about Oregon's early history for Hubert

H. Bancroft's forthcoming history of Oregon. Jesse maintained that he agreed reluctantly, but the correspondence went on for over a year. Jesse shared his thoughts on many of the figures in early Oregon history as well as his philosophy on life, religion, and death.[426] Jesse seems perplexed with Bancroft's use of the information, however:

> Mrs. Victor [who worked for Bancroft] stopped at my house for about three weeks, and in answer to some thousands of questions I gave her all the information I possessed in regard to the early history of the country. As you wish for information upon the subject Mrs. V. examined me so exhaustively and I find so little of what I gave her in her finished work. You too may find my statements unsuited to your purpose or in discord with those of others. This view of the case does not encourage me, in again passing in review the incidents of half a century many of them painful to memory and to bestow upon them the time and labor necessary to make the narrative understood.[427]

Frances Fuller Victor, a very bright, independent young woman, worked as a researcher and writer for Hubert Bancroft's San Francisco publishing house. She wrote to Jesse, the "Sage of Yoncalla," looking for information on early Oregon history, and he replied that if she wanted information, she "must come to me for it." He was very surprised when she did just that, arriving one day on the stage in the fall of 1865. He was even more surprised that she stayed for an extended period. Jesse seems to have been smitten with this very bright young lady and took great pleasure in conversing with her about Oregon's early history. He later writes his friend Elwood Evans that he "generally succeeded in escaping from male authors and think I could fight them off," but confesses that he is "no match for the ladies of the pen … Mrs. Victor pumped me so dry of historical matter that the stores of both of memory and imagination were utterly exhausted … there was nothing I could conceal or withhold from the keen scrutiny of this lady."[428] Years later, Mrs. Victor writes in a newspaper article in the Salem *Daily Oregon Statesman* that when she left Jesse's home at the end of the three weeks Jesse stated, "I should be proud if I could call you my daughter."

Jesse argued that history is of value to the student only when that history illustrates ideas that have influenced the progress of mankind, adding that in that sense, Oregon had no history, for it had added no new fact to human knowledge, had no statesman, warrior, or scholar in any branch of human knowledge that deserved to live in the memory of mankind. He went on to assert that those who wrote the word history upon a title page assumed a "grave responsibility." [429]Jesse further critiques Gray's *History of Oregon*: "I read a part of it as it came out in the Astoria newspaper. It is like the man a mere bundle of insane, and baseless prejudices—it is a loss of time to read such stuff."

Jesse does comment on a portion of Mrs. Victor's, *River of the West* that deals with some adventures in the Rocky Mountains. He disagrees with her account, but adds: "I have forborne to criticize this part of her book because she relates these adventures as they were related to her by *Meek*—They do not rise to the dignity of history and as mere romance it does not matter whether they are true or not."[430]

He goes on to promise that at some future date he will relate some stories from the time of the mountain men, stories he had heard while in St. Louis keeping books for the fur trappers, stories that illustrate "how training, simply training, in a life constantly surrounded by danger and death, will so strengthen the nerve, and the will to meet and resist them, as to amount to heroism of the highest order recorded in the annals of the past. This, too, of our own people, and of our own day and generation, but of a part of it now rapidly passing away leaving no successors."

In one of his letters to Bancroft, Jesse apologizes for being remiss in his correspondence: "I have to support myself by common labor, and as I have to make up by diligence what I lack of activity and strength I have the night only for rest and relaxation. These I must have or be unfitted for labors of the day. My hand swollen, stiff, and sore from handling the rough tools of husbandry abhors the pen, my mind is dull and torpid from excess of fatigue—and my eyes have so failed me that I can scarce read common print by the strongest artificial light." Later in this same letter, he states that he has "more interest in the hereafter than in the past and that we must seek for data for the solution of the all absorbing problem of the design and destiny of the human race." Jesse proceeds to share his views on the origin of the human race, written at about the time when Darwin's theory of evolution was gaining popularity in the common literature of the day. Darwin's basic theory introduced the concept that all related organisms are descended from common ancestors and based on the concept of natural selection of the fittest. Jesse, however, rejects this notion:

> Now so certain have we become that every germ (of no matter what) produces its king—and that each stage of the existence of every entity, as certainly and invariable proceeds and follows other stages as the climate laws of the Eternal are as himself unchangeable, that we should accept the fact of procreation as we do the laws of mathematics and others of the laws of the Creator our human intellects are capable of comprehending. It is true climate and culture will affect animal and vegetable life—but the changes are limited to variety, never extending to species. To individuals not to race and when the artificial stimulus ceases the change comes and origin asserts its original rule.
>
> I do not believe any law of the Creator ever has been or ever will be changed or suspended. The creative no more that any other—no plant or animal now exists that ever has been or ever will be some other plant or animal by any process natural or artificial…
>
> While man physically is only a man subject to all the wants appetites and vicissitudes of animal life, he also possesses a mental gift which makes him capable of progress and investigation which lifts him infinitely above all other earthly creatures. This etherian spark he never could have derived from the loins of a

Monkey or other inferior beast—not itself possessing it—and as God has not given to any creature a faculty or committed a quality necessary to the performance of its functions—men must have a higher destiny and consequently higher duties to perform that other animals—among these are duties to a moral law of which no other animal has any conception.[431]

In a Christmas Eve letter to Deady, Jesse gives us a little more insight into his views of the creator:

> Though today has been to me one of effort, as every day is, yet while I plied the shovel and mattock the brain has been busy with thoughts suggested by the anniversary of the birth of God, the God of my forefathers, whose temples cover the enlightened and civilized portions of the earth, and before it bow in solemn worship the purest and best of humanity. I believe in Christ as the greatest among moral teachers and reformers. I believe to him or her who keeps his law the present life will be happier, nor need they dread the future. But further than this, my faith does not see clearly. I have fallen into doubt with no desire to do so. In fact, I have resisted its growth by avoiding all controversial, atheistically, or deistical writings, and, what is far worse to me, ignorant preaching.[432]

During this same time, Jesse carried on an interesting correspondence with a young lady he had first met when she was a three-year-old traveling with her family on the Oregon Trail. Jesse had carried this girl, now Bethenia Owens-Adair, on his shoulders as he walked along the trail in conversation with her father. Here he describes his situation in California to her: "Your letter was brought to me at my sheep ranch, more than fifty miles from any post office. I read it sitting upon a stone, with the broad expanse of solitude spread around me, while I watched and herded another man's sheep for a living."[433]

Bethenia had remained in contact with Jesse over the years, and he became an important influence on her as he encouraged her decision to study medicine. At the time, of course, such endeavors were considered very "un-ladylike," but Jesse repeatedly told her God had given her a bright and inquisitive mind that she should not waste. Over the years that she struggled to fulfill her ambition, Jesse encouraged her in numerous letters. Late in her life, after she became a doctor, she wrote a book about her life experiences and shares many of Jesse's letters written to her while she struggled to obtain her medical education. She included the letters in her memoirs because, "they show the depth of his pure and sensitive nature, and I believe Oregon is entitled to all that enhances the greatness and goodness of this, one of her noblest sons, who served her for so long, so faithfully and well."[434]

A letter written by Jesse to Bethenia in 1876 from Clear Lake sheds light on their relationship:

> My Friend—When you told me the pecuniary success you had gained and the social standing you had reached by making yourself a physician, and I suggested to you that a further success was in your reach by making yourself eminent in the scientific department of your profession, you asked me the question, "Do you really believe me capable of reaching so high an eminence?" Upon an examination of this question it presents two aspects. Neither of them are very flattering to me. First, it expressed a doubt of my judgment, and I think I at least have a right to ask upon which ground I am to place the meaning of your question. Is there anything in our past intercourse that implies a want of sincerity on my part, I am not aware of it. True, I have said things of you and to you that were flattering and intended to be so, but they were uttered in the utmost sincerity, and intended to encourage you in pursuits calculated to elevate, strengthen, and refine you intellectually. I have had no personal end to gain by flattering your vanity, or misleading or deceiving you on any point. And you know this as well as I do, I must conclude that you think my judgment, which you have flattered me by placing a high

value on, is now failing me. Is this so? And if so, have I not earned, if in no other way, by always treating you with candor, candor in return?

... Are you going to stop in the midst of your career? Are all these sacrifices to be made, and you fall short of the goal of your ambition?

Most solemnly and earnestly do I protest against such a termination.[435]

In a letter written to Jesse from Ann Arbor, Michigan, in 1879 Bethenia writes, "Your letters always encourage me. They are filled with beautiful thoughts and sentiment, which I treasure with care by copying in a blank book... Some day they will be utilized. They must not decay."

In August of 1883 Jesse shares similar sentiments about her letters to him:

My very Dear Friend—Your kind and flattering letter, addressed to me at this place, has been received, and probably your most skillfully prepared prescription never soothed the suffering of an afflicted body more than your kind and affectionate words have cheered and comforted my somewhat drooping spirit, I have so often been the victim of misplaced confidence,—so often by misfortune, had reason to doubt the soundness of my own judgment,—my sincerity doubted, and my motives misjudged by others, that you can scarce conceive how proud I am of your good opinion and kind recollection. But my dear friend, you gravely over-rate the little I have been able to do for you. It is true, I gave you my best judgment, and my warmest sympathy, unbiased by a single selfish motive; but it is to your own strong mind, and indomitable energy that you owe your success in life; and to your merit, not to luck or accident, is due the favors that fortune is showering upon you. Be true to yourself, and firm in your pursuit of a high purpose in life, and neither man nor devils can prevent you from reaching the goal of your ambition.

I will rejoice with you in all you succeed, sympathize with you, and console you in your sorrows and misfortunes, and counsel with you in your troubles and perplexities. All this will I do, because my heart is with you. As ever yours,

Jesse Applegate[436]

Losses

As Jesse was giving encouragement to others, his own life continued its downward spiral and one of the hardest blows for him came in August of 1879: the death of his beloved older brother Charles, for whom Jesse felt a deep attachment. They were alike in many aspects of their character and belief systems, yet they often disagreed and even argued over small matters. Nonetheless, each was always the first to come to the defense of the other. Sallie Applegate Long shares in her family history that the Applegate children were "taught respect and affection for 'Uncle Charles' and never heard either parent speak an unkind word of him." In a letter written shortly after Charles's death, Jesse tells his remaining brother Lindsay that in boyhood, Charles had always been his protector and, next to his mother, his dearest friend.

> In proof that he had not failed any of the great duties of his life it may be said that to his country he was always true and loyal; to his fellow-citizens honorable, just, and generous; to his family, kind, liberal, considerate, these virtues have not been unfruitful.
>
> I am proud of him in death, and may I stand in the presence of the awful judge before whom he has been called, sustained by good acts and many, and qualities as great, balanced against faults and follies no greater.
>
> My dear brother, of our numerous family, the daughters have long since passed away; of the six brothers, one lies in Louisiana, one in Illinois, one in Missouri, one in Oregon. They have gone across the dark river in the order of their

birth. You and I alone remain—old men tottering to the brink. Without troubling ourselves about opinions and beliefs about which certainly is unattainable, we have tried to practice those duties towards God and our fellow man which internal and external evidence prove to be right. Belief is not a matter of will but of evidence, but our acts are under our own control and by them we must abide in the future as in the past.[437]

Lindsay would be the last surviving Applegate brother, dying in 1892, four years after his younger brother Jesse's death. He is buried in Ashland, Oregon.

Applegate and Deady: A Difficult Relationship

Another important figure in Jesse's twilight years was Judge Deady, even though several historians have suggested that their long-standing friendship ended after Deady ruled in the state's favor in the May case in 1874. The following letter of August 8, 1880, sheds some light on the matter:

> When before a "court of competent jurisdiction" I had been charged with both *fraud* and *forgery* by the testimony of a competent witness and pure men like yourself stood aloof of me as a person infected. I placed myself in a kind of quarantine until proved guilty or purged of these horrid suspicions and being still in quarantine I would not now write this letter if you had not again resumed your practice of sending me packages with your initials marked on the outside, showing you were not ashamed to be known as my correspondent. I have been a long time in voluntary exile—have received but few letters and answered none. I have neither received or paid visits except with my children. I have been but once to a public place (Drain) and then only to vote the Republican ticket... Being in the flesh I have periods of discontent, but they do not come very often, nor hurt me much when they do come...

I am very poor but have not yet eaten the bread of dependence. I hope my ability to labor may last as long as my necessity to eat. My thanks are due to you for the many real services, kindnesses, and attentions which have marked the years of our long acquaintance.[438]

However, relations between Jesse and Judge Deady were not yet settled. In 1883 Deady sat in on the court decision of Justice Sawyer of the United States District Court ruling that Jesse's deeds to his children were null and void since the land was encumbered by debts before the deeds were made. Furious that Deady had not recused himself from the case, Jesse gives Deady a piece of his mind in a letter of April 24, 1883:

You may feel slightly uneasy about your detection in this matter by one helpless old man whose death you have made the last atonement he can make to his injured family. But if your crime was known to the world, and the world in self-defense took away your power to harm, and put a mark upon you so you could harm no more, I think you would find the scourge of repentance a pretty lively punishment. I think it is the only kind of repentance a man who lives a lie is capable of feeling.[439]

Deady's journal entry of May 5 records his reaction to Jesse's letter:

Had a very mean letter from J[esse] A[pplegate] this week about his case, of date April 24. I don't think I shall ever recognize him again. He scolds like a drab and lies like a Cretan.[440]

Jesse's attorney demanded that Jesse apologize for this attack on Deady, but Jesse, the ever-uncouth independent, refused. A year later, still bitter, he suggested to his old friend Nesmith that it would be a "great public work" to remove Deady from his throne and expose his corrupt and partial decisions as well as his duplicity and treachery in his pretended friendships.[441] The ties between the two old friends were damaged to the extent that Deady did not even mention Jesse's death in his daily diary in April of 1888.

One Final Loss

Jesse and Cynthia were content enough in their little mountain home, puttering about with the daily chores and hoping to clear a profit from the vineyard that would enable them to pay off all remaining debts. They shared the cabin only with a cat; Jesse had never cared for dogs and did not allow one on the property. When the weather was nice, he worked outside in the vineyard and garden. When the rains forced him inside, he busied himself with his "scientific study" and reading the few magazines and books friends sent to him. Life was not what he had envisioned for himself, but he and his wife of fifty years had established a peaceful rhythm for these final days of their lives. The children and grandchildren made their way up the mountain for visits and an occasional old friend journeyed up to spend a peaceful afternoon talking over old times.

On June 1, 1881, Jesse received the biggest blow yet—his dear wife of fifty years, Cynthia Ann Applegate, died at the age of just sixty-seven. Her health had never completely recovered from setbacks that had caused them to come home from Clear Lake. From a stone found on the property, Jesse and his son Peter cut a simple headstone to mark the grave. Cynthia was carried down to the little cemetery to join her dear girls in her final resting place. The stone was placed facing north and south, although it is customary for graves to face to the east. Cynthia was laid to the north; seven years later, Jesse would be laid to rest facing south.

Jesse writes on June 3, 1881 about the loss of his wife:

> I have been stunned and stupefied by this last blow providence had dealt me, for it was wholly unexpected. We did not expect to be so long separated, but we had made up our minds

that I was the first to be summoned. Fifty years ago we joined our earthly destinies together. In the true sense of the word, in all these years she has been my helpmate. She has been the chief comfort of my life, the sharer of my toils, and my consoler in adversity. She had strong, good sense, a loving heart and a deep devotion to the right. She was a safe counselor, for her untaught instincts were truer and safer rules of conduct than my better informed judgment. Had I oftener followed her advice her pilgrimage on earth might have been longer and happier. At least, her strong desire to make all happy around her would not have been cramped by extreme penury. I have not been as good a husband as she has been wife. In the day of prosperity I did not realize at its proper value the priceless treasure, devoted and true. It requires adversity to prove the true gold.[442]

Two days later, in a letter to Mrs. Caroline Haynes, granddaughter to General Joseph Lane, he describes his situation now that he is widowed:

The day after I laid my poor, old wife with her children who had gone before her to the dread unknown I spent the day alone in our desolate little home … The stun of the blow has passed and while the anguish of it still remains and will remain till death, I am now in better condition to think of myself and others. The law of the land gives me the possession of our home while I live. But I cannot remain upon it alone. To do so would be forcing both feelings and bodily strength beyond their powers of endurance, and this morning I gave my decision to Dan, that the place should be sold.

If the place is not sold, at whatever privation I must remain upon it until enough of its present crop is realized to pay some debts. When this is done I will be free of all earthly obligations save those of love and gratitude …

It was a fixed conclusion of both my wife and myself that we could not survive another winter. She is already gone, which seems to hasten the time of my own summons.[443]

Within days of the funeral, Jesse had left the little mountain home and gone to live with his son Henry in the Clear Lake area. From Henry's home in March of 1883, he writes to his daughter Sallie: "No matter how busy I am with other matters during the day—in sleep I am with the dead, with your mother, most of the time. Last night Charley came to me. I spoke to him, but he did not answer, and when I tried to touch him, he disappeared. I do not believe the dead and living can communicate with each other."

Jesse stayed with Henry until July of 1883, when he writes: "I do not believe I shall survive another winter, and I have the human weakness to desire my body to be laid by the side of your mother. But it does not matter where the body perishes if the spirits live and know those that have been congenial to them on earth—they will meet again."

In another letter from Clear Lake, he writes, "no one should grieve for the ending of a life that has exceeded its usefulness and its happiness." Shortly thereafter, he came back to Yoncalla and the home of his daughter Sallie. Over the next five years, he wandered from one child's home to the next, even going up to the little cabin on Mt. Yoncalla to live alone for short periods.

In an article about her father, Sallie describes the joy and pain that were part of Jesse's life at that time:

While there [at Henry's] a little boy was born into the family that he named for a dear friend, Walter Thayer. He constituted himself little Walter's nurse and became very fond of the babe which was also attached to him. When he left there, it grieved him very much to part with this little child. He then made his home with me for two years after this. During this time my younger sister also lived with us with her children... She had a little girl that was just beginning to walk and talk. My father rather avoided the children and they were not allowed to annoy him, but one day I saw this baby trying to climb onto his foot as he sat with one knee laid over the other. He drew his foot away and looked sharply at her over his specks. "No, you little midget," he said, "you shall not steal your way into my heart to tear it again when sometime I shall have to part from you." The baby put on a grieved look and presently he took her up into his arms. From that time, they were great friends and she was, I think, much comfort to him. But the last tears my Father shed were over the grave of this little child. She died of Diphtheria on March 16, 1888-he died on the 22nd of April-five weeks later.[444]

Jesse's Darkest Days

Jesse drifted between the homes of his children and became more and more melancholy until finally in July of 1886 his son Robert and J.L. Drain took him before a judge in Douglas County to have him declared "unsafe to be at large." The complaint alleged that Jesse "talked irrationally on all subjects and becomes violent when opposed, striking his best friend and relatives, combative when contradicted on questions of history."[445]

The Rouge River Courier of September 17, 1886, carried an article describing Jesse Applegate on his darkest day:

> A few days ago, the southern train from Roseburg brought to Salem a stout and pleasant faced man, accompanied by a tall, wiry built man of nearly eighty years. [He was seventy-five.] The former had a pleasant smile and kindly voice, while the querulous speech and listless stare of the old man, told that his ability to reason had become dethroned, and that this big and good-natured looking fellow was his keeper on the way from southern Oregon to the state infirmary for the insane. The deputy sheriff was Clay Slocum of Roseburg, while the poor, demented old wreck at his side, was one of the grandest men of Oregon, Jesse Applegate, and "The Sage of Yoncalla" as he was called in the years that have flown by. The brave

old man whose name is part and parcel of the history of the "Times that tried men's souls" is [now] among those who are in the condition of the "living dead."

Jesse's heart would certainly have been broken had he understood that those who had signed papers for his commitment said he was, "insane and unsafe to be at large." The commitment papers state that this is Jesse's first attack of dementia and describe him as a man six feet tall, weighing 160 pounds, gray-blue eyes with sandy-gray hair. The doctor then states the cause of the insanity: "Old age, physical debilities, but chiefly worry over financial reverses."[446] His great-niece, Lillian Gertrude Applegate, would have disagreed with this statement. She writes, "It has been said that sickness before his death was caused by loss of his property. This is a mistake. He did worry, but it was over disappointment in those whom he trusted. Uncle Jesse was a born friend, and he could never understand betrayal."

Jesse stayed at the state hospital for about twelve months. He discovered one of his old friends and fellow pioneer of 1843 was also an inmate and the two spent many an hour talking about times past. Jesse was treated with great kindness during his stay at the hospital. He was deeply grateful for this kindness and after his release spoke with respect and affection of those who befriended him during this extremely trying time. One of the men who befriended him was Dr. Harry Lane.[447] In fact, Jesse's last letter was written to Dr. Lane on April 15, 1888. "I may now say I am as well off as a man in his 77th year has any reason to expect...As to my mental condition I cannot myself be the judge. I only *know* that my senses act slowly and imperfectly, as a result of which the records made upon the memory partake of their imperfections, and it may be *I only think* when I rightly receive an impression that my mind acts rightly and sanely upon it."[448]

Jesse spent the last winter and spring of his life shuttling between the homes of his sons Robert and Alexander. April 22, 1888, was a beautiful, sunny day. Jesse loved the sun and spent most of the day outside working in his favorite daughter-in-law's garden and enjoying the sun. Jesse had been called a "sun worshipper" because he loved working outside in the sunshine. In days past he had often been seen saluting the sun, particularly after it came out from behind the clouds, "Ah, there is the blessed sun."

At the end of that beautiful spring Sunday, the family sat up until 9 p.m. visiting, laughing, and talking about old times. Soon after retiring, Alexander, hearing his father breathing heavily, hastened to his bedside and found him suffering with severe pains in the stomach to which he had been subject for years. This pain lasted only a few minutes before Jesse died without a sigh or struggle.[449]

Jesse had given very clear instructions to Alexander in regards to his funeral. He wished for things to be very plain and simple: no display of ornamentation about his dress or "the box." He also made it very clear he did not want an expensive foreign headstone. When his wife died, he had helped his son quarry a plain, smooth slab of sandstone from the property and had given instructions that his name should be on one side and on the other side the name of his dear wife. "Nothing else, if anyone wants to know more, let him consult the records."[450]

Jesse's headstone

At one in the afternoon on April 24, 1888, the family carried Jesse to his final resting place on the little hill nestled at the foot of Mt. Yoncalla, placing him at the head of his dear wife, facing to the south. Finally, the grand old man could rest in peace beneath his beloved cloud-capped mountain and leave the struggles of this world to those left behind.

Applegate Cemetery-looking back across Jesse's beloved valley.

On the same day, *The Oregonian* carried the following obituary: "Death has removed another noted citizen of Oregon. Jesse Applegate bore a leading part in the settlement and making of Oregon; his individuality was a positive force; his generosity was proverbial, and his energy though given often to eccentric courses, was as marked as his generosity and other virtues. As an original character, he stood conspicuous, during forty years, in the life of Oregon, and he has an assured place in the history of those who came here as pioneers and laid the foundation of the state."[451]

Bush, noted newspaper editor, shared the following words in Jesse's obituary:

> In all that constituted useful and honorable citizenship Jesse Applegate was for forty years one of the foremost men of the territory and state. His culture and intelligence were of high

order and out of the usual run. His honor and truth no man questioned and his life was without stain. His service in the settlement of the Oregon territory was not exceeded by any other of the actors upon the stage.[452]

The obituary also carried excerpts of Colonel Nesmith's address on Applegate to the Oregon Pioneers Association of 1875:

> The services and reputation of Jesse Applegate are the common property of the Oregon Pioneers...This was the noblest Roman of them all. His life was gentle and the elements so mixed in him that Nature might stand up and say to all the world, this was a man.
>
> As a frontiersman in courage, sagacity, and natural intelligence, he is the equal of Daniel Boone. In culture and experience, he is [the] superior of half the living statesmen in the land.

General E. L. Applegate, a nephew to Jesse, wrote an obituary sketch of his Uncle Jesse, declaring that he was grateful for the opportunity to pay tribute and respect to the wisdom, the worth, and the influence of the "Sage of Yoncalla."

> He was a member of the constitutional convention. He was opposed to the extension of slavery. He was in favor of internal improvements and the protection of American industry by the general government; and upon the outbreak of the rebellion he was loyal to the very core. But in the zenith of his influence and success in life, he trusts the unworthy, he is betrayed by the designing and treacherous and struck deep with the poisoned fang of ingratitude—his property swept from him, his affairs and himself in ruin. Thus the mighty hath fallen! As the tall Pillar, or the grand Colossus, under the awful pressure of the hand of time, must crumble and fall,—must finally mingle its particles with the common

kindred dust of the plain,—so we give him up, as we must all give up each other, to a fate that cannot be stayed, to a destiny which we cannot know. Then, farewell, Uncle Jess! Thou grand man, with thy great heart, with thy bright and wonderful intellect and universal knowledge, thou prince of lofty conversation, farewell.[453]

Jesse, the Man

Even after recounting his history, I am not sure it is possible to capture a man as complex, complicated, and controversial as Jesse Applegate in the two-dimensional world of the printed page. Stories of his many deeds, excerpts of the many letters that have survived over time, and the many testimonials of his contemporaries still may not present a complete picture of this complex man, so an analysis of his character may be in order.

Jesse's story clearly shows that he was a man uniquely prepared for his role in the building of the western frontier of Oregon. His heritage was that of a frontiersman; his training in St. Louis prepared him for leadership as a lawgiver. His physical stature and personality uniquely called him to his destiny of leadership on the westward march.

Jesse was a complicated man: he was first and foremost an idealist, but he was also proud, assertive, and unyielding on his principles. He enjoyed being the "uncouth independent" that could cause all politicians, friend or foe, a little uneasiness. He had the political savvy and historical knowledge to serve his community and country but lacked the politician's art of compromise to stay long on the stage. He fought for truth, honor, and justice in all that he did. Over and over again he trusted others too easily and too well, believing others to have the same strong sense of honor he himself possessed. Frear writes, "His greatest enemies, though believing him eccentric, impractical, and stubborn, still admired his 'great intelligence ... and thorough honesty.'"[454]

Since Jesse never allowed himself to be photographed, we must rely on the sketches drawn by his nephew, Buck Applegate, and the physical descriptions given by several who knew him to form a mental picture of him. His family described him as a man of six-feet, well-proportioned, muscular, and erect in his posture. He had remarkable powers of endurance in his younger days. Once he rode his horse to Portland on business and as he started home, his horse went lame just outside of Portland. Undaunted, he walked back to Yoncalla in three days, a distance of about one hundred fifty miles. Resourceful in overcoming obstacles and displaying courage in all circumstances, he possessed a commanding personality that made men willing to follow his lead. Once he had made up his mind about something, it was hard to sway him, which caused many to call him stubborn. He tended to carry the weight of the world on his shoulders, and would blame himself for the calamities that befell those he cared for.

Francis Fuller Victor describes her first impressions of Jesse:

> I shall never forget my reception ... He stood at the gate when the stage drove up. His philosophical head close shaven, with its large ears standing almost at right angles to his face, his large mouth stretched wide in a cordial yet half quizzical smile, together with his gaunt figure and farmer's garb made altogether a most unexpected picture—for I had heard a great deal about this Oregon statesman, and looked for something different ... Of all the minds I have ever come in contact with I think his the most independent; for though stored with learning he did not draw his ideas from other men's stock

but thought for himself. As he liked to talk in his deliberate, reflective way, I only had to listen.[455]

Bancroft adds his first impressions of the man: "He is a man of medium stature, well-made, calls himself a mountaineer, and he has a slight, graceful swing to his gait. He has short, gray hair, a rather small head, wide across the eyes, large ears, nose, and mouth, penetrating gray eyes, and his voice and demeanor are mild and benignant. He is one of the finest writers in the state, a man universally respected, of sound sense, and practical sagacity, of determined energy and strict integrity."

George Riddle, fellow pioneer, says of Jesse, "I have always looked upon Jesse Applegate as one of the grandest men I ever met, unselfish to such a degree that his whole thought after arriving in Oregon in 1843 was to aid emigrants and those not so fortunate as himself. He was never at any time a wealthy man, but he was the owner of his donation land claim and personal property that stood for a competence in his old age. All his property was swept away from him through his kindly disposition to aid a man he thought his friend."

Jesse spent many years of unpaid service to his state and community, always refusing to be paid for what he thought was "one's duty" to the better good. In the end, his sense of duty helped lead to his financial downfall as it raised his esteem in the eyes of others.

Those who knew Jesse best said he was inclined to tease those he liked but was always very formal and distant towards those he disliked. Jesse's face revealed his mood to those who knew him well. When happy, his eyes were sparkling and he wore a big smile. He loved to tell amusing stories and had a quick wit, always teasing the little ones about the house. He was fond of young people, inviting them to social events in his home. Above all, he had a kind and generous heart that resulted in generosity to all he encountered, often to his own detriment.

On the other hand, when Jesse was troubled or angry, he was silent, his face dark and clouded. He never complained, never asked for sympathy—was just utterly silent. His daughter Sallie said he showed his grief by being "still and silent, a trait he has passed on to each of his children."

Jesse had a keen, inquiring mind and truly enjoyed the intellectual stimulus of sparring with those he believed to be his intellectual equal, which explains his long and extensive correspondence with people like Deady, Bates, Dr. Owens-Adair, Francis Fuller Victor, and Hubert H. Bancroft. One example of this can be seen in Jesse's great delight in his political and religious differences with Deady, who was a Democrat and Catholic, while Jesse was a life-long Whig-Republican who disdained all formal religion. Jesse felt free to ridicule, flatter, compliment, or offer what he thought was constructive criticism to those he corresponded with regularly. Because his mind was always hungry for some new information or challenge, he read all he could, subscribing to all the Oregon papers, the *San Francisco Bulletin*, the *New York Tribune*, *Harpers Weekly*, and even the *Congressional Record*. Although a profound political thinker, he also found great challenge and joy in the more mundane, such as his correspondence with the Department of Agriculture in Washington, D.C., from whom he received generous seed allotments for experimentation purposes. He took great pleasure in planting, tending, crossbreeding, and meticulously reporting on the results of his work. Once, when a census taker came to his farm, he recorded that Jesse was a farmer, upon which Jesse seized the paper, crossed out the word "farmer," and replaced it with "horticulturist."

Jesse took great pleasure in growing things but also loved wild animals, especially birds. He loved to hear the larks' cheery songs and watch the antics of the robins. He knew all the birds' names and nesting habits and often went out of his way to protect a bird's nest in the spring from the plow or other danger.

Jesse was very much a family man and enjoyed his role as father. He was a kind and indulgent father to the little children, but he was also a strict taskmaster who gave a command only once and expected obedience. However, the children had a great deal of freedom to wander about the farm and enjoy the pleasures of childhood as long as their chores and schooling tasks were finished. Sallie Long says she has no memory of her father inflicting punishment other than through words of condemnation: "He had a natural power of command that ensured obedience, a kind of dignity that enforced respect."[456]

Jesse enjoyed his family and took his role as father and provider very seriously, but he also loved his profession as a surveyor. He loved getting out and about in new country, the excitement of exploring the unknown. His daughter Sallie shares an amusing little story about her father and his relationship with his profession:

> My father had a great love for his profession of surveying, the affection he held for the implements of his craft. Once a fire broke out in the garret of our house. Papa ran inside and dragged the compass boxes out from under his bed and carried them to a safe place. He then proceeded to put out the fire. My mother with much disgust scolded him about it afterwards. He answered that as long as he has his instruments, his compass was a means of livelihood and besides he had owned it since his youth, it had been his comrade on many a long campaign and he loved it like a child. "Like a very large child," said my mother with disgust.[457]

Deady complained once to Jesse, "You are at times dangerously fractious and your extreme love of independence often makes you unmarketable and totally useless to yourself, your friends, or your cause."[458] Jesse admitted that sometimes he did have to struggle with his temper and that he would be happier and more useful to his family if he were not so sensitive to criticism. "But if they inherit an extreme love of independence, and integrity unmarketable and unpurchasable, I think in the long run they will be better off."[459]

Jesse describes himself to Captain John C. Ainsworth in 1869:

> Some call me impractical and a visionary. They greatly mistake. I am practical in all things, visionary in nothing. It is true I have erected a standard of right and wrong in my conscience from which I never swerve. I have matured in my judgment a set of political principles which I never abandon. These I cannot yield to the persuasion or pleasure of others. But in all matters of policy, in all measures intended to promote the good of the Nation, State, or County in which I live, there is no man more open to conviction or more ready to yield his private judgment and follow that of others, and in these no man more cheerfully submits to the decision of a majority, whether it be of the Nation, State, County or municipality in which I live.
>
> While I am always earnest in support of what I think right, I strive to be always fair and just to my opponents, and I never suffer my religious or political differences to interfere with my personal friendships. [460]

In a letter to his friend Bethenia Owens-Adair, whom he often addressed as "My child," Jesse gives some insight into his personality:

> Intellectually, I fall far below the standard you seem to have set up of my measure. Not from lack of a clear, discriminating mind, but from a lack of the indomitable courage and perseverance that inspires you to great undertakings, and will bear you forward to great results. Too easily discouraged and turned aside by obstacles, and influenced by strong passions and appetites my advance in the path of knowledge has not been that of a traveler determined to reach the end of his journey, but a loiterer, who follows the path for the beauty and grandeur of the scene and the rich abundance of the flowers that strewed the way.

My mind led me to the pursuit of science; it was to me an easy road to pursue. Those things difficult and abstruse to most minds presented no difficulties to mine. My remarkable progress attracted the attention of the learned. Rich men offered their patronage, and money freely tendered was not wanting to bring me forward on the road I seemed so easily to follow. But I was too proud to be dependent on any man's bounty and too poor to prosecute my studies without first procuring the means of support...Suffice to say that, like many others, the promise of my youth was not realized in manhood. The struggle for competence brought me in contact with the world. I yielded the lofty but lonely pursuit of science to its seductions.[461]

Once again, we see Jesse's pride and lack of self-confidence standing in the way of him developing his brilliant mind. We have to wonder why he traded the world of academia for the more physical pursuit of the pioneer on the cutting edge of the westward movement of America. Perhaps, as he himself once said, "It is my destiny."

In another letter to Dr. Owens-Adair, Jesse expounds on a subject that seemed important to him and gives us a window to his value system:

About hatred and jealousy I have only to say: They are base passions, which we have in common with the lower animals. Besides the evils they work to others, they are a continual punishment to those who entertain them. They cannot long remain the tenants of a pure and innocent heart. They will soon drive out innocence and corrupt purity, or be themselves driven out. I write knowingly upon this subject, because in the course of my life I have been afflicted with both. But I have earnestly struggled against them, and no struggle in a good cause is entirely barren of good results. Toleration and charity for the faults and failings of others, I am sure, may be cultivated until they will create in our soul's desire for the good of all, and a sense of being at peace with all the world. Perhaps no degree of cultivation will save us from anger when provoked by deep or sudden injury, but we need not suffer it to degenerate into hatred and revenge.[462]

Jesse became the moral compass for the emerging Oregon society through his many letters to the editors of newspapers and prominent political figures. Samuel Frear in his thesis, "Jesse Applegate, An Appraisal of an Uncommon Pioneer," gives a good summery of Jesse's impact on early Oregon society, "Jesse Applegate was important in society, not only for the deeds he accomplished, but for his role in providing comment, counsel, dissent, criticism, and loyal opposition."

Jesse was an honest, unselfish man with a love for independence and liberty. He believed that the cornerstone of all relationships was truth and honesty. He also believed it was important to be true to oneself and firm in the pursuit of a high purpose in life. Yet, he never seemed to understand that his sense of honor often hurt those he loved as well as himself. His complete trust of others and a lack of discernment of character often led to his downfall. With that downfall, he rarely faulted others, but indulged in severe self-judgment that seldom allowed him to enjoy any of his many accomplishments.

His reverence for the government established by his forefathers, and his determination to preserve it, kept him ever faithful to his principles. He always sought equity in law and defended the rights of the minority. As Lincoln steered the course of a nation, Jesse steered the destiny of a state and defined its history. His letters, preserved by others, give a true, "reflection of [his] mind without the fig leaf." One can only hope that a new generation is inspired by his faithfulness to these ideals, and his courage and vision to fight for them.

Notes

The following abbreviations are used in the notes:

- OHQ-Oregon Historical Quarterly
- OHS- Oregon Historical Society
- OHRL- Oregon Historical Research Library
- UORL- University of Oregon Research Library
- DCHML- Douglas County Historical Museum Library

Endnotes

1   Jesse Applegate to Deady, 23 March 1862. Deady Papers, MS48, OHSRL.

2   Ibid.

Chapter 1

3   John Mark Faragher, *Daniel Boone: The Life and Legend of an American Pioneer* (New York: MacMillan, 1992), 32–39.

4   Murtie June Clark, "Colonial Soldiers of the South, 1732–1774," in Cecily Merrill, *Without Papers* (Portola Valley, CA, 1999).

5   Revolutionary War Pension, United States America. Sources: Jerseymen in the Revolutionary War, 135, 143. New Jersey pension #16139.

6   Jesse Applegate to M.P. Deady, 26 July 1863. Matthew Paul Deady Papers, Mss 48, OHS Research Library.

7   KY. Court of Appeals Deed book, vol. 2.

8 Warrant 8084.

9 "Revolutionary War Soldiers in Missouri," *MOSGA* (Summer 1985): 154.

10 D. W. Applegate to O.C. Applegate, 16 March 1889. Applegate Papers, Oregon Collection, University of Oregon Library, Eugene; O. C. Applegate to Henry Applegate, 22 April 1889. O.C. Applegate Papers.

11 Sallie Applegate Long, "Jesse Applegate," OHS Research Library.

12 "Revolutionary War Soldiers," 154.

Chapter 2

13 J. M. Peck to Joseph Lane, 19 March 1852, reprinted in "Letter About Jesse Applegate," *Oregon Historical Quarterly* XV (September 1914): 208–209.

14 Applegate to Hubert H. Bancroft, 29 August 1878, in Jesse Applegate, "Notes and Communications on Oregon History," Mss. (Bancroft Library, University of California, Berkeley), copy, University of Oregon Special Collection Library.

15 Ibid.

16 Ibid.

17 Ibid.

18 Ibid.

19 Gaston, *Centennial History of Oregon* IV: 417.

20 Joseph Schafer, "Jesse Applegate, Pioneer and State Builder," *University of Oregon Bulletin* IX (February 1912); Bancroft, *History of Oregon* (San Francisco, 1886), 413.

21 Susannah Gertrude Applegate, "Jesse Applegate, Prince of Pioneers," unpublished manuscript, DCHM; Annie Applegate Kruse, personal interview, 1960.

22 Schafer, "Jesse Applegate."

23 Applegate to Edward Bates, 30 December 1861. Applegate Letters, OHSRL; *Oregon Statesman*, April 22, 1861.

24 Applegate to Deady, 30 December 1861. Applegate Letters, OHSRL.

25 Jesse Applegate to Lisbon Applegate, 9 September 1830. Jesse Applegate Papers (Manuscript of Western Americana, Yale University Library, New Haven) copies, University of Oregon Library, Eugene.

26 Book A, p. 403, Cole County Recorder's Office, Missouri.

27 Sallie Applegate Long, "Mrs. Jesse Applegate," *OHQ* IX (June 1908): 179–83.

Chapter 3

28 Ibid, 180.

29 Jesse Applegate to Lisbon Applegate, 18 July 1841. Applegate Papers, Yale.

30 Perhaps "rent" would be a better word; although Jesse tried to pay the wages to the slaves, their owners ended up collecting the money.

31 Sallie Applegate Long, "Traditional History of the Applegate Family," Mss. (OHS, Portland); Wilfred Brown, ed. *This was a Man* (North Hollywood, CA: Camas Press, 1971).

32 Jesse Applegate, "Views of Oregon History," Bancroft Library, UORL.

33 Jesse Applegate, "Views of Oregon History, Yoncalla, 1878," Bancroft Library.

34 R.O. Case, *Empire Builders.*

35 Applegate to Addison Gibbs, 18 February 1865. Applegate papers, Yale.

36 The measure passed in slightly different form in 1850.

37 Jesse Applegate to John Minto, 12 December 1883. OHRL.

38 Mary Patricia Rawe, "Winning Beekman Prize Essay on the Oregon Trail," *OHQ* XLIV (June 1943).

39 Documentary in *OHQ* II (June 1901).

40 Jesse Applegate to Lisbon Applegate, 11 April 1843. Applegate Papers, Yale University, copy at UOL.

41 *New York Daily Tribune*, February 2, 1843; John Unruh, *The Plains Across* (Urbana, Il: University of Illinois Press, 1979), 36.

42 *New York Aurora*, February 3, 1843; Unruh, *The Plains Across*, 38.

Chapter 4

43 Schafer, "Jesse Applegate."

44 That Brown Crock now sets in my kitchen.

45 Applegate to Lisbon Applegate, 15 February, 1846, Cole Library.

46 Applegate, "Views and Communications on Oregon History," (Bancroft Library, University of California, Berkeley), typewritten copy, UORL, Eugene.

47 Peter H. Burnett, "Letters of Peter H. Burnett," *OHQ* III (December 1902): 406–7.

48   Peter H. Burnett, "Recollections of an Old Pioneer," *OHQ* V (March 1904).

49   Jesse Applegate, "A Day with the Cow Column," *OHQ* I (December 1900). First published in the *Overland Monthly* I (August, 1868).

50   Ibid.

51   Documents, Letters of Peter Burnett, *OHQ* XIII (December 1902): 409.

52   Applegate Papers, DCHML.

53   Charles Henry Carey, *A General History of Oregon Prior to* 1861 (Portland, OR: Metropolitan Press, 1935), 1:392.

54   Applegate Papers, Douglas County Museum.

55   Colonel Nesmith's address on Applegate to the Oregon Pioneer Association 1875,oHS.

56   Applegate, "A Day With the Cow Column," *OHQ* I, No. 4, 371–383.

57   Shafer, "Jesse Applegate."

58   Burnett, "Recollections," 70.

59   J. W. Nesmith, "Diary of the Emigration of 1843," *OHQ* VII (December 1906): 329–30.

60   Ibid., 341.

61   James W. Nesmith, "Diary of the Emigration of 1843," *OHQ* Vll (December 1906): 342.

62   Ibid., 344.

63   Burnett, "Recollections," 82–83.

64   Sara Jane Hill, manuscript in Oregon Historical Society Library, 11.

65   Burnett, "Recollection," 82.

66   Ninevah Ford, *The Pioneer Road Makers*, 10.

67   Elwood Evans, *History of the Pacific Northwest, Oregon and Washington* (Portland, OR: North Pacific History Company, 1889), 1:258–59.

68   Burnett, "Recollections," 288–89.

69   Lindsay Applegate, "Notes and Reminiscences of Laying Out and Establishing the Old Emigrant Road into Southern Oregon in the Year 1846," *OHQ* XXII (March 1921): 72–114; Jesse A. Applegate, *Recollections of My Boyhood*, 149–59.

70   Allen Nevins, ed., *Narratives of exploration and Adventure by John Charles Fremont*, 292.

71   Jesse A. Applegate, "On the River," in Brown, *This Was a Man*, 81–92, Jesse A. Applegate, *Recollections of My Boyhood*.

72   E. L. Applegate, Obituary Sketch of Jesse Applegate, Access Genealogy.

73   Burnett, "Recollections," 65–66.

74   Lindsay Applegate, "Notes and Reminiscences," 72–114.

75   Applegate, "Views of Oregon History."

Chapter 5

76   Burnett, "Recollections," 288.

77   Nineveh Ford, "The Pioneer Road Makers," www.geocites.com/ Heartland Valley/6043/n-ford.txt.

78   Hubert H. Bancroft, *History of Oregon* (San Francisco, 1886), 1: 410.

79   Homan, *Dr. John McLoughlin: The Father of Oregon*, 150.

80   Lindsay Applegate, "Notes and Reminiscences," 12–14.

81 Bancroft/Victor, *History of Oregon* 1:417.

82 Burnett, "Recollection," 168–69.

83 Leslie M. Scott, "First Taxes in Oregon," *OHQ* XXXI (March 1930). Holman, Dr. John McLoughlin, 119.

84 Ibid., 12.

85 *Overland Monthly and Old West Magazine* 4 no. 24, (December 1884).

86 Jesse Applegate to Lisbon Applegate, 15 February 1846. Applegate Papers Yale.

87 Ibid.

88 Jesse Applegate to Lisbon Applegate, 11 October 1847. Applegate Papers, Yale.

89 LaFayette Grover, ed., *The Oregon Archives* (Salem, 1853) 68.

90 Frear, "Jesse Applegate."

Chapter 6

91 Carey, *History of Oregon*, 1:202–251.

92 Marie M. Bradley, "Political Beginnings in Oregon," *OHQ* IX (March 1908): 47.

93 Carey, *History of Oregon*, 1:318.

94 Ibid., 304, 331.

95 Ibid., 307–23; C. H. Chapman, *Story of Oregon*, Ch. XII, Applegate, "Views of Oregon History."

96 Applegate, Ibid.

97 Jesse Applegate to Lisbon Applegate, 15 February 1846. Applegate Papers, Yale.

98   Applegate to Deady, 6 November 1864. Joseph Lane Papers, Oregon Collection, UORL, Eugene.

99   Applegate, "Views and Communications on Oregon History," (Bancroft Library, University of California, Berkeley), typewritten copy, UORL, Eugene.

100 Applegate to Lisbon Applegate, 16 June 1845. Applegate letters, UOHL, Eugene.

101 Applegate to Elwood Evans, 10 October 1867. Oregon Collection, UORL, Eugene.

102 Johnson, *John McLoughlin, Father of Oregon*, 223.

103 Schafer, "Jesse Applegate."

104 Applegate to W.H. Gray, 10 July 1879. Applegate Letters.

105 Frederick V. Holman, "Brief History of the Oregon Provisional Government," *OHQ* XIII (June 1912): 126–27.

106 Ibid, 133.

107 J. Henry Brown, *Political History of Oregon* (Portland, OR, 1892), 164–66.

108 Bancroft, *History of Oregon* I: 474.

109 Applegate, "Views of Oregon History," MS 39,40.

110 Walter C. Woodward, "Political Parties in Oregon," *OHQ* II (December 1910): 340.

111 Applegate to Deady, 15 April 1866. Matthew Deady Papers, Mss 48, OHSRL, Portland.

112 Applegate to Nesmith, 20 July 1845, Applegate letters OHS.

113 In "An Act regulating the proceedings and defining the duties and powers of the Supreme Court," passed August 12, 1845. (Document 1187, Prov. and Terr. Government Papers).

114 Grover, *Oregon Archives*, 72–85; United States Congress: Abridgment of the Debate of Congress from 1789 to 1856.

115 Ibid.

116 *Oregon Laws and Acts,* 1845 (New York: N.A. Phemister & Co., 1921), 6.

117 J. A. Hussey, "Champoeg, Place of Transition," OHS, Portland, 1967.

118 Ibid.

119 Grover, *Oregon Archives*, 90.

120 Frear, "Jesse Applegate."

121 Applegate to Gray, December 1879. Applegate Letters.

122 Bancroft/Victor, *History of Oregon*, 1:474.

123 Jesse Applegate to Lisbon Applegate, 15 February 1846. Applegate Papers, Yale.

124 Woodward, "Political Parties," 348.

Chapter 7

125 Jesse Applegate to Lisbon Applegate, 15 February 1846. Applegate Papers, Yale.

126 Lindsay Applegate, "Notes and Reminiscences," 14.

127 Bancroft, Works, Vol. XXIX, 515.

128 Unruh, *The Plains Across*, 347.

129 James Collins, "From Independence to Independence," (unpublished manuscript, DCHML, 1967)

130 Ibid., Chapter 9.

131 Ibid., 128.

132   Ibid., 12.

133   Buena Cobb Stone, "Southern Route into Oregon: Notes and a New Map," *OHQ* XLVII (June 1946).

134   Ibid.

135   Lindsay Applegate, "The South Road Expedition," *OHQ* XXII (March 1921): 14.

136   Helfrich, "The Applegate Trail," Klamath Echoes, (1971), Vol. 9, 2.

137   Applegate to John Preston, June 4, 1851, National Archives-Pacific Alaska Region.

138   *Oregon Spectator*, July 4, 1846, p. 3, co1.1.

139   Charles George Davis, *The South Road, and the Route Across Southern Oregon* (North Plains, OR: EmigrantsWest.com, 2001): 114.

140   Lindsay Applegate, "The South Road Expedition," 15.

141   Collins, "Independence," 130.

142   Collins, "Independence," chapter IX; Davis, *The South Road*, 118.

143   Lindsay Applegate, "The South Road Expedition," 16.

144   Collins, "Independence," 133

145   Ibid., 135.

146   Lindsay Applegate, "The South Road Expedition," 16.

147   Collins, "Independence," 140.

148   Ibid., 142

149   William Emerson, *The Applegate Trail of* 1846 (Ashland, Or: Ember Enterprises, 1996), 27.

150   Collins, "Independence," 146.

151   Lindsay Applegate, "The South Road Expedition," 32–33.

152 Collins, "Independence," 151.

153 Helfrich, "Klamath Echoes," 2.

154 Collins, "Independence," 157.

155 Lindsay Applegate, "The South Road Expedition," 36.

156 Collins, "Independence," 158.

157 Emerson, *The Applegate Trail*, 29; Lindsay Applegate, "The South Road Expedition."

158 Collins, "Independence," 158.

159 Edwin Bryant, *California*, 196.

160 Helfrich, "Klamath Echoes," 4.

161 Ibid.

162 Jesse Applegate to Lisbon Applegate, 8 August 1846, UORL.

163 IBID., 10 August 1846.

164 Morgan, *Overland in* 1846, Vol. 2, 637,638. [New York Tribune, October 24, 1846]

165 Unruh, *The Plains Across*.

Chapter 8

166 Lockley, *Pioneer Women*, 81.

167 Ibid., 86.

168 Emerson, *The Applegate Trail*, 36; Devere Helfrich, "Applegate Trail," *Klamath Echoes*, Klamath County Historical Society, Klamath Falls, 1971, 27.

169 John E. Simmons, "In Search of the Applegate Trail," Professional Educator's Training (Vancouver, WA: PET, 1996), 31.

170 Bancroft, *History of Oregon*, 1:559.

171 Ibid.

172 Davis, *The South Road*, 69.

173 Collins, "Independence," 121, 129–30.

174 Annie Kruse, Applegate family historian, personal interview 1958.

175 Lindsay Applegate, "The South Road Expedition," 41.

176 Bancroft, *History of Oregon*, 1:561; *Sunday Oregonian*, November 24, 1946, p.5.

177 Collins, "Independence," 168.

178 *Sunday Oregonian*, November 24, 1946, p.5, cols. 4 and 5.

179 Collins, "Independence," 196.

180 Ibid., 197.

181 Ibid.

182 Ibid., 198–99.

183 *Oregon Spectator*, April 6, 1848; Jesse Applegate Way Bill.

184 Jesse Applegate to George Abernathy, OHS Mss 929(Abernethy) Box 1, file 9.

185 Bert Webber, *Applegate Trail to Oregon* 1846 (Central Point, OR: Webb Research Group, 1996), 72.

186 Davis, *The South Road*, 194.

187 Jesse Q. Thornton, *Oregon and California in* 1848, (New York, 1855), 218.

188 Ibid.

189 Webber, *Applegate Trail*, 75.

190 Collins, "Independence," 203.

191 Thornton, *Oregon and California,* 1:239.

192 Walter Meacham, "The Applegate Trail," in Brown, *This Was a Man.*

193 Thomas Holt, *Holts Journal,* first published in the *Oregon Spectator,* March 18, 1847. Reprinted in *Overland in 1846, Diaries and Letters of the California-Oregon Trail,* Vol.1.

194 Ibid.

195 Davis, *The South Road,* 210.

Chapter 9

196 *Oregon Spectator,* October 1, 1846, p. 2, col. 2.

197 Bancroft, *History of Oregon,* 1:566.

198 *Oregon Spectator,* March 4, 1847.

199 Thornton, *Oregon and California,* 1:161–62.

200 Bancroft, *History of Oregon,* 1:555, 562.

201 Bancroft, *History of Oregon,* 1:563–66.

202 Holmes, Kenneth L. *Covered Wagon Women, Diaries & Letters From The Western Trails,* 1840–1849 (Glendale, CA.: A.H. Clark Co., 1983), 51–52.

203 *Oregon Spectator,* November 26, 1846, p.3, col. 1.

204 *Oregon Spectator,* April 29, 1847, p.4. col. 1.

205 *Oregon Spectator,* May 13, 1847.

206 Jesse Applegate to Lisbon Applegate, 11 October 1847. Applegate Papers, Yale.

207 *Oregon Spectator,* November 14, 1847, p.2, col. 3.

208 Peter W. Crawford, *The Overland Journey to Oregon in* 1847 (North Plains, OR: Soap Creek Enterprise, 1977).

209 Lester Hulin, "1847 Diary of Applegate Trail to Oregon," (typescript, Lane County Historical Society, Eugene, OR).

210 Documents, Oregon Provisional Government, Legislative session 1847, in OHS library, Portland, OR.

211 Clark, *Pioneer History of Oregon*, 2: 585.

212 Burnett, "Recollections," 287.

213 Walter Meacham, *Applegate Trail* 1846 (state historical brochure, 1946), 25.

Chapter 10

214 George W. Fuller, *A History of the Pacific Northwest* (New York: Albert A. Knopf, 1945), 143.

215 Ibid., 145.

216 Eva Emery Dye, *Stories of Oregon* (San Francisco: Whitaker and Ray, 1900), 126.

217 Shannon Applegate, *Skookum: an Oregon Pioneer Family's History and Lore* (New York: Beech Tree Books, 1988), 93.

218 Oregon Archives, Journal, 233; F. G. Young, "Finances of the Cayuse War," *OHQ* (December 1906).

219 Roy H. Glassley, *Pacific Northwest Indian Wars* (Portland, OR: Binford & Mort, 1953), 13.

220 *Oregon Spectator*, January 6, 1848, p. 1. col. 1.

221 Dye, *Stories of Oregon*, 128.

222 Bancroft, *History of Oregon*, 1:670; Grover, *Oregon Archives*, 225.

223 John Minto, "Levi Scott Company in the Cayuse War, OHS Mss, Shannon Applegate, *Skookum*, 94.

224 Victor, *Indian Wars*, 180.

225 Victor, *The River of the West*, 191–92.

226 J. Henry Brown, *Political History of Oregon; Provisional Government* (Portland, OR: Wiley B. Allen, 1892), 328.

227 Glassley, *Pacific Northwest Indian Wars*, 14.

228 Oregon Archives, MS 863.

229 Oregon Archives, MS; Young, "Finances of the Provisional Government," 423.

230 Young, "Finances of the Provisional Government," 423, Victor, *Indian Wars*, 201.

231 Bancroft, *History of Oregon*, 1:679; Collins, "Independence," 228.

232 Frances Fuller Victor, *Indian Wars*,146.

233 Collins, "Independence," 228.

234 John Minto, "Capt Levi Scott Company in the Cayuse War," OHS Mss. 752.

235 Ibid., 10.

236 Collins, "Independence,"228.

237 John Minto, "Capt Levi Scotts Company In the Cayuse War," OHS Mss 752.

238 Ibid., 229.

239 Ibid., 232.

240 Shannon Applegate, *Skookum*, 98.

241 Jesse Applegate, "Views of Oregon History, etc.," Bancroft Library.

Chapter 11

242 Grover, *Oregon Archives*, 258, 266.

243 Bancroft, *History of Oregon*, 2:60.

244 Grover, *Oregon Archives*, 274.

245 Ibid., 275–76.

246 Ibid., 294.

247 Ibid., 280–83.

248 Ibid., 316–17.

249 Schafer, "Jesse Applegate," 11.

Chapter 12

250 Reese Kendall, *Pacific Trail Camp-fires* (Chicago: Scroll, 1901).

251 Claim No. 38, notification No.54, certificate No. 103, T. 22 S., R. 5 W., W. M.

252 Applegate to Archibald McKinlay, 3 May 1850. Applegate Papers, Yale.

253 Rosa Dodge Galey letter to Wm. D. Miner, Ashland, Oregon, May 1947, 3.

254 *Index to Oregon Land Claims*, (Oregon State Library, division of State Archives, Salem, 1957); Applegate to S.R. Thurston, 4 July 1850. Applegate Letters.

255 Long, "Jesse Applegate."

256 Applegate to H.H. Bancroft, 14 January 1879. "Notes and Communications," MSS.

257 Long, "Jesse Applegate."

258 This deed is at the Applegate Interpretive Center in Sunny Valley, OR.

259 Long, "Jesse Applegate."

260 Galey to Wm. D. Miner, Ashland, Oregon, May, 1947, 2.

261 Verne Bright, "The Lost County, Umpqua, Oregon and Its Early Settlement," *OHQ* VLI (June 1950), 113–115.

262 Applegate to McKinlay, 10 January 1851. Applegate papers.

263 Bright, "The Lost County."

264 Ibid., 118.

265 Ibid., 124.

266 Anne Applegate Kruse, *Yoncalla, Home of the Eagles* (Drain, OR, 1950),15.

267 Lewis A. MacArthur, "Earliest Oregon Postoffice," *OHQ* XLI (March 1940): 56.

268 Burnett, "Recollections," 288.

269 Jesse Applegate to Thomas Ewbank, commissioner of patents at Washington, D.C. December 28, 1851. Report of the commissioner of patents for the year of 1851, part II, Agriculture, 468–74.

270 *Oregon Spectator*, May 1, 1851, p. 3, col. 1.

271 Collins, "Independence," 250.

272 Ibid., 250.

273 *Oregon Statesman*, June 20, 1851; Frances Fuller Victor, *The Early Indian Wars of Oregon Compiled from the Oregon Archives and Other Original Sources with Muster Rolls* (Salem, OR: Frank C. Baker, State Printers, 1894), 277.

274 Collins, "Independence," 260.

275 Long, "Jesse Applegate."

276 P. Kearny to Adjutant General, 19 June & 29 June 1851. Quoted in Evans, *History of the Pacific Northwest*, 1:386–87.

277 *Oregon Spectator*, March 27, 1851 and April 10, 1851.

278 Frear, "Jesse Applegate," 53.

279 Applegate to John B. Preston, 1 July 1851, BLM, Box 50, National Archives-Pacific Alaska Region.

280 Applegate to Preston, 9 November 1851, BLM, Box 50, NAPAR.

281 Applegate to Preston, 9 September 1853.

282 Applegate to Lane, 17 November 1854. Lane Papers, U of O.

283 Ibid.

284 Applegate to Addison Gibbs, 30 January 1865, Mss 685, box 1, file 7, OHS.

285 Ibid.

286 Oregon Historical Society Files, File 2, "The Indian Murder in Umpqua County," *The Umpqua Trapper* (Winter 1974): 75.

287 Ibid., 76.

288 OHS, File 2.

289 "The Indian Murder in Umpqua County," 79.

290 O.C. Applegate to A.B. Meacham, quoted in Alfred B Meacham, *Wigwam and War-path* (Boston: John Dale and Co., 1876).

291 Bureau of Indian Affairs, N-670–1859.

292 OHS, File 2.

293 "The Indian Murder in Umpqua County."

294 Joel Palmer to the Commission of Indian Affairs, June 23, 1853, C.I.A., A.R., Nov.26, 1853 (Serial 710, Doc.1), 449.

295 Annie Applegate Kruse, "Yoncalla, Home of the Eagles." 6.

296 Charlotte Blake, "Jesse Applegate: His attitude Toward the Oregon Indians," Reed College Bulletin, XXI (November, 1942) 27.

297 Ibid., 5–7.

Chapter 13

298 Schafer, "Jesse Applegate."

299 Applegate to Deady, 12 February 1865. Applegate Papers.

300 Applegate to Bush, 16 November 1857. Bush Papers, University of Oregon.

301 Applegate to Bush, 25 November 1857. Bush Papers.

302 Robert W. Johannsen, *Frontier Politics and the Sectional Conflict* (Seattle, 1955), 12–13.

303 *Oregon Statesman*, June 20, 1854; Chadwick to Deady, 15 June 1854. MP Deady Papers, OHS, Portland.

304 Applegate to Lisbon Applegate, February 15, 1846, Yale University Library.

305 Applegate to Bancroft, 14 January 1879, H.H. Bancroft Papers, University of Oregon Special Collection.

306 Applegate to Medorem Crawford, 4 February 1855. Medorem Crawford Papers, Oregon Collections, University of Oregon Library.

307 Ibid.

308 The first page of this letter is missing, and the remaining five pages are not dated. Special Collection, University of Oregon Library.

309 *Oregon Statesman*, June 23, 1857 and June 27, 1857, 2.

310 *Oregon Statesman*, July 14, 1857, 2.

311 Carey, *The Oregon Constitution*, 78–85

312 T.W. Davenport, "The Late George N. Williams," *OHQ* XI (September 1910), 280.

313 Carey, *The Oregon Constitution*, 82–83.

314 Ibid., 105–6.

315 Oregon Archives, "Constitutional Convention."

316 Ibid., 175–77.

317 Collins, "Independence," 286–88.

318 Bancroft, *History of Oregon* 2:424.

319 Carey, *The Oregon Constitution*, 208–9.

320 Applegate to Deady, 15 November 1868. Deady Collection, MS48, OHSRL, Portland.

321 Woodward, "Political Parties in Oregon," 251.

322 *Oregon Argus*, March 31, 1861.

323 Applegate to Medorem Crawford, 26 December 1861. Crawford Papers.

324 W. C. Woodward, "Rise and Early History of Political Parties in Oregon," OHQ (December 1911), 336.

325 Ibid., 344.

326 Ibid., 347.

327 Applegate to Deady, 4 September 1865, Applegate Letters.

328 Schafer, "Jesse Applegate," 230.

329 Eugene, *Oregon State Journal*, December 9, 1865.

330 Ibid., December 30, 1865.

331 Ibid., January 6, 1865

332 Schafer, "Jesse Applegate," 233.

333 Samuel Bowles, *Across the Continent; A Summer's Journey to the Rocky Mountains* (New York: Samuel Bowles and Company, 1866), 176–77.

334 Applegate to George Gibbs, August 6, 1865, reprinted in the Salem *Oregon Statesman*, August 28, 1865, 2.

335 British and American Joint Commission for the Final Settlement of the Claims of the Hudson's Bay and Puget's Sound Agricultural Companies. In the Matter of the Hudson's Bay Company, Vol. VIII (Washington D.C., 1867) 265–312.

336 J. Orin Oliphant, "Old Fort Colville," Washington Historical Quarterly (Seattle), XVI (June, 1945), 94–96.

337 Applegate to Deady, 11 July 1869. University of Oregon Special Collections.

338 Schafer, "Jesse Applegate."

Chapter 14

339 The descriptions of the house were taken from three sources: Sally Applegate Long; "The House of Jesse;" Mary Wise, in Brown, *This Was A Man.*; "Jesse Applegate Mansion," from Eva Emery Dye, *The Soul of America, an Oregon Iliad.*

340 Sheba Hargreaves, "From Old Scraps of Paper," in Brown, *This Was A Man.*

341 Sallie Long, "My Sister Rozelle," in Brown, *This Was A Man.*

342 Ibid.

343 Applegate to J.W. Nesmith, 21 May 1861. Applegate papers, University of Oregon.

344   Dye, *The Soul of America*, 332.

345   Susannah Gertrude Applegate, "Jesse Applegate, Prince of Pioneers" (unpublished manuscript, DCHML).

346   Jesse Applegate to Charles Putnam, 31 October 1864. Family papers.

347   Applegate to Deady, 6 November 1864. Applegate Letters.

348   Applegate to Deady, 15 April 1863. Applegate Letters.

349   This is not the route that the railroad ended up using through this area. What Jesse describes would have by-passed Grants Pass.

Chapter 15

350   Applegate to Joseph Lane, 5 February 1860. Lane Papers.

351   Jesse's son-in-law, Charles Putnam, had worked with Greeley before coming west; he named his third child Horace in honor of his friend.

352   Leslie M. Scott, "Oregon Nomination of Lincoln," OHQ V XVII (December 1916): 205.

353   Ibid., 207.

354   Austin Mires, "Jesse Applegate and Honest Abe," *The Umpqua Trapper* IV (Summer 1968); Kruse, *Yoncalla, Home of the Eagles*, 17.

355   Applegate to Deady, 26 July 1863. Deady Papers, MS48, OHSRL.

356   Abraham Lincoln, 1809–1865: *Collected Works* vol. 6.; U. S. Military Academy, 1863, Box 82, No 184.

357   Scrapbook Number Fifty-Nine (OHS) 56.

358   The *Drain Enterprise*, 29 June 1950, ran a copy of a letter written to Governor Addison Gibbs on 5 July 1864. OHS original letter.

359   Scrapbook Number Fifty-Nine (OHS).

Chapter 16

360 *Rogue River Courier,* 6 August 1886.

361 Cover sheet on the box containing depositions, legislative jour-
nals, and other background documents in the case of Dowell v
Applegate, Douglas County Museum of History, Roseburg, OR.

362 *Dowell v. Applegate,* Douglas County Museum.

363 Clark, Malcolm, Jr., ed., *Pharisee Among the Philistines: The Diary
of Judge Matthew P. Deady,* 1871–1892 (Portland, OR: Oregon
Historical Society, 1975)

364 Secretary of State, 1872, Department of State, Salem, Oregon,
18–19.

365 State of Oregon, County of Marion, Circuit Court Case file
No.2086.

366 State Archives Vault, Salem, File Number 2344.

367 Vol. 1, Court Case- Judgment, June 1878.

368 Forty-Fourth Congress, Ch. 106–1877, Interior Department-
Surveying Public Lands.

369 Dean Deaver and Maud Deaver, "Jesse Applegate—The Man," in
Brown, *This Was A Man.*

370 Applegate to Deady, 13 June 1875. Deady Papers, MS48, OHSRL.

371 Acts and Resolutions of the Legislative Assembly of the State of
Oregon (Salem, 18740, Appendix, 1–46.

372 *Dowell v. Applegate,* Douglas County Museum.

373 The Dorris brothers did not honor the note and pay Jesse's portion
of May's debt, a mere $6,087 against their debt of $25,000.

374 Applegate to Deady, 17 June 1869. Deady Papers.

375 Applegate to W.H.H. Applegate, December 17, 1878, O.C. Applegate Papers. Deed recorded at the Douglas County Clerks Office. Vol. 11, p.75, recording 775.

376 *Dowell v. Applegate*, 8 Sawyer (U.S.) 427 (1883).

377 Jesse Applegate to Lindsay Applegate, 17 June 1883. O.C. Applegate Papers.

378 Vol. 15, The Supreme Court of the State of Oregon, March Term, 1887, and October 1887.

379 *Rogue River Courier*, 6 August, 1886.

380 Applegate to Deady, 26 June 1875.

381 Applegate to Deady, 12 September 1875, Repeated in court testimony Dowell vs Applegate, Douglas County 14, October 1880.

382 Applegate to Deady, 17 September 1875.

Chapter 17

383 Hubert Howe Bancroft, *California Inter Pocula* (San Francisco: The History Company, 1888), XXXV, 458.

384 Keith A. Murray, *The Modocs and Their War* (Norman, OK: University of Oklahoma Press, 1959), 18.

385 Bancroft Library, Statement by W.S. Kershan, 48; Meacham, *Wigwam and War-Path*, 296.

386 Murray, *The Modocs and Their War*, 27.

387 Ibid., 38.

388 Ibid., 38–39.

389 Ibid., 35.

390 Ibid., 49.

391 Murray, *The Modocs and Their War*, 41.

392 A. B. Meacham, Supt. Of Indian Affairs in Oregon to F. A. Walker, Com. Of Indian Affairs, Washington D. C., 27 January 1870. N.A. Ft. Klamath, Letters, Shaw Library, Don C. Fisher Papers, Volume 1.

393 Don C. Fisher Papers, Volume 1, Shaw Library, Klamath Falls, OR.

394 Jesse Applegate to A.B. Meacham, Supt. Indian Affairs, 27 July 1871, Don C. Fisher Papers, Vol. 1, Shaw Library, Klamath Falls, OR.

395 Meacham, *Wigwam and War-paths*, 350.

396 Ibid.

397 Ibid., 351,52.

398 Ibid., 354.

399 Ibid., 356.

400 Bancroft, *History of Oregon*, 2:564–65; John Meacham to A.B. Meacham, 21 August 1871. S.F.P., D. C., 1873 #1811.

401 Applegate to A. B. Meacham, February 1, 1872

402 Letter to A. B. Meacham and General Canby from concerned citizens of Lost River, Don E. Fisher Papers, Vol. 1, Enclosure 7, Shaw Library.

403 Edwin N. Thompson, *Lava Beds NM: Modoc War*, 5.

404 Ibid, Ch 2, 5.

405 Murray, *The Modocs and Their War*, 94.

406 Ibid, 135.

407 Meacham, *Wigwam and War-path*, 415.

408 Peter Cozzens, *Eyewitnesses to the Indian Wars*, 1865–1890, 174.

409 Murry, *The Modocs and Their War*, 143.

410   Ibid, 177.

411   Governor Grover to Canby, 10 February 1873, Oregon Superintendent, 1873, Office of Indian Affairs, Shaw Library, Don C. Fisher Papers.

412   *Yreka Union*, February 22, 1873.

413   Applegate to Clum, 26 February 1873, Oregon Superintendent, 1873, Office Indian Affairs.

414   Bancroft, *California Inter Pocula*, 519–520.

Chapter 18

415   Robert B. Johnston, "Two Jesses and The Modoc War," *Journal of the Shaw Historical Society* 1, 5 nos. 1 and 2, Oregon Institute of Technology.

416   Ibid., Enclosed in a letter of Jesse Carr to Hon. Will Drumond, Commissioner General Land Office.

417   Applegate to Deady, 17 September 1875. Deady papers, University of Oregon.

418   Burnett, *Recollections of an Old Pioneer*, 230.

419   Applegate to Deady, 2 November, 1875. Deady Papers, MS48, OHSRL.

420   *Pharisee among Philistines*, 240.

421   "Document—Letter, Jesse Applegate to W. H. Rees, Secretary Oregon Pioneer Ass.," *OHQ* XX (December 1919).

422   S. F. Chadwick to Deady, 21 January 1876. M. P. Deady Papers, MS48, OHSRL, Portland.

423   Applegate to Deady, 10 April 1877. Deady Papers, MS48, OHSRL, Portland.

424 Jesse Applegate, interview notes by A. Bowman for H.H. Bancroft, OHS MF 176, Reel 7, copy film from Bancroft Library, UC Berkleley.

425 OHS, Address by Hon. J. Quinn Thornton, Oregon Pioneers Association of 1878, 69.

426 Applegate, "Views of Oregon History, etc., Yoncalla, 1878," (copied from manuscript material in Bancroft Library, University of California).

427 Jesse Applegate, "Views of Oregon History, etc.," Bancroft Library.

428 Applegate to Elwood Evans, 13 October, 1867, Elwood Evans Papers.

429 Ibid.

430 Applegate, "Views of Oregon History," Bancroft Library.

431 Applegate to Bancroft, 9 December , 1879, H.H. Bancroft Papers, University of Oregon Library Special Collection.

432 Applegate to Deady, Christmas night, 1877. Applegate Papers, DCM, Roseburg.

433 B.A. Owens-Adair, *Some of Her Life Experiences* (Portland, OR, 1906), 287.

434 Ibid, 283.

435 Dr. Owens-Adair, *Some of Her Life Experiences*, 289–90.

436 OHS, Bethenia Owens-Adair, Mss 503.

437 Jesse Applegate to Lindsay Applegate, 11 August, 1879. Lindsay Applegate Papers, University of Oregon.

438 Applegate to Deady, 8 August, 1880. Deady Papers, MS48,0HSRL.

439 Applegate to Deady, 24 April 1883. Deady Papers, MS48, OHSRL.

440 Pharisee Among Philistines, The Diary of Judge Matthew P. Deady, 1871–1892.

441 Applegate to Nesmith, 6 January 1884, Applegate Letters.

442 Applegate Papers, DCHML.

443 Applegate to Caroline Haynes, 5 June 1881, Letter found in Susanna Applegate papers, DCHML.

444 Long, "Jesse Applegate."

445 Jesse Applegate Commitment Papers, Applegate File, Douglas County Museum, Roseburg.

446 Applegate File, Douglas County Museum, Roseburg.

447 Long, "Traditional History of the Applegate Family."

448 Applegate to Lane, 15 April 1888. Nina Lane Faubion Papers, Oregon Collection, UOL.

449 "Jesse Applegate, Sudden Death of the 'Sage of Yoncalla,'" Morning *Oregonian*, Tuesday, April 24, 1888; Long, "Traditional History of the Applegate Family."

450 Long, Ibid.

451 "Jesse Applegate, Sudden Death," in Harvey W. Scott, *History of the Oregon Country* (Cambridge: Riverside Press, 1924), 5:297.

452 *The Oregonian*, April 24, 1888.

453 "Jesse Applegate, Obituary, General E. L. Applegate," ancestor. com, retrieved March 16, 2004.

Chapter 19

454 Frear, "Jesse Applegate," 140.

455 Jim Martin, *A Bit of Blue: Life and Work of Frances Fuller Victor* (Salem, OR: Deep Well Publishing, 1992), 57, 58.

456 Long, "Jesse Applegate."

457 Ibid.

458 Deady to Applegate, 15 November 1868. Deady Papers, MS48, OHSRL.

459 Applegate to Deady, 9 August 1868; Frear, "Jesse Applegate," 102.

460 Jesse Applegate, "A Philosophy of Politics," from a letter to John C. Ainsworth, in Brown, *This Was A Man*.

461 Owens-Adair, *Some of Her Life Experiences*, 289.

462 Ibid.

Bibliography

Books

Applegate, Shannon. *Skookum: An Oregon Pioneer Family's History and Lore*. New York: Beech Tree Books, 1988.

Bancroft, Hubert Howe. *California Inter Pocula*. San Francisco: The History Company, 1888.

———. *The Works of Hubert Howe Bancroft*, vols. I & II. San Francisco: The History Company, 1888.

———. *The History of Oregon*. 7 vols. San Francisco: The History Company, 1890.

Bland, T. A. *Life of Alfred B. Meacham*. Washington, D.C.: T.A. and M. C. Bland, 1883.

Bowles, Samuel. *Across the Continent; A Summer's Journey to the Rocky Mountains*. New York: Samuel Bowles and Company, 1866.

Brown, J. Henry. *Political History of Oregon; Provisional Government.* Portland, OR: Wiley B. Allen, 1892.

Brown, Wilford H., ed. *This Was A Man.* North Hollywood, CA: Camas Press, 1971.

Brown, William. *California Northeast:The Bloody Ground.* Oakland, CA: Biobooks, 1951.

Bryant, Edwin. *What I Saw In California.* New York, 1849.

Carey, Charles Henry. *The Oregon Constitution.* Salem, OR, 1926.

———. *A General History of Oregon Prior to* 1861, 2 vols. Portland, OR: Metropolitan Press, 1935.

Case, Robert Ormond. *The Empire Builders.* New York, Doubleday, 1947.

Clark, Malcolm, Jr., ed. *Pharisee Among the Philistines: The Diary of Judge Matthew P. Deady,* 1871–1892. Portland, OR: Oregon Historical Society, 1975.

———. *Eden Seekers: the Settlement of Oregon,* 1818–1862. Boston: Houghton Mifflin, 1981.

Clarkey, SA. Pioneer Days of Oregon History, 1905.

Cordano, Vira. *Levi Scott, Oregon Trailblazer.* Portland, OR: Binford, 1982.

Cozzens, Peter. *Eyewitnesses to the Indian Wars,* 1865–1890. Mechanicsburg, PA: Stackpole Books, 2002.

Coffman, Lloyd W. *Blazing A Wagon Trail To Oregon.* Missouri: Echo Books, 1993.

Crawford, Peter W. *The Overland Journey to Oregon in* 1847. North Plains, OR: Soap Creek Enterprise, 1977.

Davis, Charles George. *The South Road, and the Route Across Southern Oregon.* North Plains, OR: EmigrantsWest.com, 2001.

DeVoto, Bernard. *The Year of Decision,* 1846. Boston, 1943.

Dye, Eva Emery. *The Soul of America: An Oregon Iliad.* New York, 1934.

Emerson, William. *The Applegate Trail of* 1846. Ashland, Or: Ember Enterprises, 1996.

Evans, Elwood. *History of the Pacific Northwest, Oregon and Washington,* 2 vols. Portland, OR: North Pacific History Company, 1889.

Faragher, John Mark. *Daniel Boone: The Life and Legend of An American Pioneer.* New York: Macmillan, 1992.

Good, Rachel Applegate. *History of Klamath County, Oregon.* Klamath Falls, OR, 1941.

Gray, W.H. *A History of Oregon,* 1792–1849, *Drawn From Personal Observation and Authentic Information.* Portland, OR, 1970.

Grover, La Fayette. *Report of Governor Grover to General Schofield on the Modoc War.* Salem, OR: Mort Brown, State Printer, 1874.

Hill, William E. *The Oregon Trail, Yesterday and Today.* Caldwell, ID: Caxton Printers, 1994.

Holman, Frederick Van Voorhies. *Dr. John McLoughlin—the Father of Oregon.* Oregon: The A.H. Clark Company, 1907.

Johansen, Dorothy O. and Charles M. Gates. *Empire of the Columbia; A History of the Pacific Northwest.* New York: Harper and Row, 1967.

Johannsen, Robert W. *Frontier Politics and the Sectional Conflict; The Pacific Northwest on the Eve of the Civil War.* Seattle, WA, 1955.

Johnson, Robert C. *John McLoughlin, Father of Oregon.* Portland, OR: Binfords & Mort, 1935.

Kearny, Thomas. *General Philip Kearny, Battle Soldier of Five Wars.* New York, 1937.

Kruse, Anne Applegate. *Yoncalla, Home of the Eagles.* Drain, OR, 1950.

Kendall, Reese. *Pacific Trail Camp-fires.* Chicago: Scroll, 1901.

Martin, Jim. *A Bit of Blue: Life and Work of Frances Fuller Victor.* Salem, OR: Deep Well Publishing, 1992.

Mattes, Merrill. *The Great Platte River Road.* Nebraska State Historical Society, 1969.

Meacham, Alfred B. *Wigwam and War-path.* Boston: John Dale and Co., 1876.

McGlashan, C. F. *History of the Donner Party.* Stanford, CA: Stanford University Press, 1968.

McLynn, Frank. *Wagons West.* New York: First Grove Press, 2002.

Morgan, Dale, ed. *Overland in 1846: Diaries and Letters of the California-Oregon Trail.* Lincoln: University of Nebraska Press, 1994.

Murray, Keith A. *The Modocs and Their War.* Norman, OK: University of Oklahoma Press, 1959.

Nevins, Allan, ed., *Narratives of Exploration and Adventure by John Charles Fremont.* New York: Longmans, Green & Co.,1956.

Owens-Adair, B. A. *Some of Her Life Experiences*. Portland, OR, 1906.

Riddle, Jeff C. *The Indian History of the Modoc War and the Causes That Led to It*. Privately printed, 1914.

Rucker, Maude A. *The Oregon Trail and Some of Its Blazers*. New York, 1930.

Schafer, Joseph. *A History of the Pacific Northwest*. New York: Macmillan, 1926.

Thornton, Jesse Q. *Oregon and California in* 1848, 2 vols. New York, 1849.

Victor, Frances Fuller. *The Early Indian Wars of Oregon Compiled from the Oregon Archives and Other Original Sources with Muster Rolls*. Salem, OR: Frank C. Baker, State Printers, 1894.

Watson, James F. *Brief and Argument of Plaintiff B. F. Dowell vs. Jesse Applegate in Circuit Court of the United States for the District of Oregon*. Portland, OR, 1882 (Pamphlet).

Webber, Bert. *The Oregon & Applegate Trail Diary of Welborn Beeson in* 1853. Central Point, OR: Webb Research Group, 1987.

———. *Applegate Trail to Oregon* 1846. Central Point, OR: Webb Research Group, 1996.

———. *The Pig War: The Journal of William A. Peck Jr*. Edited by Brewster Coulter and Bert Webber. Central Point, OR: Webb Research Group, 1993.

Weldon, Willis Rau. *Surviving Oregon Trail* 1852. Pullman, WA: Washington State University Press, 2001.

Woodward, Walter Carleton. *The Rise and Early History of Political Parties in Oregon, 1843–1868*. Portland, OR, 1913.

Unruh, John D., Jr. *The Plains Across*. Urbana, IL: University of Illinois Press, 1979.

Diaries, Manuscripts and Manuscript Collections

Applegate, Colonel Howard Rex. The Applegates of Oregon, Their Ancestors and Descendants. El Cerrito, CA, 1956.

Applegate, Jesse. *A Day with the Cow Column*; reprinted in Jesse A. Applegate, *Recollections of My Boyhood*. Edited by Joseph Schafer. Chicago, 1934.

————. Papers, 1832–1849. Yale University Library, New Haven. [Microfilm, University of Oregon research Library.]

————. Papers, 1850–1858. Miller Collection, Yale University Library, New Haven. [Microfilm, Special Collection Department, University of Oregon Library.]

————. Papers. Letters, 1843–1888. Oregon Historical Society, Portland.

————. "Notes and Communication on Oregon History," 1878. Bancroft Library, University of California, Berkeley. [Typed Copy, Special Department Collection, University of Oregon.]

Applegate, Lindsay. Papers, 1863–1891. Special Collection Department, University of Oregon.

Applegate, Oliver. Papers, 1842–1848. Special Collection Department, University of Oregon.

Applegate, Susannah G. "Jesse Applegate, Oregon's Prince of Pioneers." Unpublished manuscript, Douglas County Museum, Roseburg, OR.

Bush, Asahel. Papers, 1850–1870. Special Collection Department, University of Oregon.

Collins, Dean. "From Independence to Independence." Unpublished diary/memoir of Levi Scott.

Crawford, Medorem. Papers, 1842–1860. Special Collection Department, University of Oregon Library.

Deady, Matthew P., "Judge Deady's Letters re Oregon, to San Francisco *Bulletin,* 1862–1867." Scrapbook Collection, Oregon Historical Society, Portland.

———. Papers, 1854–1880. Oregon Historical Society, Portland.

Dowell v. Applegate. 1869–1883. Manuscript Collection, Bakken Research Library, Douglas County Museum of History.

Evans, Elwood. "Notebook of Annotated Clippings, Copies of Pamphlets, and Correspondence, 1859–1882." Oregon Collection, Special Collection Department, University of Oregon.

Frear, Samuel. "Jesse Applegate: An Appraisal of an Uncommon Pioneer." Master's thesis, University of Oregon, 1961.

Faubion, Nina Lane. Papers, 1888. Special Collection Department, University of Oregon.

Fisher, Don C. Collection of papers concerning the Modoc Indian War, vol. 1. Shaw Historical Library, Oregon Institute of Technology, Klamath Falls.

Grover, La Fayette, "Notable Things in Public Life in Oregon," 1878. Bancroft Library, University of California, Berkeley. [Typed copy, University of Oregon Library.]

Helfrich, Devere. "Applegate Trail." *Klamath Echoes*, Klamath County Historical Society, Klamath Falls, OR, 1971.

———. "Applegate Trail II." *Klamath Echoes*, Klamath County Historical Society, Klamath Falls, OR,1976.

Hill, Sara. Hill manuscript in Oregon Historical Society Library.

Hulin, Lester. "1847 Diary of Applegate Trail to Oregon," Typescript, Lane County Historical Society, Eugene, OR.

Kruse, Anne Applegate. "The Applegate Story." Special Collections Department, University of Oregon.

Lane, Joseph. Papers, 1854–1885. Oregon Collection, University of Oregon.

———. Papers, 1851–1887. Oregon Historical Society, Portland.

Long, Sallie Applegate. "Jesse Applegate." Oregon Historical Society, Portland.

———. "Mrs. Jesse Applegate." Oregon Historical Society, Portland.

———. "Something About the Sage of Yoncalla." Oregon Historical Society, Portland.

———. "Traditional History of the Applegate Family." Oregon Historical Society, Portland.

Meacham, Walter. *Applegate Trail* 1846. State of Oregon Historical Brochure, 1947.

Merrill, Cecily. *Without Papers*. Portola Valley, CA, 1999.

Miller, Emma. "A Memory of the Sage of Yoncalla," 1889. Oregon Historical Society, Portland.

Miner, William D. "Jesse Applegate: Oregon Pioneer." Master's thesis, University of Indiana, 1948, OHS.

Oregon Superintendent of Indian Affairs. Records of the Oregon Superintendent of Indian Affairs, 1848–1873. Microcopy 2, RG 75, National Archives, Washington, D.C.

Oregon Supreme Court. B.F. Dowell, et al. vs. D. W. Applegate, et al. File no. 4517 (1892), Oregon State Archives.

Papers of the Provisional and Territorial Government, 1841–1859. Oregon State Library, State Archives, Salem.

Pringle, Virgil. *Overland in 1846: Diaries and Letters of the California-Oregon Trail.* Edited by Dale Morgan, vol. 1. Lincoln, NE: University Of Nebraska Press, 1993.

Preston, John B.-Jesse Applegate. Letters, BLM Records-49, 1851–1853, National Archives-Pacific Alaska Region.

Schafer, Joseph. *Jesse Applegate: Pioneer and State Builder.* Eugene, OR: The University of Oregon Bulletin, 1912.

Simmons, John E. "In Search of the Applegate Trail." Professional Educator's Training, PET 1996, Vancouver, WA.

Waldo, Daniel. "Critiques," 1878. Bancroft Library, University of California, Berkeley. [Typed copy, University of Oregon Library.]

Periodical Articles

Applegate, Lindsay. "Notes and Reminiscences of Laying Out and Establishing the Old Emigrant Road into Southern Oregon in the Year 1846." *Oregon Historical Quarterly* XX, No. I (March 1921).

Blake, Charlotte. "Jesse Applegate, His Attitude toward the Oregon Indians." *Reed College Bulletin* XXI (November 1942): 17–27.

Bradley, Marie M. "Political Beginnings in Oregon." *Oregon Historical Quarterly* Vol. IX, No. 1(March 1908).

Bright, Verne. "The Lost County, Umpqua, Oregon, and Its Early Settlements." *Oregon Historical Quarterly*, Vol. LI, No.2 (June 1950).

Burchard, Mildred Baker. "Scott's and Applegate's Old South Road." *Oregon Historical Quarterly*, Vol. XLI, No.4 (December 1942).

Burnett, Peter H. "Recollections and Opinions of an Old Pioneer." *Oregon Historical Quarterly*, Vol. IV, No. 1 (March 1904); Vol.V, No. 2 (June 1904): 151–198; VI, No. 3 (September 1904): 272–205.

Davenport, T. W. "Slavery Question in Oregon." *Oregon Historical Quarterly* IX, No.3 (September 1908): 189–253.

———. "The Late George N. Williams." *Oregon Historical Quarterly* XI, No.3 (September 1910).

Delano, Alonzo. Reprinted in *Klamath Echoes* 9, (1971) Klamath County Historical Society, Klamath Falls, OR.

"Excerpts from the New Orleans Picayune from January 3, 1843 to April 27, 1844." *Oregon Historical Quarterly* II, No. 2 (June 1901): 187–203.

Fenton, William D. "Political History of Oregon from 1865 to 1876." *Oregon Historical Quarterly* XV, No. 4 (December 1914): 89–139.

Garrison, A. H. "Reminiscences of Abraham Henry Garrison— Over the Oregon Trail in 1846." *Overland Journal* (Oregon California Trails Association) Vo1.2, No.2 (Summer 1993).

Holman, Frederick V. "A Brief History of the Oregon Provisional Government and What Caused Its Formation." *Oregon Historical Quarterly* XIII, No. 2 (June 1912): 89–139.

"Jesse Applegate, New Light Thrown upon his Early Life by a Letter from J.M. Peck to Gen. Joseph Lane, Delegate in Congress from Oregon." *Oregon Historical Quarterly* XV, No.3 (September 1914): 208–209.

Johnston, Robert B. "Two Jesses and the Modoc War." *Journal of the Shaw Historical,* 5 nos. 1 and 2, Shaw Historical Library.

"Letter, Jesse Applegate to W.H. Rees, Secretary, Oregon Pioneer Association." *Oregon Historical Quarterly* XX, No. 4 (December 1919): 397–399.

"Letters of Peter H. Burnett." *Oregon Historical Quarterly* III, No. 4 (December 1902): 398–426.

McArthur, Lewis A. "Earliest Oregon Postoffices as Recorded at Washington." *Oregon Historical Quarterly* XLI (March 1940): 53–71.

Mills, Hazel E. "Travels of a Lady Correspondent; Frances Fuller Victor's Comments on the Northwest Frontier, 1861–1878." *Pacific Northwest Quarterly* XLV (October 1954):105–115.

Mires, Austin. "Jesse Applegate and Honest Abe." *The Umpqua Trapper* IV (Summer 1968).

Nesmith, J. W. "Diary of the Emigration of 1843." *Oregon Historical Quarterly* VII, No. 4 (December 1906): 329–359.

Odgers, Charlotte. "Jesse Applegate, Study of a Pioneer Politician."

Reed College Bulletin XXIII (November 1944): 7–20.

Overland Monthly and Old West Magazine 4, no. 24 (December 1884), San Francisco.

Penter, Samuel. "Recollections of an Oregon Pioneer of 1843." *Oregon Historical Quarterly* VII, No. 1 (March 1906): 56–61.

Rawe, Mary Patricia. "Winning Beekman Essay on the Oregon Trail." *Oregon Historical Quarterly* XLIV, No. 2 (June 1943).

Sargent, Alice Applegate. "A Sketch of the Rogue River Valley and Southern Oregon History." *Oregon Historical Quarterly*, Vol. XX, No. 1 (March 1921).

Scott, Harvey W. "The Formation and Administration of the Provisional Government of Oregon," *Oregon Historical Quarterly*, Vol. II, No.2 (June 1901): 95–118.

Scott, Leslie M. "First Taxes in Oregon, 1844." *Oregon Historical Quarterly* XXXI, No 1 (March 1930): 1–24.

Schafer, Joseph. "Jesse Applegate; Pioneer, Statesman and Philosopher." *Washington Historical Quarterly* I (July 1907): 217–233.

Schafer, Joseph. "Jesse Applegate, Pioneer and State Builder." *University of Oregon Bulletin* IX (February 1912).

Stone, Buena Cobb. "Southern Route into Oregon: Notes and a New Map." *Oregon Historical Quarterly*, Vol. XLVII, No. 2 (June 1946).

"The Indian Murders in Umpqua County." *The Umpqua Trapper* X (Winter, 1974).

Woodward, Walter Carleton. "Political Parties in Oregon." *Oregon Historical Quarterly* XI, No. 4 (December 1910).

"The Rise and Early History of Political Parties in Oregon." *Oregon Historical Quarterly* XLI, No. 1 (March 1940): 40–52.

Young, F. G. "Finances of the Cayuse War." *Oregon Historical Quarterly* VII, No. 4 (December 1906): 418–432.

Miscellaneous

Book A, Cole County Recorder's Office, Missouri, 403.

British and American Joint Commission for the Final Settlement of the Claims of the Hudson's Bay and Puget's Sound Agricultural Companies, *In the Matter of Hudson's Bay Company. Testimony on Part of the United States,* 4 vols. Washington, D.C., 1867.

Deady, Matthew P., "The Annual Address." Transactions of the Third Annual Re-Union of the Oregon Pioneer Association, (Salem, 1876), 17–41.

Documents, Oregon Provisional Government, Legislative Session 1847, in library of Oregon Historical Society, Portland.

Nesmith, J. W., "The Occasional Address." Transactions of the Third Annual Re-Union of the Oregon Pioneer Association (Salem, 1876), 42–46).

Lincoln, Abraham, 1809–1865: Collected Works, Volume 6; U.S. Military Academy, 1863, Box 82, No 184.

Revolutionary War Pension, United States America Sources: Jerseymen in the Revolutionary War, 135, 143. New Jersey pension #16139.

Personal Interview with Margaret Brown Vescogni, Great-granddaughter to Rozelle Putman, March 2006.

Newspapers

Ashland Daily Tidings, 1877–1879.

Boonville Herald, Boonville, Missouri.

The Drain Enterprise, Drain, Oregon.

Klamath Falls Express, Klamath Falls, Oregon.

Iowa Territorial Gazette

Mail Tribune, Medford, Oregon.

New York Aurora

New York Daily Tribune

Oregon Argus, Salem, 1855–1863.

The Oregon Journal

The Oregonian, Portland, Oregon.

Oregon Sentinel, Jacksonville, Oregon.

Oregon Spectator, Oregon City, 1847–1853.

Oregon State Journal, 1865–1866.

Oregon Statesman, Salem, Oregon.

People's Press, Eugene, Oregon.

Rogue River Courier, Rogue River, Oregon.

The Sacramento Bee, Sacramento. California.

The Yreka Union, Yreka, California.